Check out his Amazon Author's Page (Jim Hoffmann) for a listing of all of his major works including but not limited to…

Come and Get Your Love: A Celebratory Ode to Redbone (Revised Edition), Pat "Redbone" Vegas and Jim Hoffmann, Susquehanna Road Publishing, 2023, 615 pages.

The Boy in the Box: America's Unknown Child (3rd Ed.) – My Obsession with America's Greatest Crime, Susquehanna Road Publishing, 2018, 442 pages.

Conversations with
David S. Lifton

Best Evidence to *Final Charade*

Jim Hoffmann

CONVERSATIONS WITH DAVID S. LIFTON: *BEST EVIDENCE* TO *FINAL CHARADE*
COPYRIGHT © 2023/2024 JIM HOFFMANN

Published by:
Trine Day LLC
PO Box 577
Walterville, OR 97489
1-800-556-2012
www.TrineDay.com
TrineDay@icloud.com

Library of Congress Control Number: 2024945258

Hoffmann, Jim.
–1st ed.
p. cm.

Epub (ISBN-13) 978-1-63424-478-7
Trade Paperback (ISBN-13) 978-1-63424-477-0
1. David Samuel Lifton (1939-2022). 2. Kennedy, John F. 1917-1963 Assassination. I. Hoffmann, Jim. Title

FIRST EDITION
10 9 8 7 6 5 4 3 2 1
Disclaimer: Mr. Lifton was an expert in his field – perhaps more than any other likewise. He was very specific about his theories and inferences and relied wholly on evidence he had uncovered. Mr. Lifton was not one to make wild accusations or assumptions.

Therefore, I want to be clear to the reader that I present his statements about his theories as clearly as possible with accompanying explanations. However, Mr. Lifton is gone, and any errors in transcriptions hereof, or interpretations thereof, are wholly mine.
Front Cover Photo Credit: Robbie Romero.
Back Cover. Photo Credit: Esteban Monroy

Printed in the USA
Distribution to the Trade by:
Independent Publishers Group (IPG)
814 North Franklin Street
Chicago, Illinois 60610
312.337.0747
www.ipgbook.com

If it were done when 'tis done, then 'twere well
It were done quickly. If the assassination
Could trammel up the consequence, and catch,
With his surcease, success; that but this blow
Might be the be-all and the end-all here,
But here, upon this bank and shoal of time,
We'd jump the life to come. But in these cases
We still have judgement here, that we but teach
Bloody instructions, which being taught return
To plague the inventor. This even-handed justice
Commends the ingredients of our poison'd chalice
To our own lips. He's here in double trust:
First, as I am his kinsman and his subject,
Strong both against the deed; then, as his host,
Who should against his murderer shut the door,
Not bear the knife myself. Besides, this Duncan
Hath borne his faculties so meek, hath been
So clear in his great office, that his virtues
Will plead like angels trumpet-tongued against
The deep damnation of his taking-off,
And pity, like a naked new-born babe,
Striding the blast, or heaven's cherubin horsed
Upon the sightless couriers of the air,
Shall blow the horrid deed in every eye,
That tears shall drown the wind. I have no spur
To prick the sides of my intent, but only
Vaulting ambition, which o'erleaps itself
And falls on the other—

– William Shakespeare
MacBeth, Act 1, Scene VIII

I wholeheartedly dedicate this work to the honor of the late, great, David S. Lifton, author of the groundbreaking, bestselling book on the Kennedy Assassination, Best Evidence: Disguise and Deception in the Assassination of John F. Kennedy,[1] and one of the original founding fathers of the JFK Assassination Research community; and to his loving family, his followers, and his supporters worldwide. As I told you during our many conversations, Mr. Lifton, you were my inspiration to become a writer in the first place, my natural mentor, and my friend. I can never repay you for that depth of caring and kindness.

I also dedicate this to the memory of Lee Harvey Oswald, and to his family. May you follow the example set by the children of Malcolm X and seek legal relief for the undue harm caused to you by this miscarriage of justice. No one understood this better than David S. Lifton.

And to my family.

---

1   Lifton, David S. *Best Evidence: Disguise and Deception in the Assassination of John F. Kennedy.* NYC: Carroll & Graf Publishers, 1992, 13th ed., 755 pages. Originally published by Macmillan, Inc. in 1981. *Best Evidence* was on the *NY Times* Bestseller List for twelve weeks in 1981 (February 15-May 3) and was also a Book of the Month Club selection. It has been published by four publishers since 1981: Macmillan, Dell, Carroll & Graf, and Signet.

ACKNOWLEDGMENTS

I would like to thank the public school students and staff who helped create the groundbreaking student documentary, David Lifton Project, back in 2018.

The schools include Canyon Ridge High School and Shadow Ridge School, Hesperia Unified School District, Hesperia, California (in So-Cal), and their principals, Mr. Scott Alghren (CRHS), and Mrs. Kelly Maxwell (SRS), but also my cohort, Robbie Romero (Teacher at CRHS), and most importantly the some twenty students from both schools who spent countless hours in production of this all-important film. The next generation of Americans deserves the truth which Mr. Lifton provided unequivocally through his Herculean research efforts into the Kennedy Assassination.

I would also like to thank my mother, Linda J. Emmering, and my late Father-in-Law, Norman Arthur Dombrow (1944-1999), for encouraging my research into the JFK Assassination by instilling in me a deep love and respect for President John F. Kennedy.

Lastly, I would like to thank some of Mr. Lifton's greatest friends – Mr. Bill Alexander, Nathalie Apteker, Brent Holland, and Vince Palamara – for their contributions to this work.

Epigraphs

"When you ride in a car, [and] you look in the rearview mirror, you see an accurate picture of where you've been.

That's what the rearview mirror is for. But today, when our country looks in the rearview mirror, we have a false history because we don't know what happened in 1963. Now, if it was just a matter of a footnote – if it was a second or third assassin – that's not true. If this body was altered, basically what I've discovered in … [my research], we've had a coup. We had a coup: a secret plan to make Johnson president and to remove Kennedy from office under the – with the appearance of an historical accident when in fact it was a very carefully planned conspiracy. When I mean conspiracy, I am not talking simply about a second or a third shooter. I'm talking about fraud in the evidence. The creation of a false reality. So, it looks like an historical quirk of fate:

Kennedy got killed, Johnson became president – and, oh yeah, by the way, the next year the war in Vietnam got escalated. And you can go to the Vietnam War [Memorial] in Washington and see the [names of] the 58,000 people that died – Americans, but what about the [one] million in Asia. So, it changed the whole nature of the country. OK. That's what happened [with JFK's Assassination] and … that's the result of a crime."
– David S. Lifton, Friday, February 9, 2018[1]

"Homework should merely push a man over the border, not lift him out of the grave."
–Cornell Visiting Math Professor Kasimatis – as told humorously by David S. Lifton)

"Hey, hey, hey, hey, hey, wait a minute!
Who ya gonna believe – me or your own eyes?"
– Warren T. Rat, *An American Tail*)

---

1   Canyon Ridge High School/Shadow Ridge School Production. "David Lifton Project." YouTube, 2018, 1:29:08 minutes (circa 1:10:10-1:11:27). Retrieved 6/30/2023: https://www.youtube.com/watch?v=ms0BJlxfaqw&t=3702s

"The legal approach [of the Warren Commission] gave me the creeps. Sometimes I thought that if lawyers had invaded the field of mathematics, two-plus-two-equals-four would have been a compromise, worked out after a jury had heard both sides – one arguing the sum was three, the other that it was five."
– *Best Evidence*, Chapter 6, "Redefining the Problem: the Autopsy as 'Best Evidence,'" page 129

"Was your life ever in danger?" asked Lifton research assistant Nathalie Apteker. "Yes. My father threatened to kill me if this book failed."

"That night [Tuesday, November 1, 1966] I made the decision to devote full time to the case. Somebody had to follow up this hypothesis, to analyze the medical data from this new viewpoint ... I thought the project would take about six months. I never dreamed I was embarking on something that would preoccupy me for the next fifteen years."
– *Best Evidence*, Chapter 10, "The Liebeler Memorandum," page 240

"You've got to turn it into a narrative. It's not just to have data. You have to make it a good read."
– David S. Lifton, 2020

"Whereas the beginning is the end, so is the end the beginning."
– Unknown

CONTENTS

FOREWORD

I met David Lifton back in 1992, after moving to Los Angeles from Maryland for a job opportunity. I'd always liked historical films and books and after seeing the Oliver Stone film *JFK*, I became interested in the JFK Assassination. I purchased a few books, and *Best Evidence* was one of them. I read the book in just 5 days. I remember staying up all night. I couldn't put it down. It was truly one of the best books I'd ever read, and I had to learn more after finishing it.

I decided to write David a letter just stating that I read his book, and I'd love to do some volunteer work. He also lived in Los Angeles, so I thought I'd try. We met for lunch, he loved that I was originally from Israel, and we had lots to chat about, and that's how we connected. Initially, I was just volunteering, and then he offered me a full time position. I worked for him at his Olympic Boulevard office for over three years. Working with David changed the course of my life – my career, because I ended up doing a lot of research for him, gained computer experience working for him, and then I ended up in software development, and later real estate.

David and I spent a great deal of time together, he enjoyed eating out at Junior's Deli and we'd have our morning or midday sessions at Junior's. He told me that he started down this road based upon the Zapruder Film, and how that evidence of a frontal shot contradicted the way the Warren Commission stated that Kennedy was shot from the rear. The crime could not have physically happened that way. In reality, it turned out that the film was doctored and spliced up which is why the timing could not work. Furthermore, the crime could not have been accomplished as they claimed in that short amount of time, but that's what started David on his journey. Because David had a science background, all his work was always fact-based, which I very much respected.

I think David was a brilliant researcher – the best – but he was too much of a perfectionist. And because he was science-based, and science is always changing and new information becomes available, he was always waiting for that additional pack of documents that were needed. I always would say to him, "Even if it's 95% – get it out there. You can't be 100%.

You'll never get all of the pieces." This explains why *Final Charade* was not finished in time. David was a perfectionist, and he just kept working on his research, and tweaking it, and getting more information.

People should know that David's original publisher – Macmillan – spent a long time validating his research for *Best Evidence*. They were quite worried about getting sued. They checked every single footnote. As David told me, it was like the Talmud. That's how serious they were, and they spent months validating the footnotes. They checked the accuracy of *Best Evidence* as if it was an historical document. Besides David's special care in documenting the evidence in his book, the publisher had a number of lawyers looking over the manuscript before it was published. *Best Evidence* went through a very thorough review. It was a big deal for Macmillan to go ahead and publish something that was in a sense accusatory of the government.

I think whether it's young people or old people who are interested in the JFK Assassination topic, I think *Best Evidence* is the best book on the market. It's a non-emotional book. Rather, it's a very scientific-based book. It's so well documented and footnoted. It's not somebody's theory. The way David worked is that evidence drew him to the conclusion – not the other way around. Most researchers started with a hypothesis and tried to get pieces of evidence to fit into their individual hypotheses. David worked differently. He let the evidence lead him to the conclusions.

On the other hand – forget the historical aspect of *Best Evidence* – it is plain and simple a great "onion peeling, layer by layer" mystery. As mentioned, I read the whole book in 5 days, often reading the whole night, I couldn't put it down. It's a masterpiece!

Through my work with David, I was able to meet the giants in the JFK Assassination Research Community like Mark Lane, John Newman, Patricia Lambert, and Marina Oswald. In fact, I participated in multiple interviews with Marina while working with David. With David S. Lifton's passing, the world misses one of the giants of the JFK Assassination Research Community. I miss my friend.

Nathalie Apteker
Research Assistant, Friend, Benefactor
Sunday, October 29, 2023

PROLOGUE

In the JFK assassination community, I hold several works as seminal that take precedence over all others:

- "The Zapruder Film" (without question)
- Mark Lane's *Rush To Judgment* (both book and documentary)
- *JFK* Oliver Stone's ground breaking cinematic masterpiece
- David Lifton's cutting edge book *Best Evidence.*

The reason, to their credit, all revived the fading topic of the JFK assassination and ushered it back to the forefront on a mass scale where it belongs.

I have interviewed David Lifton many times over the years for my show *Night Fright* on You Tube. David and I always got along famously. His vast knowledge of the assassination was tantamount to the viewer's expectations and always exceeded them. And, of course, in the JFK community he is considered a founding father and legend. David's quick mind also blessed him with a rich, witty sense of humour, which brought with it a great many howls.

MY SHOWS WITH DAVID

David, I, and our dear friend and colleague Bill Blackwell, shared a show in December 2021 that would sadly turn out to be David's final interview. We discussed David's new research, at great length, that was slated to be included in his new to be released book titled: *Final Charade.* To view the shows with David, Google: "David Lifton JFK Playlist You-Tube JFK Files."

DOWN THE RABBIT HOLE

David told me that he was lured away from entering his family's business of selling "lighting fixtures to wives" because: "…two things beckoned that were very exciting. First of all, I was part of the Apollo Program. And I can assure you, I mean they're nice people, but that didn't compare to going to the moon." [We all howled]. (And there, my friends, is an example of David's sense of humour).

David continued: "Second of all, I got involved with Professor Liebeler over at UCLA."

Wesley J. Liebeler, Professor of Law, Emeritus (1931-2002) was an assistant counsel to the Warren Commission. When the WC ended he was offered a position at UCLA in 1965 which he readily accepted.

While attending UCLA himself, David hooked up with Liebeler. During Lifton's research of JFK related documents, David unearthed a shocking never before released document: "I found this remarkable FBI report that said the President' Body had been altered PRIOR to autopsy."

This led David "down the rabbit hole," one that all researchers plunder down. His research culminated with the 1981 release of his bestselling book: *Best Evidence: Deception and Disguise in the Assassination of John F. Kennedy."* The rest, as the cliché goes, is history. What amazes me and still does, are how many researchers I have had on my show reference *"Best Evidence"* as one of their main reasons for getting involved in their own JFK research. *"Best Evidence"* was so profoundly influential on a global scale, even the average person that had little knowledge of the subject, could cite the title and parts of the book. In short it caused a "critical mass" of people that suddenly became aware, more than ever, that something was amiss with the JFK assassination.

Indeed, the book became a hot topic at office water cooler conversations and at coffee shops. The Canadian Broadcasting Corporation (CBC) even did a segment on their premiere investigative series *The Fifth Estate* titled: "Who Killed JFK" which was broadcast on the anniversary of JFK's death November 22, 1983. It was jaw dropping and left people once again demanding answers. Even in Canada. Another anomaly that always sparks my curiosity is how many Canadians have taken up the mantle of researcher. This author included.

The reason being, JFK was a global figure, one of unity and peace. Above all, HOPE. When Kennedy was gunned down and just two days later, his purported assassin, Lee Harvey Oswald, was silenced by Jack Ruby, a known mob associate, the world knew it wasn't a lone nut assassin but that the assassination was the result of a conspiracy. The first rule of assassination is silence the assassin lest they talk. To this day, mainstream media shudders from the truth looping all in the JFK community as "conspiracy nuts" who they assume must also believe the world is flat. Not so.

(It's corrugated…)

David understood this and fought for the truth. I must admit, I admire all researchers for their convictions, even those whose theories I vehemently disagree with. Their quest for the truth reaps them no benefits financially or publically.

TED SORENSEN

David remains the only researcher that understood the profound impact and role of JFK Special Assistant Ted Sorensen. Most media and JFK researchers overlook Sorensen's essential contributions to the Kennedy administration. They will readily acknowledge his speech writing and ignore the rest of his contributions to the Kennedy administration. Speech writing was only one of a multitude of assignments JFK levied Sorensen with.

I had the opportunity to interview Ted Sorensen twice. I have since turned those interviews into two feature length documentaries. I had sent a private copy to David of an early screener. He called me and raved about Sorensen. "It was all Sorensen!" he exclaimed. "JFK wouldn't have been JFK without Sorensen." He got it.

Google: *"Ted Sorensen A Life With JFK Inside Camelot"* and *"JFK Assassination The Oval Office To Dealey Plaza"*

ANTI-SEMITISM

It never ends. It is older than the proclaimed "oldest occupation." From day one, Jews have been subjected to murder and hate for no other reason than being Jewish.

David's family fled Russia to America in 1893 because of the Russian Pogroms, essentially an open license to rape and murder Jews that resulted in the horrific killing tens of thousands of Jews.

Jews make up 0.2% of the world's population. Yet, they get blamed for everything. Everything. Hitler blamed Jews for WWII and set upon the world an entire industry, complete with spreadsheet lists which included colour of hair, intricately scheduled train transports (in the middle of a war!) and ultimately extermination camps set up with huge gas chambers to murder en mass and of course, the furnaces contracts which were awarded to the highest bidder. By 1945, 2 of 3 European Jews had been killed. There has always been the lunatic fringe associated with the JFK conspiracy. Does anyone remember Ice bullets? Jackie killed JFK? Now the latest is Jews killed Kennedy. Somehow, someway, all unexplained of course, Israel and the Mossad managed to orchestrate and conspire to kill Kennedy. Oye!

Unfortunately, those who know better in the research community, big names, ones you would recognize instantly, perpetuate the lie. David and I discussed this new travesty against the Jews at great length. Both of us vehemently denounced and condemned it. I will continue to rail against those that unjustly demonize Israel and Jews.

THE QUEST FOR THE TRUTH

David spent every waking moment of his life seeking the truth in the murder of the 35th sitting president of the United States, John F. Kennedy. Day in, day out. During his lifetime, David has been researching new witnesses, new theories and new evidence. All to culminate in his new book *Final Charade*.

David passed away on December 6, 2022, leaving behind his unfinished manuscript. His close friend and attorney Bill Blackwell had warned and urged David to make arrangements for his research and manuscript just prior to his death, "just in case," specifically so that they would not be lost. David said he would, but never followed through. Tragically, as of this writing, his computer, his research and his manuscript have disappeared. Their whereabouts are unknown. It is Bill's and my fear that they may be lost forever. We both refer to David's interviews on my show as perhaps the only reference to his research on his book: *Final Charade*.

LEGACY

The bottom line, if it wasn't for David Lifton, the quest for truth in the John F. Kennedy assassination would have faded decades ago in the 1970s. He revived it and brought it to the forefront. David asked the uncomfortable questions mainstream hide from AND he demanded answers from those in the know. We, as a community, owe a great debt to David and all the pioneers that came before us. We call that Chutzpah.

Brent Holland
Producer/Host of *Night Fright Show*
Friend
Saturday, November 4, 2023

* * *

I first learned of David Lifton in 1968-1969 while attending Arizona State University when my father Fred Newcomb told me about this fascinating researcher that was very provocative and different from the rest of the group of researchers in Los Angeles at the time. Lillian Castellanos, Ray Marcos, Mike Farrell (the actor), Steve Jaffe, and others would gather every so often and share their research. Dad was the photographic and graphics expert that participated, and he and David exchanged their information with each other.

Although they eventually parted ways over personality conflicts, David had an enormous impact on my father's basic thinking on the case. Dad had been in the orbit of Jim Garrison, and when Jim lost his case against Clay Shaw, he became disillusioned with the whole New Orleans conspiracy scenario.

But, David was talking more about the forensic evidence and chain of custody, also – and most importantly – how the evidence in Dallas changed when it got to Washington, DC. Dad didn't know it then, but he soon switched from looking at the case as a conspiracy from the outside to more of an "inside job" involving the Secret Service and Lyndon Johnson. Eventually he and Perry Adams wrote *Murder From Within* (1974) and David Lifton would eventually write the *New York Times* bestselling book *Best Evidence* released in 1981.

Tyler Newcomb
Friend
Sunday, October 29, 2023

INTRODUCTION

David S. Lifton is one of the founding fathers of the JFK Assassination research field and author of *The New York Times* bestselling book, *Best Evidence: Disguise and Deception in the Assassination of John F. Kennedy*. In awe of him and his work and with reverence and respect, I always addressed him as "Mr. Lifton." He was my literary idol, indirectly induced me to start writing in 1996, and later became my mentor, and friend. Thus, I will continue to pay homage to this great man by addressing him likewise throughout this work as I did in life.

Mr. Lifton is the smartest man I have ever met. As a researcher, he was very particular about what he theorized and stated as possibilities. He was a scientist. He was an engineer. If Mr. Lifton couldn't prove something, he would not entertain the idea any longer. That is what Cornell University gave him through their Engineering Physics School: a truly evaluative and analytical mind.

I first met Mr. Lifton in person on Friday, February 9, 2018, at his home in Dana Point, California, south of Los Angeles. The purpose was to allow my public school students to interview him for a documentary about him, the *David Lifton Project*. The specific focus thereof was to have Mr. Lifton explain his work to young people, the next generation, a documentary film which could then serve as a bridge for future generations who wished to know the truth, to know what really happened that tragic day in Dallas, Texas, so many years before.

Fact is, I actually corresponded via post with Mr. Lifton back in the early 1990s, and spoke twice on the phone with him as well. As I discuss below in our conversations, I never gave the Kennedy Assassination much thought growing up. The first time I came face-to-face with the spectre of a conspiracy was when, back during the Summer Session of 1985 at Eastern Illinois University, in our roach-infested rental home, my astute roommate Craig (S.) read from Mr. Lifton's book about the "Head Snap" and a "Grassy Knoll Assassin." I remember quipping to Craig something like, "Grassy Knoll Assassin? What are you talking about?"

Fast forward to 1993 when I was a young teacher at Waubonsie Valley High School in Aurora, Illinois. One of my students came up to me during class, held up *Best Evidence*, and asked me if I had ever read this book. "Well, no," I replied. She then told me she was going to a lecture by Mr. Lifton later that night in downtown Chicago. I told her to please get a picture with him and show me the next day – which she proudly did.

Not long after that day, I bought and read one of the most important books anyone can read. *Best Evidence*, quite honestly, changed my life. It opened my eyes to the harsh reality that not all is as it appears – especially when told "a story" by the U.S. Government.

I was so moved by his work, and the notion that President Kennedy's murder was more than just the modus operandi of a "lone nut," I sought to read every book I could get my hands on, be its thesis one of a lone gunman or a conspiracy. My thinking was that the truth probably lay somewhere in the middle. Naturally, without doubt, I now know the harsh truth is that Oswald was set up as "a patsy" – just as he said he was.

Needless to say, my wife quickly soured on the idea of my quest for knowledge, primarily due to the prohibitive cost of my quest, but also due to her practicality in the matter: "Kennedy's dead. Nothing will bring him back. Why bother?" I'm an historian. My brain does not allow such thoughts to percolate inside my brain.

Around 1993, I ordered a copy of his documentary, *Best Evidence: The Research Video*. I even went so far as to write Mr. Lifton a letter asking him if he could come speak to the students at Waubonsie Valley High School, to which he assented. Unfortunately, I was not able to raise any more than five dollars from my students, and I had to cancel. Boy, was he mad! Mr. Lifton told me he had already rearranged his schedule, and that if I wanted to reschedule, I was to call 1-800-Lecture. Do you know, that was so embarrassing – even now as I write this – that I never brought that up to him? Ever.

However, it all worked out in the end. I kept the correspondences he sent me, and one day in 2017, after speaking to my friend and colleague, Robbie R., about the idea of having our students interview Mr. Lifton, I reached out to him – and the rest is history.

Again – the point of the *David Lifton Project* was to share his all important research with the next generation of Americans, the youth of our nation; students sharing the importance of Mr. Lifton's work with other students. Though much of the student film covers the thesis of *Best Evi-*

dence, midway into the film, Mr. Lifton discusses the seeds of *Final Charade* – which sprouted in March of 1980.[1]

Point of fact, Mr. Lifton praised our students who interviewed him and later told me that he had been interviewed hundreds of times by professional news crews, and that the Hesperia USD students did as good a job as any of the previous professionals did. That was quite stunning to hear from such a prominent figure. But, our students are great!

Because of this project, Mr. Lifton and I ended up speaking every week at times, sometimes twice a week, though in the end (Late October 2022 until his passing on December 6, 2022), sadly not at all. Our initial conversations would revolve around updating his GoFundMe account – which I helped him to set up back on Friday, September 4, 2020, including the formal thanking of his contributors. Generally, our conversations would then revolve around his research past (*Best Evidence*) or present (*Final Charade*), but sometimes segue into personal discussions about my family, his family, etc.

One thing I will always remember was that Mr. Lifton liked to keep notes on his conversations. I would hear him typing away on the keyboard of his Mac Air as he would ask me to repeat my daughters' names and who did what for a living. The funny thing is, he constantly got my elder daughter confused with my younger one.

Sadly, I believe our last conversation on the phone was in mid-October of 2022. Thereafter, we communicated via text or email. I'm eternally grateful to Mr. Lifton for sharing his time and his knowledge with me.

I truly believe that Mr. Lifton's life would make quite a biography. After all, he is one of the top researchers and one of the Founding Scribes of the JFK Assassination Community. The following list includes the most prominent researchers which I would expect Mr. Lifton to agree with: Edward J. Epstein, Barry Ernest, Mary Ferrell, Jim Garrison, Robert Groden, Mark Lane, Jim Marrs, Sylvia Meagher, Fred T. Newcomb, Vince Palamara, Josiah Thompson, Col. L. Fletcher Prouty, Cyril Wecht, Harold Weisberg.[2]

Knowing a biography of this man may never happen, I include the following information to help enhance the historical record. Mr. Lifton was

---

1   Ibid. For the trailer, see: Canyon Ridge High School/Shadow Ridge School Production. "David Lifton Project." YouTube, 2018, 1:00 minute. Retrieved 6/30/2023: https://www.youtube.com/watch?v=IsrLgtFQjmQ.

2   Wikipedia: Category: Researchers of the Assassination of John F. Kennedy. Though this is an incomplete list, it's a start. A note to the reader: Wikipedia is not the best source for any topic, and although I would not "bet my life" on its veracity as a wholly truthful source, it is always my "go to" starting point for context whenever researching; thus its reference throughout this work. Hence, when cited, it's for providing the reader with said context only.

born (Wednesday, September 20, 1939)[3] and raised in Rockaway Beach, New York, on the western end of Long Island. He later moved to Los Angeles, Beverly Hills, Dana Point (Orange County, California), Dallas, and Las Vegas. For the longest time (Circa 1981-1995), he had an office on West Olympic Boulevard in Century City.

Now regarding his address in Las Vegas, Mr. Lifton's West Las Vegas apartment number was 1122. 1122! (He lived off of West Desert Inn Road.) I asked Mr. Lifton if he found that strange. He replied that he did not, and that he had not recognized the significance of the apartment number until our conversation. I then asked if he believed in fate – if that apartment was "meant to be" or "a sign" viz-a-viz numerology to which he replied, "No." He later survived a carjacking at night while returning home to this same apartment which he discusses below.

The following biographical information comes from our Wednesday, December 15, 2021 (58:40:23), conversation, in which Mr. Lifton delves into his life as a young man.

He had a girlfriend named Gina, a Marxist, whose dad was the youngest member of the Abraham Lincoln Brigade during the Spanish Civil War. Somehow he traveled to Miami. While in Miami at a youth hostel, a stranger asked "Does anybody want to go to Havana tomorrow?" Mr. Lifton obliged the stranger and stayed at the famous Hotel Nacional in 1958 – a few months before Castro took over.

In the Summer of 1961 (21 years old), Mr. Lifton used his Bar Mitzvah money to travel to Rotterdam, then Paris, via the Holland America Line.

He traveled to the Volkswagen factory in Wolfsburg and spent about $950 dollars for a brand new Beetle. Mr. Lifton used the VW to travel around Europe. He kept that car for sixteen years.

While in Paris, Mr. Lifton studied the French Language everyday at the Alliance Française de Paris.

Mr. Lifton saw the headline in the *International Herald Tribune* when the Berlin Wall went up on August 13, 1961. He later drove through the East German "transit corridor" and visited the wall.

The same week that Soviet Cosmonaut Yuri Gagarin (Wednesday, April 12, 1961) made his space flight, Mr. Lifton drove to Rome.[4]

He took a student charter to Israel, and then to the southern tip at Eilat where he went snorkeling in the Gulf of Aqaba.

---

3   DayoftheWeek.org.

4   Wikipedia: Yuri Gagarin.

As Mr. Lifton will describe in detail below, at the end of his sojourn to Europe, he brought his car to Marseilles, France, for shipment to the United States. He took a student flight via President Airlines, but it developed engine trouble and had to land in Shannon, Ireland. Mr. Lifton had to wait two or three days for the engine to be repaired.

Since there were two large groups waiting for the plane, there was a coin toss, and the student group lost out to the German farmers. The plane took off and crashed into the muddy River Shannon with no survivors. As Mr. Lifton reflected, he had no fear at the time, as all youth tend to sense no danger; they feel "invincible."

When his plane landed in Newfoundland, he remembered thinking that the European adventure was exciting, but he also felt that he did not have to travel anymore – because he had "been there, done that."

When Mr. Lifton finally arrived back at Cornell University, he felt that it was like a "human zoo"; a rat race of sorts.[5] The experience of traveling made him ask himself, "Why am I doing engineering physics?"

At Cornell, an elite school, Mr. Lifton was ranked 18/125 engineering students but graduated 35/37 in his class. Some of his fellow students were "super smart" – his words: Michael Hauser, later of NASA, and Malcolm Beasley, later a Stanford Provost. Mr. Lifton sarcastically noted that such students knew calculus before the other students even took the course, and that they "must have been reading the *Scientific American* when they were 7 years old."

He noted that he made it through the coursework successfully, and was glad he was part of the Engineering Physics School at Cornell University. Though he was not good enough to be Phi Beta Kappa, Mr. Lifton noted that he did pretty well, and "those [Cornell] professors were amazing."

Mr. Lifton was absolutely smitten with California, and UCLA was like "Heaven on Earth." UCLA was a great experience. He loved it and was proud to have attended there, however he realized that Cornell was harder than UCLA. As Mr. Lifton indicated, "I flunked courses at Cornell."

According to Mr. Lifton, physics is like applied mathematics. He remembered reading a lot of books at Cornell, including the one by Max Born the famous physicist.[6] By flunking courses, he learned to teach himself. Like "Martin Eden," Jack London's famous character, Mr. Lifton was an autodidact.

---

5   See Cornell.edu.
6   Wikipedia: Max Born.

Mr. Lifton had a paid internship at the North American plant in Downey, California, for NASA – however it was nothing short of a boondoggle according to him, where "guys were selling real estate" to while away the time. When he tried to leave out of boredom and a sense of integrity, his boss told him that he needed this vital experience in the field in order to get a job after he finished his master's degree at UCLA. To that, Mr. Lifton quipped, "experience doing nothing?"

Harrison A. Storms was Mr. Lifton's boss at NASA who later was fired due to the Apollo 1 tragedy in 1967.[7] Storms did not know what to do with Mr. Lifton at NASA – who was an idealist and actually wanted to work and learn something. Mr. Lifton stated that he was once assigned a "project to measure the boiling point of water."

When he needed to procure a device that measures temperatures using light (Pyrometer), Mr. Lifton found out that he had to order the device, and that it would take six months to get it. So, he figured out a way to get the part at North American's Los Angeles Division. When Mr. Lifton went to pick up the part, it was surreptitiously placed into a paper bag. This memory always made him laugh.

Regarding his parents, Mr. Lifton recalled how "my mother would make chopped liver for me – just as we had it on Friday nights. She would send it [by] express mail. It would just be defrosting as it arrived in Downey [from New York]. So, I had my chopped liver." His parents loved him very much.

Mr. Lifton's favorite quote was from a visiting Cornell professor, Mr. Kasimatis, and discusses the context below. He mentioned it 4-5 times during our conversations and laughed every time: "Mr. Lifton. The homework is meant to push a man over the border, not lift him out of the grave." Yes, Mr. Lifton devoted his life to the serious understanding of what really happened to President Kennedy, but he also knew how to laugh amidst the tragedy of his life's work.

THE CONVERSATIONS

Editor's Note: The recorded conversations between Mr. Lifton and I encompass a lot of information and topics – from his research, to his GoFundMe page, to my family, to my kids (He always asked how my kids were doing! Once, he even tutored my youngest child in Calculus over the phone.), to the weather, to politics, etc. Some of it is not related to Mr.

Lifton's research and thus the needs of this manuscript. I certainly do not want to waste time, money, or space in the book on such conversation.

Furthermore, Mr. Lifton was a meticulous and deeply thoughtful writer and would typically go over and over each sentence. I saw this with my own eyes during our sometimes weekly or even bi-weekly meetings which usually centered around updating his GoFundMe account, thanking his donors, updating his Facebook and Twitter accounts, etc.

He would repeatedly state and restate sentences he was preparing to post on his account to make sure they sounded correct. When this occurred in our JFK conversations, I omitted the repetitive stylistic gesticulations unless it added to the topic at hand.

Therefore, it's important to note that – where possible – with the use of ellipses, I truncated those parts of our conversations which I considered superfluous to the purpose at hand.

Lastly, I'm grateful that I had a chance to become friends with my mentor, and literary idol. Mr. Lifton had dedicated his life to the truth about the JFK Assassination, and stressed that there needed to be a modern, thorough investigation. That being said, our conversations were held in the sunset of this great man's life (age 81-83), and his memories were not as sharp as when he was younger. This he stated several times during our conversations.

Thus, and I state this with much love, reverence, and respect for my friend and mentor, what you are about to read and contemplate are Mr. Lifton's thoughts and theories which are clouded by the natural declinations of age – like faded old drapes drawn across America's window of history clumsily blocking a bright sun of pulsating truth – yet substantively as shocking, truthful, and clear as if Mr. Lifton is speaking to you in the present day.

For Jim Hoffman
1-6-21
David S Lifton

Praise for *Best Evidence*:

"*Best Evidence* is a prolix medical thriller that examines every shred of evidence several times over and serves at the very least as a comprehensive narrative of assassination, fact and theory . . . Much of Lifton's evidence is compelling. *Best Evidence* is a disturbing book." —*The Washington Star*

"A blockbuster . . . insistent and inescapable . . . David Lifton just grabs you by the throat and refuses to let you loose." —*The Washingtonian*

For Jim Hoffman,
Let's change
history
David S Lifton

(Inscription of My Copy of *Best Evidence*)

2020

SATURDAY, NOVEMBER 7, 2020

JH: One of the things I have been interested in since I was in my … 30s was – well, you already know this story, and I'll just say it quick[ly] … I'm interested in a lot of things, but one of the things that I'm really interested in is the Kennedy Assassination. A lot of reasons I can tell you, and I know you know this. My mother, I could call her up right now and say, "Kennedy," and she will start crying. [It's] very emotional for her….

DSL: Wow. Yeah….

JH: You know, she loved him … She was twenty one when he was killed. I was alive, but I was in her womb. So, I-

DSL: (Laughs)

JH: Was two months away [from being born], and I read an account somewhere that talked about this notion, but I do feel like [this connection to JFK, too].[8] I mean, I was alive – I was alive as a human entity, and I do feel … connected to that event … I know my mom cried for many, many weeks.

DSL: Yeah.

JH: And that had to have an impact on me.

DSL: Sure.

JH: And … I thought nothing of the Kennedy Assassination. I went to school, and I read the [text]book, "Lee Harvey Oswald shot Kennedy." End of story. Until 1985 when I was sitting in my college – our little [roach infested] house, and my friend [and roommate] Craig – I'll just use his first name – was reading your small…

---

8   This is not the article, but I do recall it being an opinion piece from Time magazine circa the release of JFK on December 20, 1991. See: Corliss, Richard. "Oliver Stone: Who Killed JFK?." Time, December 23, 1991. Retrieved 9/17/2023: https://content.time.com/time/subscriber/article/0,33009,974523-1,00.html.

DSL: Paperback edition....

JH: Paperback edition. It's real thick. And he's reading *Best Evidence*, and ... he was telling me about the Head Snap, the Grassy Knoll Assassin, and I'm like, "What are you talking about?" And I was a History major. So, I'm embarrassed to say, I knew *nothing* about that.

DSL: I don't know what they're doing today, but it's a shame if they don't teach the alternative interpretation of ... [the Kennedy Assassination]....

JH: Oh, no, they do not. Fast forward to about 1990, and I had a student at a school I was working at as a social studies teacher.[9] I remember her face, I remember her talking to me, and I just can't remember her name – which is fine. But, she came up to me [one day] and said, "Oh, my God, Mr. Hoffmann, have you seen this book?" And it was *Best Evidence* ... I said, "No ... I kind of remember because of the college days." But, I won't get into why I don't remember much from my college days. (Laughs) But ... [the student] was telling me, "Oh, yeah, I'm going tonight to Chicago to meet the author, David Lifton, and I'm going to hopefully get a picture with him." And as I recall, she showed me that picture the next day ... [The student] got to meet you ... Because of that student, I went out and bought *Best Evidence*. [My passion's] never ended ever since.

DSL: Yeah.

JH: I read the book. I've read it at least two or three times ... I've done more than just read it, I've studied it, and I teach the basic principles from it. Because of that book, I ended up reading ... *every book* [about the JFK Assassination] I could get my hands on just to be able to say, "I'm open-minded about this ... [and] not narrow-minded."

DSL: Right.

JH: Let me just list a couple of books that I've read ... I'm sure you know a lot of these guys. For example ... the second book I bought was *Rush to Judgment* by Mark Lane.[10]

DSL: Good book.

JH: I then, now this would be around 1992-93, when Oliver Stone's film [*JFK*/1991] came out. And I read *High Treason* by Robert Groden.[11] I read-

9   Waubonsie Valley High School in Aurora, Illinois, a part of Community Unit School District #204 – 40 miles west of Chicago.
10   Lane, Mark. *Rush to Judgment: A Critique of the Warren Commission's Inquiry into the Murders of President John F. Kennedy, Officer J.D. Tippit and Lee Harvey Oswald*. Holt, Rinehart and Winston, 1966, 478 pages.
11   Groden, Robert J. and Livingstone, Harrison Edward. *High Treason: The Assassination of*

DSL: Yeah, yeah, right. Go ahead….

JH: I read *Plausible Denial* by Mark Lane. I read, of course, *On the Trail of the Assassins* by Jim Garrison.[12] And as you … told me before, you met Jim Garrison and worked with … [him]?

DSL: Yes. I met him. I spent an evening with him….

JH: OK … I don't know how you feel about this, but I read *what I thought* was an important book by Col. L. Fletcher Prouty, *JFK: The CIA, Vietnam, and the Plot to Assassinate John F. Kennedy.*[13] I felt that was an important book for various reasons, one being he talked about how the Pentagon was connected to that [event]. And then of course, you know-

DSL: You left out *Six Seconds in Dallas*….14

JH: You know what? That's one book I haven't read. Of course, it's one of the most important books. And also-

DSL: It was an important book … I think we've gone beyond that with *Best Evidence*. But, yeah, it was an important book.

JH : And wasn't Epstein's book as well, would you say?

DSL: Yes!15 The book…. What happened was [that] the Warren Report was published in September [of] '64…. And then came the 26 Volumes of the Warren Commission in November [of] '64. And then the first – what we call the – books about the Kennedy Assassination in my thinking begin in July 1966 with Epstein's *Inquest* and then two months later, Mark Lane's *Rush to Judgment*….

JH: And I will admit, I did not read the whole thing, but I read most of the summary of the Warren Report.[16] I did not – I know you've read every volume….

DSL: Well, well, yeah, it's like buying a set of encyclopedias…. Yes, I have read most of them because once I made the discoveries that I did [e.g. "surgery of the head area"], [and] that there's photographic evidence of

President John F. Kennedy: What Really Happened. Conservatory Press, 1989, 469 pages.

12   Lane, Mark. *Plausible Denial: Was the CIA Involved in the Assassination of JFK?* Thunder's Mouth Press, 1991, 393 pages. Garrison, Jim. *On the Trail of the Assassins.* Sheridan Square, 1988, 342 pages.

13   Prouty, Col. L. Fletcher. *JFK: The CIA, Vietnam, and the Plot to Assassinate John F. Kennedy.* Carol Publishing Group, 1992, 366 pages.

14   Thompson, Josiah. *Six Seconds in Dallas: A Micro-Study of the Kennedy Assassination.* B. Geis Associates, 1967, 323 pages.

15   Epstein, Edward Jay. *Inquest: The Warren Commission and the Establishment of Truth.* The Viking Press, 1966, 220 pages.

16   Warren Commission. *The Official Warren Commission Report on the Assassination of President John F. Kennedy.* Doubleday & Company, Inc., 1964, 888 pages. Note that several corporate publishers like Doubleday, The Associated Press, and *The New York Times* published the summary volume.

assassins firing from the front – which I believed I could see with my own eyes in some of the enlargements, then I bought the 26 volumes.... But, let's not leave out the most important ... event which was [when] I was at UCLA, and I met this law professor who had been on the Warren Commission [i.e. Wesley Liebeler].... He and I struck up a relationship, and I made regular meetings and visits to his office.... Basically, he was my dialogue opponent.[17] He asked me to attend his class. Then, in October of 1966, when I had known him for about a year, a year and a half, I make this whopping discovery that ... really is the solution to the crime – which is that the president's body was altered. I mean, anybody who watches *Law & Order* understands the importance of the autopsy *in any murder*.[18] The autopsy is a description of the body at the time ... [of] death, and it describes the wounds and the cause of death ... by basically deconstructing the body, opening it up, finding the bullets and all that ... The notion that you can have a conspiracy, the autopsy report was falsified ... sounds a little bit weird, if not possible because you'd have to recruit all [of] these people connected with the ... [crime]. But the fact that instead of ... falsifying the autopsy report, this crime was engineered on the idea of falsifying the foundation for the autopsy report. That is, what were these people examining in [the] autopsy? The body of the president. So somebody had the bright idea that if we kill the president, and we want to falsify the autopsy, we don't have to go and recruit all [of] these doctors. We just have to get to the body, take the bullets out, mess with the wounds – which renders the body a medical forgery, and send it to the autopsy room. And then the doctors there, if they believe what they're seeing, will be honest ... [for] they've been deceived by an altered body. That's what *Best Evidence* is all about....

JH: That's....

DSL: *Best Evidence* is based on the idea of my discovery that Kennedy's body was altered in the five hour period between the time of the shooting at 12:30 PM, Central Standard Time in Dallas, and the time the autopsy was conducted at 8 o'clock at the United States Naval Hospital at Bethesda, Maryland. In between those two points in time, the president's body ... was rushed to the hospital after the shooting. He was pronounced dead, then his body was placed in a coffin. That coffin was brought out to Love Field in Dallas [and] placed aboard Air Force One. Then, the nation was [mourning] ... Walter Cronkite – everybody was commenting on

17   Wikipedia: Wesley Liebeler.
18   Wikipedia: Law & Order.

what happened in Dallas. There were wire service reports. The plane lands at 6 o'clock. The whole nation watches as the coffin is put on a forklift or mechanical lift–

JH: Yeah....

DSL: And it's lowered from the rear entrance of Air Force One down to the ground level.... On that lift is Jacqueline Kennedy and Bobby Kennedy, and it's placed into a Navy ambulance which went to Bethesda Naval Hospital where the autopsy began at 8 [PM]. So, this is like a magician's trick. I discovered the evidence that between those two points in time, when the murder occurred ... and the observation at Parkland Hospital, and the time of the Bethesda autopsy five and a half hours later, *somebody altered the body*. The bullets were removed and there was surgery. And by that surgery, I don't mean clinical, life-saving surgery, it was what they call *pathological surgery*. Surgery done during an autopsy to remove the top of the head, take out the brain, [etc.].... And that's where my story starts where I understood something happened to the body in that period. I discovered the FBI report that says that when the body was taken out of the coffin at Bethesda Naval Hospital, it was ... "apparent that there had been surgery of the head area, namely in the top of the skull." And, that's where my story begins. I brought that to Professor Liebeler at UCLA, who I had now known [for] a year and a half, and we were arguing about what this evidence meant ... the head snap, and the smoke on the Grassy Knoll – and he was just blown away.... He was astounded. Two things: First of all, that I made the discovery.... But, second of all, that there in the public record ... in an FBI report was evidence of post-mortem, illegal surgery to the body of Kennedy – prior to the autopsy.

JH: I've got a couple of questions.... He [Liebeler] kept saying to you, "But, David, there's no evidence of that." And so, when you brought this to him, evidence of a – something other than Oswald shot him, that helped to add to the fact he was astounded. Because here you're showing him actual evidence that the body was altered. Is that correct?

DSL: Well, let me be specific here. What happened during our year and a half relationship before I made the discovery was [that] we went back and forth on the evidence of whether Oswald acted alone, or whether he was even involved at all. And what happened is that ... Liebeler and I were walking down a path together you might say, and he got interested just like I was. I was quoting the autopsy report to show that the wounds must have been altered.... He was also looking at the same thing.... There 21 was this conundrum: How could this ... have happened? And then ... I made a discovery in an FBI report that the FBI said "that there had been surgery of the head area." And that's what blew him [Liebeler] away – not just the concept that it had been done. Sometimes, I think that he may have even conceived of it before I did. That was part of the puzzle. The other part was that it was in the public record. This FBI report had been released a year before and was at the National Archives. And there it was, buried in the sentence in the third page of the report written by the two FBI agents who attended the autopsy.[19] That when the body was taken out of the coffin at Bethesda, end of the line, it was quoted [by the FBI agents as stated above]. What the Hell did that mean? I ... called up the FBI agent who wrote that report almost immediately; as soon as I read it ... November [2], 1966. I read it to him, and he said he couldn't comment on it because of, you know, the Bureau's regulations. But, he said, and this was unforgettable – and it's in my book. He said, "The report stands." *He stood behind that report.*[20]

JH: Yes.

DSL: So, then the question becomes, "Well, what did it mean?" And then, within a month – I'm skipping a lot of detail here – I learned *what it meant.* That the report was written based upon the FBI agents [Sibert and O'Neill] taking notes in the autopsy room at the time the coffin was opened.... It [what they wrote] represented what lawyers would call an "oral utterance." In other words, if you say something, and I'm making notes, then I write a report about it ... I'm recording *in a report* your oral utterances. Of course, if I had a tape recorder, it would be a perfect transcript.... That's what happened. These FBI *agents not understanding what it meant–*

JH: Yeah.

DSL: Made notes that when the body was taken out of the coffin, it was quote, "apparent that there was surgery of the head area." And it turns out that the reason they wrote those things was because the chief autopsy surgeon who was right there [Humes] and conducting the examination said it. And so then I called up the autopsy surgeon and that's a chapter – that's all in *Best Evidence* [Chapter 10].... And I read it to him, and he was as-

19   James W. Sibert and Francis X. O'Neil. Though they sent a teletype to FBI Headquarters a few hours after the autopsy, their famous report was dictated on Tuesday, November 26, 1963.
20   Wednesday, "November 2, 1966, had been extraordinary" according to Mr. Lifton. (Page 246) On that one day, he contacted both Commander James J. Humes (autopsy doctor) and James W. Sibert (FBI agent). See Chapter 10 of *Best Evidence*, "The Liebeler Memorandum," pages 240-246 of the Carroll & Graf edition. See also Chapter 12 of *Best Evidence*, "An Oral Utterance," pages 301-304 of the Carroll & Graf edition.

tounded. He was astounded because he didn't know it was in the record. And I said, "Well, what are you going to say when there's a new investigation?" He says, "I don't know what I'm going to say." (Laughs)

JH: Wow. Let me say this: You spent a lot of time and money interviewing key witnesses to support your contentions, and your theories, and the facts that you present in *Best Evidence: The Research Video*.

DSL: Correct.

JH: That is *fascinating*. I used to use that [the video] in the classroom. It's fascinating to watch them [eyewitnesses].... [Through their statements] you show how the body was altered from Point A – Dallas to Point B – Bethesda Naval Hospital. Correct me if I'm wrong, when the coffin came off the plane, in your book – which blew me away, [you state that] that coffin was actually empty....

DSL: Yeah, by that time ... the people involved in this affair had gotten hold of the body, and I can prove that the body was not in that [ornamental] coffin.... It [body] arrived twenty minutes before the coffin. So, if you had a camera positioned at Bethesda Naval Hospital, first would arrive a black hearse with some men in plain clothes who quickly run into the [autopsy] room (Laughs) with a shipping casket. That's the body entering Bethesda Naval Hospital. Then, twenty minutes later, a Navy ambulance coming from Andrews Air Force Base drives up with Jackie Kennedy and Bobby Kennedy next to the big Dallas coffin – which unknown to them *is empty*.... So, I made a timeline and showed what was going on here – that somehow the body had been removed from the casket prior to the takeoff of Air Force One in Dallas.

JH: To make a point of distinction. The men in "plain clothes" were carrying a cheap shipping casket that you'd-

DSL: Yes.

JH: Ship a body in. And when Jackie came [to Bethesda], she had a ten thousand dollar ornamental casket.

DSL: That's right.

JH: Totally different.

DSL: Yes, a totally different casket....

JH: Totally different. So, I'd like to just say this ... if you haven't ever read a book *about* the Kennedy Assassination and you're interested, *absolutely* start with *Best Evidence* and then go from there. If you've read different books, but you haven't read *Best Evidence*, you *must read it*. It's the lynchpin. That's the most important book ... I've read all [of] these different books. This is the *one book* that's not been refuted. This is the lynchpin [of the solution] to the whole thing. Also, I will add – I'm kind of a fan of Joe Rogan–

DSL: Yes.

JH: [And] he has millions of fans, and he says ... [this] with Oliver Stone [in his studio]. They both say they've read the book.... Joe Rogan says that [he was blown away] ....[21]

DSL: Well, you know, I think – I'd like to add one thing here ... a student of science or engineering – will find it [*Best Evidence*] an easier read than those who are not. Because in science and in physics or engineering [disciplines], they have what they call "before and after" situations. So ... the professor's up there and [says in lecture] "Here's a black box," and he draws it on the blackboard. "Now, I've put a signal in at the input end, and something else comes out at the output end. And, what happens in between can turn the original signal into a different signal." OK? That's what I call a "before and after" situation, and it occurs in physics when two particles collide.... They say, "Well ... before there were these two particles, and then they collided, and then we get this rainbow effect." ... They compare the before and the after. This whole business with the body struck me as relatively easy to understand because it was simply another before and after situation. Only, instead of a black box with an electronic signal, it's the flesh and bones of *the President of the United States*. The wounds started out this way, and then at this later point in time it was another way. And so, it was a before and after and kind of like, I was a detective out there looking for the transfer function.[22] .... You could say, "Well, you were just looking for evidence of body alteration – *and that's true.*" But, the analogy to what I learned in engineering and specifically in engineering physics was *absolutely applicable* point by point because conceptually, this was a before and after situation on the ... body of the President of the United States.

21   JRE Clips. "Joe Discusses the JFK Assassination with Oliver Stone." YouTube, 2020, 09:24. (Circa 05:10-05:40) Retrieved 10/10/2023: https://www.youtube.com/watch?v=nQuEUsvy8nM. JR: "Did you read David Lifton's book, *Best Evidence*?" OS: "Years ago, yeah." JR: "That's what got me into the Kennedy Assassination." OS: "Yeah." Rogan later says that reading the book made him "so depressed" because it was true.

22   Wikipedia: Transfer Function.

JH: OK. So, let's go to January 1981 – *Best Evidence* was published. It was on the *New York Times* Bestseller List for something like nine weeks.

DSL: Three months. Three months.

JH: Three months. It had been published by four separate publishers….

DSL: Now the importance of the Carroll & Graf Edition [1988] was that's when I had obtained the autopsy photographs … I published them as an appendix, and then wrote about how I got a hold of them – which is an interesting story…. And *that's* what blew people away. So, now I had a whole second audience. The first audience, I am sure in '81, was interested in and fascinated by the idea that there had been what they call a "strategic deception" executed in Dallas on November 22. A strategic deception is much more involved than simply saying, "Oh, there was a second assassin." It's the falsification of the *entire appearance* of the crime at the time, and then the records left behind. And they did that by focusing on the body. Then, I come along and get these pictures years later. I included them in the Carroll & Graf Edition, and that got me a whole new generation of readers who now could look at the pictures at the back [for corroboration of body alteration]. And also the advent of the Internet cannot be ignored. Roughly 1994 or … [1995] when, for the first time, instead of arguing with your neighbor about this, or somebody you knew at a coffee shop, *it's world wide*. And so there were discussion groups, and it's – it's all over the Internet [these] discussions about this issue.

JH: I want to get to *Final Charade* – your next book, but before that, just a quick comment. When I was at Waubonsie Valley High School in Aurora [IL] from '86 to 1995–[23]

DSL: Yeah.

JH: Every year with another teacher, a guy named Mark [P.] … he was a trained X-ray technician during the Vietnam War.

DSL: Yeah.

JH: We would present [the JFK Assassination] … in May in honor of President Kennedy's birthday which is in May – May 29th, 1917. I would present the historical evidence using your book. He [Mark] would present the medical/scientific evidence using the pictures from your book.

DSL: Yeah. (Smiles)

---

23   Wikipedia: Waubonsie Valley High School. The school is located some 40 miles west of Chicago.

JH: Man, we blew those kids away.[24] We would have literally about a hundred and fifty kids an hour.

DSL: Wow.

JH: All day. Back in those days, they [school officials] allowed you to do stuff like that: free thinking-

DSL: Yeah.

JH: Kind of like [the] Berkeley Free Speech Movement. And so, we would probably service … five hundred kids a year.

DSL: Wow.

JH: We did that for probably … [4] years … something like that.

DSL: But, what I had discovered was the essence of the deception. It was not altering the type-written autopsy report, but what the report was based on: the body. So, the crime of killing Kennedy … consists of killing him, that is putting bullets *into his body*, and then covertly extracting them prior to the start of the autopsy by eight o'clock that night.… But, that's the principle of it. The body was altered prior to autopsy, and that lawyers are trained to go with the best evidence, and that the best evidence in a murder case is the body of the victim.

JH: So, *Final Charade,* you actually – I was shocked – you started it around the time [that] *Best Evidence* was published. Is that correct … ?

DSL: Umm, about – yeah within a year. Yes … The publisher took me to dinner. You know, they loved the book. They were so happy with the commercial success. Now, we want you to write another one. (Laughs) A sequel. And I … honestly, I didn't want to. But, they gave me money, and I had to pay the rent, and I said, "OK." I guess in the sequel, I will focus on – and my primary objective in the beginning was – the shooting of [Governor] Connally … I had to come up with an explanation for why his body looked the way it did. And one thing led to another, and so, that's what happened.… You're right. It started within a year. But, if I were to type out a chronology of everything that happened since … when I really got to work on the sequel seriously [approximately mid-1990s], and the breakthroughs – it's a whole story, another whole story of breakthroughs and insights. And … yes, so that's … gone on for many years, and now

---

24   This annual JFK Assassination presentation was started around 1992 and continued until 1995 when I left Illinois for California. Mark and I would present the material all day in what I facetiously dubbed the "Entertainment Center" – which was a large room equal in size to about 4 classrooms or so. As the presentation spread in popularity, by 1995, we probably educated on average 500 plus students per day for four years. I'm still very proud of this feat.

we have this book called *Final Charade* – which … doesn't suggest a solution. I think it *is the solution* to the Kennedy Assassination because it tells the full story of Lee Oswald. Who he was? How he got involved in this thing? … You have to really understand what's going on with the CIA files [on Oswald], and how they got him. Here, you have a kid who wants to go to the Soviet Union … for a personal adventure – which he does. Instead of coming back and writing up this manuscript about his personal adventure, he ends up getting pre-selected as the assassination patsy in a murder that's gonna take place a year and four months later.[25] That's what happened. That's the tragedy of Oswald. He was a U.S. Intelligence agent with a personal agenda to start a career as a writer….

JH: I'd like to add … that at one point you were really close with his widow, Marina Oswald. Is that correct?

DSL: Yes. Oh, she used to call me all the time once *Best Evidence* was published – many, many times…. She understood that *Best Evidence* proved that her husband was innocent. She understood that. And she was always – I mean, she was wracked with guilt. She'd turn on the TV, and there was … somebody making a joke … it was in the culture to make jokes about Oswald as the … assassin. And she knew her husband loved President Kennedy. So, she [Marina] reached out to me. We got to know one another. Subsequently, she sat for a filmed interview done by a very competent and well-known cinematographer. He posted some of those interviews on *Hard Copy*, and they are available … on the Internet today.[26]

JH: Correct me if I'm wrong … there was a movie made about Marina Oswald, and you were in that film as a [real life] character. Because you … were friends with her. Were–

DSL: Yeah….

JH: You part of the – did you help write the screenplay for that?

DSL: *Fatal Deception*.[27]

JH: That's right, *Fatal Deception*….

---

25   As discussed in more detail below, Mr. Lifton believed that Lee Harvey Oswald, a fan of Jack London, read his book, *Martin Eden*, and it inspired him to become a spy, defect to the Soviet Union, and then write a book about the experience.
26   The specific descriptions of these interviews are cited below.
27   Wikipedia: *Fatal Deception: Mrs. Lee Harvey Oswald*. Though a TV drama, I highly recommend watching it. Helena Bonham Carter and Frank Whaley readily capture the spirit of Marina and Lee which makes the movie powerful. The story encapsulates Marina's life – including the friendship between Mr. Lifton and Marina Oswald.

DSL: What happened was, I was approached by a producer in Hollywood who wanted to do a story. He sat down, and we talked … I said, "Look. I'll tell you what I know, but you have to pledge [to] me not to put all this in your project because then I won't have a book."

JH: Right….

DSL: So, we … got to talking, and he wrote the script, and then at some point he said to me, "You know, we want to put you in the script." (Laughs) So, I said, "OK." … Of course, it's greatly compressed. You cannot – in a hundred and twenty page script – capture … something that was going on for a decade and a half…. So, Marina's in it … and it captures her angst… She had the same problem I had as a researcher in the beginning. I mean … she knows her husband loved President Kennedy, and [yet] she's in a culture where she turns on the radio and TV everyday – and he's portrayed *as this monster*. Well, he wasn't a monster. [Lee Harvey Oswald] was a very idealistic American who wanted to be a writer and went to the Soviet Union *to have an adventure* … I went to Europe the summer he was in Russia in 1961 … *I had an adventure*. I was in Berlin the week after the wall went up … I drove through Checkpoint Charlie and spent an afternoon in [East Berlin].[28]

JH: If I'm not mistaken, is that when you tried to fly back, and you almost died in a plane crash? Or is that a different [trip] …?

DSL: No, no, no. That's … the same trip. I was there, and then I flew back. I was in … Europe and to France, Germany, Rome, flew to Israel. Spent two weeks in Israel. Then [I] had to take my Volkswagen which I purchased … at the factory for nine hundred and fifty dollars.

JH: Wow.

DSL: Then, I had to bring it to Paris for shipment back to the United States … for … the beginning of the fall term of my senior year at Cornell. And I had to get on a charter flight. The flight developed engine trouble over the English Channel. They had to "feather" the engine [and] land at Shannon, Ireland, and for two days we were there while the engines were fixed…. There were two planes and both [with] President Airlines…. They were fixed, and they had a coin toss to decide who would get on the first flight…. The coin went up, and if I was making a movie, I'd show that coin going round and round and landing. And it was the other group, the German farmers, [who won the toss]. So, they got on the plane-

28 Wikipedia: Checkpoint Charlie.

JH: Wow.

DSL: And it took off and crashed into the Shannon River – and everybody died.... That's on [the front page of] *The New York Times*, September 10, 1961.... I took the next flight. We all got on the next flight, and there was a lot of nervousness, you know....[29]

JH: Oh, yeah....

DSL: Yeah. That's what happened.

JH: So, I want to ... bring ... [the conversation] up to modern times. You've been working on *Final Charade*. A couple of things. My partner and I, Robbie [R.] ... we interviewed you with some students....

DSL: I liked that.

JH: [The film] was screened in London.[30] ... Also, you have a GoFundMe page....

DSL: Yeah.

JH: You're what, 81 [years old] now?

DSL: Yeah.

JH: You're ... up there in years ... [and trying to] finish this important research. Basically, it's [*Final Charade*] gonna be ... in my opinion, the last book that's ever gonna be written that really will tell us what really happened that day. Now, you don't give names, but you're gonna give "The How?" of this plot.

DSL: Correct.

JH: Most importantly now. You called me up a couple of days ago and you said, "My, God! This happened to me." I wanted to share this with the audience because it shows that ... even though you're 81 [years old], you've got all [of] this energy-

DSL: (Laughs and smiles)

JH: You're still kickin' ... What happened to you? Can you tell us the story?

DSL: Yeah, I was carjacked.

JH: And you live in Vegas right?

DSL: Right now, I live in Vegas … I lived in Dallas for a year. Did an oral history with the Sixth Floor Museum. Got a lot of work done … I had my reasons for wanting to move to Vegas.… I've been working like the Dickens on the book. And when you say "working on *Final Charade*"– it's not always writing chapters. It's … continuing the research-

JH: Yeah….

DSL: On the assassination and figuring out, "Well, how the Hell am I going to tell this part of the story?" You've got to turn it into a narrative. It's not enough just to have data. You have to make it a good read. So, I'm living here in Vegas and my habit everyday – I'm a night person. I go to bed at five in the morning [and] get up at noon; whatever. One o'clock, then I'm workin'. Well, anyway, I like to get away from here, from the residence, so I go to this diner … I do my work for three to four hours and now it's ten o'clock [PM], [and] the waitress says, "You know, David, it's time to go. Close it up." So, I get in my car, [and] I leave with my computer bag … I get into the car, and it's about 10:05. I just did a chronology on this earlier today. And I get into the car. Make a phone call to a friend. We talk for about twenty five minutes.… And then I started the engine and drove the *five minutes* back to the *gated community* where I live.… So, I pull up [and] punch the digital code into the little device. The gate raises, and I drive my car through to my assigned parking place … I pull into my … space, cut the engine, get out of my car with my computer in my left hand – the bag – and the car keys in my right hand, and as I walk away from the car, there are these three guys I noticed when I pulled in. They looked like the residents there.… But now, one of them is facing me, and he has a drawn gun … a 9mm Glock.[31] I'm looking right down the barrel of a Glock.

JH: My God.

DSL: And he says, "I want your car keys." So, I had to give him my car keys cause it was a simple choice: I mean if I (Laughs) tried to argue about it, I'd be dead. Then, he says, "I want you to lie down on the ground right here on the asphalt." And … while I was lying down on the asphalt, and the other guy had the gun still on me, one of his associates placed a paper mask over my license plate. So, it made it impossible to identify my car by its license plate – cause they put on fake alpha-numeric numbers-

JH: Hmm….

31   Wikipedia: Glock.

DSL: Across my license plate. And then … they got into the car, and … the last thing he shouted … [was], "Stay lying on the ground!" You know, implying that I'd get hurt if I tried to get up. But as soon as I heard the engine go away from the area … I immediately got up and walked over to the sidewalk … and I said to this guy who was walking his dog, "Did you see what just happened to me?" And he (Laughs)-

JH: (Laughs)

DSL: I don't think he comprehended. But I immediately dialed 911, and the Las Vegas Police Department – a patrol car came over. And then the next day, they brought me these – a scrapbook full of pictures … I immediately identified the assailant. There he was … I have a question for them [LVPD] next week.… Why the Hell don't you arrest this guy again – cause he already had a mugshot? And find out: What did they do with David Lifton's car?

JH: (Laughs)

DSL: You know (Laughs) because I don't have wheels right now, and … I don't want to buy a car if I don't have to buy a car. On the other hand, maybe these guys stripped it of all its parts. I don't know what they did with it. The officer tried to say, "Oh, they just wanted to go joyriding." I don't think so because I did some Internet research and there have been other – what they call – "parking lot carjack[ing]s in the area."

JH: Hmm.

DSL: So, this is not new to this area [West Las Vegas]. So, these guys cased the area … [and] these cars lined up … hundreds of cars around the residential complex, and it's like an open jewelry box. That's what it is. It's like an open jewelry box … It was only ten o'clock, ten … forty at night. The police were there very quickly … but what could they do…?

JH: I hope it gets resolved. Well, thank God you're OK.… I'd like to say, you know for me, I'm … in my mid-fifties, I really appreciate [you]. You devoted your whole life to this. If it wasn't for you, and some of these other … [researchers], we would not know … anything really about Kennedy's assassination … When I was in high school, [I] just assumed, "Oh, Oswald shot Kennedy." End of story.

DSL: Correct. Yeah.

JH: It's [much] more than that. So, I appreciate from the bottom of my heart what you've done.… I can imagine you've made a lot of sacrifices to do this research and to write *Best Evidence,* and you're now in the process of trying to wrap up *Final Charade....* As I said, as Robbie said, my buddy Robbie and I, when we interviewed you [with the students], we cannot wait to read that book! (Laughs) So, anyway, do you have anything you'd like to add, to say...?

DSL: Well ... I think the thing I'd like to say ... is that when President Kennedy visited Dallas on November 22, 1963, and as he was walking down the steps with Jackie from the rear part of the plane ... [think of the paradox of] the roaring crowd that was there to greet him ... [yet] in that crowd and on his Secret Service detail, were people who were prepared *to murder him....* [People] who were involved in the original crime. And to them ... Kennedy was misrepresented and misunderstood to be someone who was selling out the country, doing bad things. You know, the crime was probably pitched on the idea that he [JFK] wanted a treaty with the Soviet Union, that he was [therefore] a traitor. All [of] this garbage ... that's believed by these extremists.... Therefore, they approached this as something that was a *good thing to do.* Important because Kennedy was a communist; a secret communist. And that's a bunch of garbage. And it's junk. And it comes from ignorant people. But anyway ... the thing that we're dealing with in arranging his murder, was a very, very clever modus operandi.

JH: Uhh, huh.

DSL: Which comes from the highest levels of [U.S.] Intelligence. Who the heck ever thinks of falsifying a body to conceal the murder? I mean, in history, I know of one case where they falsified a body in World War II and floated ... it ashore in Spain-[32]

JH: Correct.

DSL: To mislead the Nazis as to where the Invasion of Sicily would occur.

JH: Yes.

DSL: That's the closest I know. But anyway, so in that group at the airport ... and I've spoken to some of those agents – and I have my own beliefs about who was involved in this.... Most of them have passed away. Luckily, I'm living at 81 [years old].... Of course, I want to finish *Final Charade.* But, if you listen to the Dallas Police Radio Transmissions, which I've studied very carefully, there's a tremendous *drama* about it *to me* because you hear this crime [unfold].... After all, they've arranged for Oswald – the

32   Wikipedia: Operation Mincemeat.

man who lived in the Soviet Union for two and a half years – to be in Dealey Plaza in the building. This whole thing has been arranged … Kennedy was invited to Dallas. Then, "Are you gonna have a motorcade?" "Yes!" He wants a motorcade. The whole thing is arranged so [that] it's a crime with a built-in cover up.… It was planned from the outset to falsify the evidence and sell this false story to the American public.… If you want to see how that's done, you read the original UPI and AP dispatches – just as they rolled off the ticker.[33] And, I have them. And you see how it [the plot] worked.… Some of the mystery is removed. But, you realize that during Kennedy's thousand days [in office], when he was planning to have peace with Russia, and not have a nuclear war, these people were planning *to kill him*. I mean, it's really amazing. His [JFK's] whole life was devoted, at that time, to making sure that we don't have a nuclear war … and he *succeeded*. No nuclear war. Peace treaty with … Russia. Avoiding nuclear war in the … Caribbean in October '62 – the Cuban Missile Crisis.

JH: Uhh, huh….

DSL: But, *these guys* – they also were carrying briefcases, and they also had papers, and they were planning *how to get rid of President Kennedy* and make Lyndon Johnson the president. I mean, that's kind of a historical synopsis of what's going on here.

JH: You mentioned the military intelligence, and it definitely sounds like an intelligence operation, without a doubt – to me anyways.

DSL: Yes.

JH: I had a student when I was at Waubonsie Valley High School where I used to give those [JFK] presentations. He had an [interesting] uncle, and I remember the kid's name, Jason – I won't use his last name.… One day, he came up to me and he said.… "My uncle works in the Pentagon – in … black ops."

DSL: Sure.

JH: Whatever that's called. I said, "Really?" And he said, "Yeah. And … [my uncle] told me this story … He said … in the early to mid-1960s, it was after Kennedy had been killed, my uncle told me [that] he went into the cafeteria" – there's probably several in the Pentagon – "and he said he sat down … and there was all this brass … everywhere–"

DSL: Yeah.

JH: Admiral[s], general[s], whatever. And you have to know this kid. He's "a card." He was a … [comedian], and I can imagine his uncle was the same way. "And he [my uncle] just said out loud, "So, who shot Kennedy anyways?""

DSL: Yeah.

JH: And he [my uncle] said, "You could hear a pin drop," and all these–

DSL: (Laughs)

JH: "Brass stared at him with the 'death stare.'"

DSL : Yeah.

JH: "And he [my uncle] said, 'I never brought up the subject again.'" (Laughs) So–

DSL: Well, I will … .

JH: Speaks volumes.

DSL: (Laughs) That's very interesting. I'd like to say again that another conclusion I have come to is that this was primarily a Dallas plot. I mean, it's Dallas officials who were involved. The Dallas Police Chief. The Dallas Deputy Chief [of Police].… It's certain people at Parkland Hospital. In other words, you could not have done this scheme in Boston and Cambridge where Kennedy was much beloved. Or in New York City. It's not gonna happen.… William Manchester, although he had the wrong particulars completely, was correct about the Dallas climate being hate filled.[34] If you pump all of this poison into the [situation] … I think it was pretty easy to recruit for this plot-

JH: Hmm, hmm.

DSL: Because … the population at large had been sold this bill of goods that Kennedy was this *terrible person*. Well, he wasn't–

JH: Right.

DSL: That was just not the truth at all. Most of these folks were alive because Kennedy avoided a nuclear war during his thousand days. And that's something that's generally appreciated. When you look at the rearview mirror to history, *until this crime is resolved*, the nation cannot get back to what it … originally was.

JH: Hmm, hmm.

---

34   Manchester, William. *The Death of a President: November 20-November 25, 1963.* Harper and Row, 1967, 781 pages. See also: Wikipedia: William Manchester and *The Death of a President.*

DSL: It really can't. Because … we can go through the Johnson Administration. You can't study the Johnson years without realizing that the [Vietnam] War was escalated suddenly-

JH: Hmm, hmm.

DSL: Within a year … Kennedy had no intention of going into Vietnam like that. Then you go down the [ensuing] presidents one after another after another. But, I'm not saying that any of those guys – subsequent presidents – were involved in any kind of a cover up.

JH: No.

DSL: I'm just saying that the foundation of this building called … "our history" or "our government" has been … soiled with this fake history.

JH: Hmm, hmm.

DSL: So, it's illusory. It's not the truth about what happened. When this is solved, we can maybe get back to the business of telling the truth – cause then we'll have a genuine history even though it will have a very dark spot in Dallas....

JH: So, I'm gonna throw this at you. I know you don't agree with me, but believe … that Kennedy's … burial vault is empty. What do you think about that?[35]

DSL: No. I believe it contains the altered body of Kennedy just as it was placed in there … at his funeral on November 25, 1963. I don't see [any reason for this].... In other words … the deception occurs by altering the body which then can be examined, buried, whatever. It's not necessary to rob the body a second time – it's already been altered. You know what I mean?

JH: Hmm.

DSL: The evidence has been altered once at autopsy. It's finished … on the night of eleven twenty two.

JH: I just feel like if they [plotters] were to get rid of the body, then they could always – like the brain disappeared – they could say, "Oh!–"

DSL: The brain did disappear.

JH: "What happened? Oh, wow!"

---

35   See: Arlington National Cemetery. "President John Fitzgerald Kennedy Gravesite." Retrieved   10/13/2023:   https://www.arlingtoncemetery.mil/explore/monuments-and-memorials/president-john-f-kennedy-gravesite. See also: Wikipedia: John F. Kennedy Eternal Flame.

DSL: (Laughs)

JH: "We'll never know now." You know …

DSL: Well–

JH: Maybe they buried him [JFK] at sea or something. I don't know.

DSL: No, no. No, no. I think … his altered body [is there]. Look. The Kennedy case. This will never happen. He will never be exhumed in my lifetime – if ever. But, if they did exhume, Jim, they would find the body that was reassembled and put together-

JH: Wow.

DSL: At the end of the false autopsy on the night of November twenty second.

JH: Wow.

DSL: That's the crime. The crime is altering the body before the autopsy, and then for the photographs doing some "monkey business" at the back of the head-

JH: Hmm, hmm.

DSL: You know, to make it appear [legit]. So they could photograph it and call these the [official] autopsy photographs.

JH: Yeah, yeah.

DSL: But, that's the body that's buried there.

FRIDAY, DECEMBER 18, 2020

JH: The way I write today is based on how you write.

DSL: Hmm….

JH: I use you as a model in terms of trying to be very analytical and one hundred percent accurate as much as possible; not sloppy. So, I wanted to tell you that. Your writing style influenced me….

DSL: I got my writing style [from] Peter Shepherd – my agent[36] … [He] told me [the following] when I visited him in New York … [after] I first sent him the manuscript, the original version, which was [written] like a

---

36   Interestingly, Peter Shepherd was still alive when we had this conversation. He did not pass on until December 28, 2021 – one year and twenty two days before Mr. Lifton. See: Somers, Erin. "Obituaries: Ben McFall, Peter Shepherd." PublishersMarketplace.com, January 3, 2022. Retrieved 8/21/2023: https://lunch.publishersmarketplace.com/2022/01/obituaries-ben-mcfall-peter-shepherd/.

scientific report: basically he said it was too antiseptic. He said, "What I want you to do is share your experience." And what he said to me – I'll never forget: "When you're writing, I want you to ... grab the reader ... by the necktie ... bring him over your shoulder and show him how you solved it." That's what he said to me. He ... [added], "You've got to capture your experience on the page so that the reader can see that."

JH: Wow....

DSL: And then ... I said, "Are you telling me I should write this in the first person?" And he [Shepherd] said, "Yes!" I said, "Peter that's ridiculous in the first person. Einstein doesn't say, 'Oh, look at this equation I was thinking of!'" No, no, no! A scientist presents his evidence. He [Shepherd] says, "No, no, no. This is different." (Laughs) He gave me this whole formula for doing it, and he said, "I want you to write it in the first person." ... I went back to my residence in Rockaway Beach [Long Island, New York]. I wrote whatever it was [sample he wanted]. And then he calls me up one day and says, "I've been reading this. This is very fine until you get to page 14 over here [and] suddenly you're breaking into this scientific mode again. I want this in the first person." (Laughs)

JH: Yeah.

DSL: Well, that's how it happened.

JH: Well, your style includes, for example, charts–

DSL: Oh, yeah! Absolutely.

JH: Sketches and–

DSL: Oh, sure....

JH: That's ... what I do, too. I love the charts ... and then the timelines that you created....[37]

DSL: Oh, the timelines are very important.

JH: Yes! And ... you did that. Yeah, he [Shepherd] told you to do first person, but you created that style.

DSL: But, don't other books have timelines....?

JH: No, no ... I've read *a lot* ... of books – not as many as you, but I've read a lot. And many of them ... are in the historical genre, because that's what I like ... and, no, your book is laid out [particularly]. It's pretty unique.

---

37   Examples include (Carroll & Graf edition): Elm Street Map, page 72; Humes' Perspective on November 22, page 159; Beveling, page 249; The Parkland/Bethesda Conflict, page 310; Timeline for Clandestine Intermission Hypothesis, page 628.

DSL: Well, that's because I'm charting, I'm illustrating a deception....

JH: I know, but it [this unique writing style] also has to do with your scientific and mathematical background....

DSL: I would call it "system engineering" and "flowcharting."

JH: Exactly! That's exactly, that's what I'm trying to say.

DSL: You don't think lots of other books do that for whatever they're describing...?

JH: I just read uhh that thick ... the one on Robert Kennedy's assassination.... It was a great book.[38] I gave it to my buddy ... to read. I found about – literally ... fifty errors (Laughs) in the book, and I wrote 'em down. I can't help myself – I write ... [the errors] down ... and I send it [list] to the publisher, and say, "Hey, you need to fix this." By the way, when I read your book, I don't think I found any errors.[39]

DSL: We were so careful with that, yeah....

JH: Your editor did a great job. One of the things I notice today is that the books aren't really closely looked at ... [Vladimir] Lenin said, "Shoot the editor if there are any mistakes." ... I think he was somewhat joking, but he took his writing seriously.

DSL: I never heard of this quote. Lenin has a quote where he talks about shooting the editor?

JH: Yes. If the book has got errors – shoot the editor....

DSL: He said that? (Laughs)

JH: He took his writing seriously.

DSL: Didn't he say he submitted a manuscript that didn't have errors or did he expect his spelling errors to be corrected...?

JH: He [Lenin] did most of his writing – if not all of it. So, I think ... he took the responsibility ... I've read a lot of his books ... I don't remember seeing errors in them either – and they're technical books.

---

38   Pease, Lisa. *A Lie Too Big To Fail: The Real History of the Assassination of Robert F. Kennedy.* Feral House, 2018, 512 pages. In my humble opinion, this is the book to read about RFK's Assassination. I think I read it in about 5 days, working two jobs. It was that good. I mean no disrespect to Ms. Pease regarding the errors. Books today do not follow the conciseness expected years ago. Interestingly, Russian Revolutionary Vladimir Lenin once said to the effect that if a book has errors, the editor should be shot. All books should be as precise as possible – grammar-wise and formatting-wise, but in today's climate, with author's doing more of the work, that is difficult to achieve.

39   I recently reread *Best Evidence* (Summer of 2023), and I found only two errors that I recall.

DSL: Oh, yeah.

JH: It's [Lenin's books] written like *Best Evidence* to a certain degree ... [with] all the footnotes. ... I'm getting off the subject, but ... your book is definitely unique ... it's influenced me, and I want to thank you for that ....

DSL: Oh, OK. But, the timelines, I think, come from systems engineering ... electrical engineering, control theory, always draw timelines. ... For example ... I don't know how an English major would deal with this. ... An English major would write a paragraph like, "Consequently, duh, duh, duh, duh, duh, duh." Whereas David Lifton would say, "Consequently, see diagram," and there's a timeline to illustrate what I mean by "consequently." ... Also, I was deeply influenced by studying engineering physics and ... electrical engineering. The whole concept of the *before and the after* [emphasis added].

JH: Yeah ....

DSL: You know, the before – you have an arrow going into the box and then an arrow coming out. So, the signal comes into the black box, and another signal comes out ... like a stereo. ... And if you put the output over the input, you make a fraction, that's called a transfer function. So, I viewed it as applying control theory – a transfer function, only instead of [applying it] to a signal, [I applied control theory] *to the body of President Kennedy and the wounds.* ... There's an "in" and an "out." ... I actually did that and very early on, I said, "Oh, they're reversing the trajectories." (Laughs) I remember sitting on a chair in my apartment on Dorothy Street [Brentwood, Los Angeles] in December '66, and saying, "Oh, this is like a transfer function. It's just trajectory reversal ...." (Laughs)

JH: Yes! Yes. So, that was an "aha moment" for you.

DSL: Well, yeah. The idea was the similarity in math analogy ... the before and after on the body. So ... I don't know ... to the extent to which it's affected other books. But, I mean, I would assume ... if you're doing FDR's history ....

JH: I've read ... David Kennedy's book ... [*Freedom from Fear*] ... It's a great book, but it's ... nothing like yours.[40] You have to be mathematical because you're dealing with-

DSL : With the body. Exactly ....

---

40   Kennedy, David M. *Freedom from Fear: The American People in Depression and War, 1929-1945.* Oxford University Press, 2001, 936 pages. I read the paperback edition. This work was originally published in hardcover in 1999.

JH: Measurements and … trajectory. And I'm saying that your book is … definitely unique … I've told you this: It stands above the others … It's never been debunked because you put all that hard work into showing – visually and then verbally … this is what happened….

DSL: Well, yes, and I think the fundamental concept is that the body is evidence. It wasn't obvious in the beginning….

JH: Another interesting … element of your research is, you have the book, and you tell it verbally, and then you tell it visually with your charts, your sketches, and you also have that excellent video – and audio-visual tool. So, anyone that reads your book, you approach it from different angles [i.e. learning modalities], so … you're going to be able to reach people whether they're a verbal person, or a mathematical person, or [an] auditory person…. No book does that, certainly not in the Kennedy Assassination [genre]. No book does that where … the way you presented the evidence and your research – it's multi-faceted, and that's … [why] it stands above.

2021

FRIDAY, MARCH 12, 2021

DSL: But I've been working on this for a few days, and I'm putting it in the beginning of the book.... When you read Mark Lane's book [*Rush to Judgment*/1966] ... do you remember the business about Oswald being picked up by a station wagon?

JH: I do, yes.

DSL: Before I go further, let me ask you, "How did you react to that?"

JH: Oh, there's no doubt – I never understood how he could get so fast from Dealey Plaza to his rooming house–

DSL: No, no, no, no – Here's the question: You do know that the Commission's version is that he left Dealey Plaza walking east–

JH: Yeah, he took a bus–

DSL: Right. OK. How did you react to the news that the Warren Report says he took a bus, then they took the station wagon–

JH: I think the station wagon makes more sense, and I understand that when he was in interrogation he said, "That belongs to Mrs. Paine. Keep her out of this." Or something like that.

DSL: That is correct. Now, here's David Lifton's version which I've had for 30 or 40 years. Are you ready?

JH: Yeah.

DSL: He [LHO] was supposed to be shot in the building.

JH: I believe that. Yeah. I've heard that.

DSL: So, now, they've got what they call in the trade [assassinations] – they've got to exfiltrate him from the area. He was given the instructions: "We're sending a station wagon over there [Elm Street in front of TSBD]. Get the Hell into the station wagon." So the station wagon comes by, he [operative in station wagon] let's out a whistle – this is in the testimony. The wagon pulls over, he jumps into the wagon, OK. Now, here's what you may not know. The wagon then goes into the Triple Underpass – that's in the testimony – and then it goes up Stemmons Freeway [South] to the first exit which is Continental Avenue, loops around, then drops him off five blocks [from TSBD] where he got on the bus. So, the station wagon was a way of getting him out and telling him something like, "Go home. Do this. Whatever." And they looped around and he gets on the bus. So, they're both true. It's just like the wounds. It's true that he left in a station wagon and it's true that he got on the bus. It was the station wagon that took him to the bus. And I have all kinds of wonderful maps of this. It [the trip from TSBD to the bus stop via car ride] takes all of 2 minutes. Back in 1970 when I visited Dallas, we drove this repeatedly to test the hypothesis, because I understood that both were true, and I wanted to see how long the drive was. And I figured it was 2 minutes – and that's all it was! So, he gets into the station wagon [with] whoever sent the wagon, loops around and gets on the bus! And that's the end of the conflict. It shows that he [LHO] has a handler, and that they're now dealing with the fact that he's still alive. It's really a great thing. Anyway, I don't want to get into it, but I have maps of that, and I've been drawing little maps.

JH: Have you ever seen that picture of the car where the license plate is torn off of the back in the picture?

DSL: Yes. That's one of those [Warren Commission] exhibits where uh, yes, I have–

JH: That's not the same car though you're talking about right?

DSL: No, no, no. That's a very interesting issue. That has to do with the car seen on the night of the [General] Walker shooting on April 10 [1963].

SATURDAY, OCTOBER 2, 2021 (01:06:35)

DSL: I knew him [Fred T. Newcomb] very well. He's the one ... who originated the theory – this was 20 years ago.[41] I didn't believe it and then I changed my mind after a while. I don't think you were aware of this ... [He] is the one who first said that there was shooting in the car.[42]

---

41   Fact is, FBI Agents Sibert and O'Neill interviewed SSA William Greer at the White House *to verify his physical description*. The proverbial "tin foil hat" aside, this is really strange – unless it has something to do with "Godzilla," or two drivers – Driver X who supposedly climbed in from the follow up car after Connally shot the original driver. (I suppose William Greer could be considered the third driver in the mix.) "Godzilla" is explained in detail in the text below. See Chapter 19 of *Best Evidence*, "Certain Preliminary Examinations," pages 488-489 of the Carroll & Graf edition.

42   Newcomb, Fred T. and Perry Adams. *Murder from Within: Lyndon Johnson's Plot Against President Kennedy*. Authorhouse: 2011, 340 pages.

JH: Really?

DSL: Yes, oh, yeah. [Newcomb's son] … and I occasionally talked and we kind of joked about my transformation. But, I can't say anything about it publicly because I'm still worried about it being too unbelievable. I'm sure there was shooting in the car now.[43] There is no question in my mind. Connally shot [someone], and then there was an agent – there's a lot of stuff in the car. But, if I talk about that, it's going to overshadow everything else I'm doing [*Final Charade*].

JH: Yeah. People will think you lost your mind or something.

DSL: That's right, but that's going to change someday.… We [Newcomb's son and Lifton] have a codename for it: "Godzilla." (Laughs) Did I ever tell you that?

JH: You did … so he [Newcomb's son] knows what that is?

DSL: Oh, yeah, yeah – shooting in the car … [While continuing to fill out "thank you notes" to his GoFundMe page] I think I saw Nathalie Apteker's name here.… She came to work for me in 1993 or 8 – I forget which year. She was a kid from Israel that read *Best Evidence* – and she wanted to work for me. So, I said, "Sure!" She [Nathalie] came to my office everyday [in Century City] and put in hours, and I gave her money; it was modest. But, here's the thing: she made a discovery.… She came running into my office and she said, "David, David, I figured out something!" I said, "What?" And she said, "I figured out who typed" – You know about the typed version versus the handwritten version of the Oswald Manuscript?

JH: I've heard of it, yeah.

DSL: "I figured out who typed the manuscript!" I said, "Who?" She says, "Oswald!" (Laughs) I said, "Really?" And she showed me the evidence, and God d*mn it – she [Nathalie] hit the nail on the head. That whole business of Oswald taking typing lessons. You may know about that?

JH: No. I didn't know that.

DSL: Yeah. He was taking typing lessons. He's the one that typed the damn manuscript. That's the reason it has all these funny errors in it; spelling errors.… [While discussing what to do with his 45 file cabinets, such as donating them to The Sixth Floor Museum at Dealey Plaza, UCLA, or

---

43   Though not directly related, examine JFK Researcher Jack White's excellent work on the doctoring of the Zapruder Film. YouTube has several of his presentations available. He compares the known photographs of the event with corresponding frames to the Z Film and found that – Voila! – they do not match.

Cornell, his alma mater] This business of the steam and the smoke and everything [behind the Grassy Knoll], that – to me – that ranks up there almost with surgery of the head area. I mean, this discovery that in the railroad yard right behind the fence [on the Grassy Knoll] was a backhoe? I mean, give me a break! I mean, that is just a really damn big important discovery.

JH: Yeah.

DSL: But everything about this case, Jim, is so weird that if you don't have a book or something to establish credibility, it sounds like you're "off your rocker." Shooting in the car. Are you kidding, you know?

JH: Yeah.

DSL: Anyway, I just wanted you to know that...

JH: So, you graduated from Cornell with basically a Masters Degree.

DSL: Basically, yes. It was a five-year program ... and then I graduated in 1962. And then, I started at UCLA in the extension school- extension classes – a few months later and then converted to full time and then made the discovery of the surgery and I got out of there [UCLA]; started writing the book [Best Evidence].... My class [at Cornell], if it was a four-year program, would have been 1961. But because it was a five-year program, it was called Class of '62. So, all the people on campus graduated in 1961, but the small little group of engineers and physics people – which I was one – our graduation date was June '62.... [While discussing how he pranked a radio show in Los Angeles, I mentioned that I had heard some people do something similar while listening to radio in Chicago] You grew up in Chicago?

JH: Yeah. [specifically Glendale Heights, some 30 miles west of the city]

DSL: When I was on my book tour ... Chicago-

JH: I know you did. Remember I told you that the [public high school] student I had ... she went and saw you and got a picture with you.

DSL: Oh!

JH: She [my U.S. History student] came back and said [to me], "Here's the picture. I've met David Lifton." ... Maybe you were at [the University of] Illinois Circle Campus which is Chicago.... But anyway, she came back and said, "Have you ever read this book?" I said, "No." I do remember it from summer school [Eastern Illinois University in 1985] when my roommate Craig ... was reading *Best Evidence* – the little tiny paperback ... and he's talking about the Grassy Knoll, and I'm like, "What?"

DSL: (Laughs)

JH: And the head snap, and I'm like, "What are you talking about?" I ... [placed that information] in the back of my mind and forgot about it – until she reminded me. And I said, "You know what, I'm going to buy that book." That's the first book I bought [about the JFK Assassination]. It was *Best Evidence*. Right after that was when *JFK* came out – the movie and all these books came out.... I made a point, and my wife got sick of it – I'm going to read every book whether it's for or against [the idea of a conspiracy] ... with the truth somewhere blended into the middle ... Yours is definitely the best – without a doubt. No question. It's never been debunked.

DSL: I know, but I've got to tell you my true beliefs ... of course I believe there was alteration of the wounds. It's the other part of it [that] I've really not emphasized other than touched on it because I'm afraid of it. I'm afraid that I'd be – I don't want to be branded a "kook."

JH: You're talking about "Godzilla."

DSL: Yeah, "Godzilla." The whole business of shooting in the car. But, I know that it happened now. You can see Connally rise up with something in his hand, and he thrusts his head towards the front [of the car]. And then there's a big explosion at the windshield. So, he had a gun. I'm sure of it. There's no question in my mind. But, I have to censor myself. So, the "heavy lifting" in that area ... was done by Fred Newcomb.... [While discussing the RFK Assassination in June of 1968.[44]] I was coming out of the UCLA pool and this friend of mine ... says, "David. I'm glad you're here tonight. I want you to meet somebody," and she gave me the [phone] number of *one of the witnesses that she happened to know*. So, I called him up. His name was Irwin ... [Stroll]. He was one of the guys hit [by a stray bullet] ... I acquired a number of conversations with him.

JH: What did that guy think? Were there multiple shooters?

DSL: Yeah, I think he did. And that caused me to go and order the grand jury transcripts. That's how I came to order the RFK evidence which I

44   The best work on RFK's Assassination bar none is *A Lie Too Big to Fail: the Real History of the Assassination of Robert F. Kennedy* by Lisa Pease and James DiEugenio, Feral House, 2018. After reading this book, I mailed it to Mr. Lifton. I'm not sure if he was able to read it. However, I would also recommend *The Assassination of Robert F. Kennedy* by William Turner and Jonn Christian, Basic Books, 2006.

studied for a month or two and then finally forced myself to stop.... It would be another huge distraction ... I was very suspicious of the ice machine which was reported as being "not functioning" in the press. But, Kennedy's head wound was a contact wound.

JH: Yes.

DSL: It ... [was created] within a couple of inches [of the head] ...

JH: Yes.

DSL: The witnesses do not say that Sirhan was two inches away from Kennedy's head. The damn evidence tells the story.... He [Sirhan] was up against the ice machine, and I was interested in whether that room had been booby trapped – and whether there was someone inside the ice machine.

JH: Or the guy behind Kennedy – Cesar ... the guard.

DSL: I know all about him, but I don't ... think he's part of anything sinister.[45] ... There was something going on with the environment. You know, it's like bringing Kennedy to Dealey Plaza and then booby trapping the area – which they did do.

JH: The thing is – you said it – the contact wound – it was the powder burns on his head.

DSL: That's correct.

JH: So, that gun had to be really close.

DSL: That means the witnesses don't have him that close or when he [RFK] was up against the ice machine there was somebody inside that enclosure which still looked like an ice machine but was providing hidden cover. I don't know....

JH: Do you think Kennedy's assassination was more than just Sirhan?

DSL: Yes. [We segued back to the issue of the steam and the smoke behind the Grassy Knoll] The very least I could do [on the GoFundMe platform] is say that ... this has come up. It's something new, and it's gonna be in *Final Charade*.... Guns don't smoke! *Guns do not smoke* – not with

45   I wholeheartedly respect Mr. Lifton's opinion on security guard Thane Eugene Cesar and his alleged involvement – though I disagree. Note that I only read a couple of books about it, whereas he studied the case. It's interesting to note that even RFK, Jr. believes Cesar was the killer of his father. For example, see Chris Spargo's article, "Robert F. Kennedy was Assassinated by Thane Eugene Cesar...," DailyMail.com, September 12, 2019." Retrieved 6/30/2023: https://www.dailymail.co.uk/news/article-7456521/Robert-F-Kennedy-assassinated-Thane-Eugene-Cesar-Sirhan-Sirhan-says-RFK-Jr.html.

modern ammunition. So, what's causing the smoke? And the answer is the damned – what do they call it again – backhoe. And you can see an outline of the backhoe on the [Wilma] Bond Slide and you see it in the [Phil] Willis Slide … It looks like an inverted … "U" behind the fence…

JH: That would definitely make sense, and it fits with the photograph where they have the … [apparent image] of the construction worker with the [hard] hat.

DSL: Oh, yeah….

SATURDAY, OCTOBER 23, 2021

DSL: [Typing GoFundMe message as he speaks] I've been continuing the work pertaining to the backhoe, and the source of the smoke, and then I could also say … years ago I wrote a screenplay *Best Evidence* … I took it off the shelf [recently] – I don't know, I'm afraid [alluding to the backhoe and the true source of the smoke on the Grassy Knoll]. I mean, people-

JH: Oh, no, no! That's a good thing – you could say, "I don't know if you are aware of this, but years ago my screenplay was turned into a movie," and then "the title of the movie was about Marina Oswald." A lot of people don't know that. I didn't know that. [At this point, I'm confusing the screenplay and film about Marina with a separate unpublished screenplay based upon *Best Evidence*.]

DSL: Well hold it, hold it! The screenplay was not turned into [a film] … Marina Oswald is a separate project entirely.

JH: You wrote that, didn't you? The one with Marina Oswald….

DSL: Oh, yeah, yeah, yeah, yeah, yeah. The Marina story – I did a lot of work on that, yes…. That's the movie [in which] they actually dramatized her life.[46] I was a serious consultant on that with the screenwriter….

JH: [We're still contemplating the wording of a note to all GoFundMe contributors] You could say, you know, "I worked on the screenplay … and that helped me become really close friends with Marina Oswald."

DSL: No, no, I already knew Marina…. The screenwriter said, "She knows you so well we want to make you a character in this movie about her."

JH: That's awesome…!

---

46   Wikipedia: *Fatal Deception: Mrs. Lee Harvey Oswald*. The entire film (aired November 1993), starring Helena Bonham Carter as Marina Oswald, is available on YouTube in clips. Mr. Lifton was portrayed in the film due to his unique and close relationship he had had with Mrs. Oswald over the years.

DSL: So, then they had a person [Robert Picardo] play David Lifton ... [Now discussing the film *Fatal Deception: Mrs. Lee Harvey Oswald* and contemplating the wording of a note to all GoFundMe contributors] We portrayed Oswald as basically innocent – caught in some kind of governmental "spider web."

JH: Yeah. Innocent, but caught up in a black op....

DSL: Yeah, but caught up in some sort of intelligence operation which led to him [Oswald] being framed.... In the aftermath of the original January 1981 publication of ... *BE* [*Best Evidence*], contrary to the normal establishment view.... Here's what happened. It's not just the way she [Marina Oswald] was portrayed. As a consequence, for years we spoke many times a week, and I persuaded Marina of her husband's innocence.... In effect, I found myself deprogramming Marina from all the nonsense she had been told.... And it was an honor to do it.... Let me tell you what happened back then. It was so exciting back then. The person who ran *Hard Copy* was named Peter Brennan[47] ... and I had all of the film footage ... [of Marina Oswald].... We negotiated ... I was very proud, you know. I got Marina to ... sit for more filming [interviews]. It was very nice. I don't know what she's doing today.... I've just lost track ... too much time has gone by.

JH: Would you talk to her if she wanted to reach out to you?

DSL: Oh, of course. Yeah.

JH: I mean, I might be able to-

DSL: I was saying things like, "Marina, this is all going to be straightened out in another year." Of course, I was optimistic. That this thing [film about her life] was just going to [lead to the truth being exposed]-

JH: Well, the pressure of the government is enormous....

DSL: Right. It's not like we're modifying a Word Document ... [Now discussing the issue of the government's control of "the narrative" through the media, Hollywood, educational institutions, etc.] The real radical thing is to ... watch the *Best Evidence* video and understand the issues.[48]

---

47   Wikipedia: Peter Brennan (Producer).

48   *Best Evidence* Research Video. *Best Evidence: The Research Video.* YouTube, 2014, 36:28 minutes. Retrieved 7/7/2023: https://youtu.be/oAWFvcrp-ao. Originally recorded in October of 1980 and published by Rhino Video in 1989.

FRIDAY, OCTOBER 29, 2021

DSL: Here's the important thing about *Martin Eden*. *Martin Eden* ... [has] a theme to the book.... This is David Lifton's ... synopsis in one sentence ... quote: "Live your life as an adventure so that you can write about it."

JH: Right, right.

DSL: In other words, the whole idea is, use your life as material and go on and write. So therefore, he can go on a boat, he can go to Alaska ... Look, writing is turning experiences into words. So, he [Oswald] basically decides, "OK, I'm going to live my life as an adventure to accumulate the experience in my brain and out will come a novel."

JH: Can you imagine if Oswald could have written a book – what he would have been able to write about? All the connections-

DSL: Oh, absolutely! Are you kidding? He would write the whole book of his own defection. He would write the book that I'm trying to write – the biography [of Oswald][49] because his life was this adventure. Are you kidding? He gets trained in radar. He comes up with the idea [write a book about his defection]. It's the height of the Cold War. He wants to see the Soviet Union, and he has to pose as a defector [to do so]. And, in addition, he happens to get an intelligent assignment[50] ... [Oswald's] able to go there both because he's hawking this intelligence assignment about radar ["secrets"] ... and he wants to live his life and meet Soviets. And, you know, and then he wants to marry this woman and bring her out. Yeah, absolutely! He lives his life as an adventure so that he can write about it *unaware that because of what he was doing, he was being set up to take the fall in a presidential assassination.* [Italics added for emphasis.]

JH: If you don't mind ... I have a question for you.

DSL: Yeah, sure.

---

49   Note that Mr. Lifton's original plan was to write a biography of Lee Harvey Oswald, but that, due to the newly found evidence of how the plot against JFK was supposed to happen, it morphed into *Final Charade* – with Oswald's life being a part of the entire work.

50   Wikipedia: James Jesus Angleton. Admittedly, this page is what I would dub, "censored" or "white washed." It avoids Angleton's connection to the JFK Assassination, although in a tangential way (Soviet KGB defectors Anatoliy Golitsyn and Yuri Nosenko as they connect to Oswald). For example, he was responsible for the "false defector" program – for which Oswald was recruited. Mr. Lifton believes that James Jesus Angleton, Chief of Counterintelligence for the CIA (1954-1974), was the main official who took notice of Oswald and placed him in the intelligence track he followed as a supposed communist (with various handlers) – including becoming the "patsy" for JFK's state-sponsored murder.

JH: Do you … knowing that Oswald went to Russia to develop – to have the experience to write about, do you think he really loved Marina? Or, do you think he needed her as part of the experience? I hate-

DSL: That's a good question. Look. I gotta answer your question. He had two children with her.

JH: Right.

DSL: I mean, you know (Laughs)…. First of all, you never met Marina?

JH: No.

DSL: She's a very sensual woman.

JH: Yeah.

DSL: It's very easy … there's your answer. I mean-

JH: Yeah, yeah. OK….

DSL: When he was dancing with her at the dance that night [Friday, March 17, 1961], she was probably one of the prettiest girls there….[51]

JH: Talk about the guts that he [Oswald] had [to go to Russia]….

DSL: Oh … absolutely! I mean, that's amazing in a way.

JH: The sad part is he got hooked up with evil individuals, and it ruined his life.

DSL: That's correct. That's correct. He got hooked up with the likes of James Angleton. In other words, at some point he became the pre-selected patsy in the murder plot of a president he adored.

JH: Yeah.

DSL: It's really, it's very sad – that part of it.

JH: It is! And I don't think it'll ever really truly be rectified. Where people will go, "Yeah, Oswald was actually a hero." He will be heralded as a hero….

DSL: Yeah, I know. Oswald was a writer, and he was living his life as an adventure – and then realized that's how he was set up. He wasn't a guy that said, "Gee, I want to be a cook. I'm going to learn all of these menus. I want to be a cook in a kitchen." His hero – *his role model* – was Jack London. That was the big – I forget when I really came to that conclusion, but it was at least 20 years ago. I remember realizing that people have role models. I was reading about the psychology of role models. And he had a role model. And his role model was *Jack London*!

 51   Wikipedia: Marina Oswald Porter.

JH: Did you ever bring that up with Marina?

DSL: I did.

JH: Did you mention Jack London or anything...?

DSL: I tried to. I don't remember what she said.... Do you remember the song, I don't know if you remember, "The Great Pretender?"[52] Well, he [Oswald] was living that kind of life. He was always on stage. He was a pretender.... That's the way he was, living his life as an adventure. He had a view of reality and himself where he was ... creating material to write about. And the person that you could get the most insight about this.... His best friend was the older man who he identified with as a father figure, George de Mohrenschildt.[53] So, if you can get yourself de Mohrenschildt's manuscript ... you will get there the writings of a man who loved Oswald like a son, and Oswald loved him as a father....

JH: Do you think – I mean de Mohrenschildt must have known that Oswald was set up?

DSL: Well, he felt that way....

JH: He probably realized that, "I was used so that they could use Oswald...."

DSL: That's a very important concept *if it's true* [Italics added for emphasis].

JH: [During our Zoom, I shared my screen and the famous backyard photo of Oswald holding the rifle.] I need your opinion on this ... I look at this picture and if you put a ruler right here [Vertically bisecting Oswald from head to toe], and you went down the center of gravity ... look at the bend in his leg-

DSL: I know, I know.

JH: To me, this photo's fake.

DSL: Yeah, but, remember-

JH: Do you agree with that?

DSL: Of course, I agree with it. And second of all, are you aware that the time that this photo was made, he [Oswald] was working at Jaggars-Chiles-Stovall, that very sophisticated photo lab in Dallas. He probably made this photo himself.

---

52   The Platters. "The Great Pretender." The Great Pretender, 1955.
53   Wikipedia: George de Mohrenschildt. This manuscript is now available commercially: de Mohrenschildt, George. *Lee Harvey Oswald As I Knew Him*. Lawrence, KS: University Press of Kansas, 2014, 416 pages.

JH: A colleague of mine ... said, "It [Oswald's strange posture] looks to me ... the original guy [body] was leaning against a wall ... with his [right] shoulder against the wall" ... That would explain the buckle in the right knee.

DSL: What he did is, Oswald made the pictures himself at the photo lab. And the way he did it is, he created – do you remember at an amusement park where you can stick your head in a hole?

JH: Yes.

DSL: That's what this is all about. He created a negative and blew it way up ... That's how he did it [placed his hands through a hole], I believe. And then he either stuck his face on there as a separate photographic alteration, or maybe he stuck his face through a hole.

JH: If he did it himself, why didn't he make the image look legit? I'm telling you, the body – there's no way you can stand like that....

DSL: No, no ... you're bringing up a matter noted in 1964. Yes, Mark Lane ... would talk about this picture and all of the anomalies connected with it.

JH: But, you think he [Oswald] made this himself....?

DSL: Oh, I'm sure of it because he had Marina take the picture. It's in her testimony, and I talked to her about it....

JH: So, I'm guessing his handlers said, "Hey, Lee, we need a picture of you" – knowing that that was going to be on [the cover of] *Life* magazine in a few months....

DSL: No, no, no. It's better than that: "We need a picture of you because we're going to create the picture of you as an assassin." He thinks he's an undercover agent who's posing as a leftwing radical. That's the whole schtick. They're going to use it to create the photographic evidence of the possession of the rifle – because that is really the rifle. That is the rifle from Klein's [Sporting Goods].[54]

JH: So ... There are people that believe that that's his head, but it's not his body.[55] You believe that really is him....?

DSL: I believe that it's really him....

---

54   Wikipedia: John F. Kennedy Assassination Rifle.
55   There are some researchers who believe that neither the head nor the body is that of Lee Harvey Oswald. Check out Jack White's research into the photographs and Zapruder Film.

JH: According to what I understand, they didn't record his interrogations, but one of the things I read is that he said [when shown the picture], "That's my face but not my body."

DSL: No, no. He said, "That's my picture, but my face has been pasted on someone's body." He never said, "I did that (Laughs) as part of my assignment." ... It was during the police interrogation that he realized the stuff that he'd been playing around with was dynamite. He didn't know that they–

JH: You think he was lying just to try to cover up the fact that he actually is the person in the photo....?

DSL: Yeah, right. Yeah, he's trying to create the appearance that he's greatly shocked and someone's trying to frame him, but he doesn't say, "Oh, by the way, I was asked as part of my assignment to pose for this picture."

JH: Don't you think at one point in the interrogation that he said, "Hey, listen. I'm working for James Angleton."

DSL: No. He never said that. There were 6 or 7 people in the interrogation room.... He never made that statement. He never-

JH: What I'm asking is, do you think there was a point where he said, "Guys, listen. I was an agent"

DSL: No.

JH: Never....

DSL: As far as we know, no.

JH: Let's assume that he did, [but] that they would just lie about it, and say he never said that. That would make sense to me why they never kept notes [of the interrogations] – or, I'm sorry, they never recorded it. They kept notes, but it was extemporaneous....

DSL: Well, they never recorded it because they didn't know what the Hell he was going to say. He was not supposed to live to be interrogated. He was supposed to die in the [Texas School Book Depository] building.... Suppose he [Oswald] said ... just for example ... "I don't know what this is all about. I need to be brought to Washington and be debriefed by the Attorney General. I'm a government agent working under the guidance of Robert Kennedy[56] ... So, you can all go screw yourself. Send me to Wash-

---

56   Wikipedia: David Atlee Phillips. Mr. Lifton believed that Oswald was told this by his handler – *in my opinion* David Atlee Phillips, the CIA's Chief of Operations for the Western Hemisphere. It made his undercover work seem that much more important – ironically so.

ington because I've got a story to tell." And then they'd say, "We know you were a government agent because you were reporting to 'Joe Smith.'[57] 'No, no, no, my handler's 'Frank Jones.'" And then they'd want to know, "Well, who's 'Frank Jones?' We never heard of any 'Frank Jones.'" In other words, he had a handler who deceived him.

JH: I see.

DSL: That's what I think. He had a handler who deceived him, and who was … another one of these alternate father figures.

JH: Maybe David Atlee Phillips perhaps?

DSL: Or whatever. They never said, "My name is David Atlee Phillips" or "My name is James Angleton." No, no, no. He [Oswald] would never know the true name [of his handler]. But, he was set up by a father figure.

JH: Wow….

DSL: And that's what's so sad, because – and you may not know this – his father died four or five weeks before he was born. His father died in August 1939, and then Lee was born on October 18, 1939.

JH: So, you're saying they were *afraid* of what he [Oswald] was going to say.

DSL: Yeah, right. That's a good point. Yes…. First of all, we don't know completely what he said, but there were so many people in the room taking notes that we have a pretty good idea. But, they [interrogators] were afraid…. All he had to do to … [screw] up the whole thing was to say, "I don't know what you people are talking about. Sure, I ordered a gun … I was working as an undercover agent for Robert Kennedy." And at that point, we wouldn't have to wait 2-3-4-6 years [for] people like Mark Lane to say, "Oh, boom! There's the plot. That's the structure. He [Oswald] thinks he's working for the attorney general. No wonder he's doing all this stuff–"

JH: So, the reason he didn't do that is…?

DSL: Because he didn't think he was in jeopardy.

JH: Do you think he was instructed at all costs not to say anything – "We'll get you out of this?"

DSL: Yeah. Well, I think that he was probably spoken to in the jail when he was arrested. And they said, "Look … go along with your cover story.

We'll get you out of this by Monday. This wasn't supposed to happen." You know, that kind of thing....

JH: Now, there are some witnesses [who claim] ... Oswald and Ruby knew each other. You don't think they did....?

DSL: I do not believe he knew Ruby at all.... Starting on Friday ... Oswald was arrested alive – which was not supposed to happen, OK? So, now they've arrested the patsy alive instead of killing him in the theater....

JH: And you think it was ... the police officer when he ran into him [Oswald] in the second floor lunchroom – he [was supposed to] have killed him there....?

DSL: [Dallas Motorcycle] Officer [Marrion L.] Baker.... He runs up the stairs [with Roy Truly, TSBD Superintendent], and then he almost catches Oswald at the Coke machine.[58] He has a gun in his ... [stomach]. And then [Roy] Truly, who's not ... in the plot at that level, says, "No, no, he works here." (Laughs) So, then they go up along the stairs to the roof, and this is in the testimony, and ... Baker says to Truly, "We must be careful. This man can blow your head off." (Laughs) It's in the Warren Commission testimony...[59]

JH: Meaning Oswald....

DSL: Yeah, yeah, Baker is into this idea that Oswald is a "Cracker Jack" assassin. Truly doesn't understand what the Hell's going on.

JH: If Baker had gone up the stairs by himself, Truly was not with him, do you think he would have tried to kill Oswald?

DSL: Oswald – especially if he [had] found Oswald running down the staircase that he was running up.

JH: And you think that Baker ... was instructed to do this?

DSL: Yes.[60] Baker's story is ... [he was told] that "There's a communist in town; this sharpshooter who's going to try and kill Kennedy. We're going to let him do it, but we want you to go and nail the communist." ... Have you heard of the play *MacBird*? It's written by this genius woman from Berkeley, Barbara Garson.[61] OK, [her husband] Marvin Garson was one

58   Wikipedia: Timeline of the John F. Kennedy Assassination.
59   See Chapter 14 of *Best Evidence*, "Trajectory Reversal: Blueprint for Deception," pages 350-351 of the Carroll & Graf edition.
60   I honestly don't know what to make of this information. I always believed Baker's story at face value, but Mr. Lifton had studied the case since 1966.
61   Wikipedia: *MacBird*. It uses Shakespeare's *Macbeth* as a template for the JFK Assassination and was published in *Ramparts* magazine in December 1966. See also Wikipedia: *San Francisco*

of the original Mark Lane investigators and he interviewed people like Zapruder...

JH: I didn't know that.

DSL: And Marvin Garson got the witnesses, and he wrote stuff under the ... [title] *Grassy Knoll Press* ... Barbara [Garson], whom I knew, she actually interviewed Zapruder in '64. So, when you look at the evidence very carefully, these people dressed as police ran past Zapruder onto the train and [it] pulled out. There's a whole story about the train.... So, Barbara asks Zapruder innocently, "Well, Mr. Zapruder, these police you saw running behind you, were they ... from the Dallas Police Department?" He goes, "Um, (clears throat), where else would they be from?" (Laughs)

JH: Wow. Wow. Crazy. Like you said, the whole thing [JFK Assassination] was set up like a movie script.

DSL: Yeah. It was set up like a movie script. When these cops, you know, five, or six, or seven that ran behind Zapruder, they're some of the extras. They're sinister as Hell, but they're some of the extras.

JH: So, you were saying that ... you saw a picture ... [of] Oswald near the ... Grassy Knoll – a picture of him standing there....

DSL: That's in the [Mary] Moorman Photograph.[62] On the right hand side.... If you look in the book *Four Dark Days in History*, you can see Oswald right there – standing at the pergola – inside, or in front of it, or whatever.[63]

JH: And then you said he [Oswald] was told or instructed by someone to "Get back into the building."

DSL: Yeah.... That was a mistake. He shouldn't have been photographed (Laughs) at the time of the assassination.... Now who the Hell knows about it except me.... We found that picture in '65. We blew it up.... We said, "Look at that man in the pergola." But we never said, "That's Oswald!" Lisa Marcus, Ray Marcus' wife ... [made the discovery]. I remember we were at her house in LA near the Fairfax Area [border of Hollywood].... Here's what I think: [Oswald thinks] they're staging a theatrical event which Kennedy is shot at, but it's all pretense. They're staging a fake assassination. I ... [can't see it] any other way. Because, the fact that Oswald's

Express Times and Barbara Garson.

62   Wikipedia: Mary Moorman.

63   Matthews, Jim, Morse, C. Franklin, et al. *Four Dark Days in History: A Photo History of President Kennedy's Assassination* (Collector's Copy). Los Angeles: Special Publications, 1963, 64 pages.

there tells me – because he loved Kennedy – he's not going to partake in a murder of Kennedy.

JH: Yeah, I read that book, *Appointment in Dallas*.[64]

DSL: Is that what they say in there?

JH: That's what it says – that it was a staged assassination, but that he [Oswald] was in the window, and that he was supposed to fire blanks from the window. Someone was going to shoot him [Oswald] ... and he would die and [presumably] fall out the window.

DSL: The problem is, we know from the Moorman photograph, he was *not* in the window.

JH: Right, right....

DSL: We don't know who was in the window, but it couldn't have been Oswald because Oswald is [outside] at the monument [i.e. pergola].... The real thing is that he's in the monument. He's right in that cubicle. So, therefore, he's then told to "get your a** over to the lunchroom." Which he did.

JH: At that point [after interacting with Officer Baker], you said then Oswald went out....

DSL: Then Oswald got the Hell out of the building.... He ran down the little grassy slope to Elm Street, somebody whistled *loudly*, and a station wagon, or Rambler, pulls over – as reported by Roger Craig.[65] It went under the Triple Underpass [got on the Stemmons Freeway southbound], and then circled around on ... that first exit, Continental Avenue, goes over a half a mile, and he's now at ... [North Lamar Street] ... and he gets on the bus at Murphy Street [and Elm Street].... He comes to Murphy [Drive] ... and runs down Murphy ... and bangs on the bus [of Cecil J. McWatters][66] ... He takes it a couple of blocks, gets off, and gets into the [William Wayne] Whaley cab.

64   McDonald, Hugh C. as told to Geoffrey Bocca. *Appointment in Dallas: The Final Solution to the Assassination of JFK.* Toronto, Canada: Pinnacle, 2013, 224 pages. Originally published by Zebra Books, 1975.
65   During our Monday, December 27, 2021, discussion, Mr. Lifton notes that *Oswald* made the shrill whistle, and that "I never knew he could whistle so loud." I think he was in error. Oswald didn't whistle – the driver did. For an interesting look at the significance of Dallas Deputy Roger Craig's testimony about what he saw, see: Steve Cameron Productions. "Roger Craig Sees Oswald Run From TSBD and Get Picked Up by Man Driving Getaway Car," YouTube, 2022, 9:42 minutes. Retrieved 7/13/2023: https://www.youtube.com/watch?v=9VygTEwbdl0&t=21s.
66   According to a modern day map of the intersection of Murphy Drive and Elm Street, it no longer exists. However, if Oswald was dropped off at North Lamar Street and Elm Street, it was only three blocks west of the bus stop.

JH: And then the Whaley cab takes him like a couple blocks past his ... [rooming house]...?

DSL: Yeah, one block past because he's very wary by that time. He [Oswald] wants to make sure he's not being followed. He runs back one block, runs into the ... [rooming house] and gets his [jacket and] gun.

JH: And then he leaves and then – do you believe that....

DSL: And then there's a cop car there.... Then they try to kill him at 10th and Patton and that doesn't work.

JH: Do you think Oswald killed Tippit?

DSL: No, no, no. He's there, though.

JH: Who do you think killed Tippit?

DSL: Whoever the hitmen are in this plot.

JH: Yeah. Why did they kill Tippit...?[67]

DSL: He's going to be the "cause célèbre" to [finally] arrest Oswald.

JH: They're going to throw him [Tippit] "under the bus" just to be able to tie Oswald to this whole mess.

DSL: That's right. He's a cop killer.

JH: Wow... Why do you think he [Oswald] went to the theater – because he was told to go there? Or...?

DSL: I don't know. But, he was very intelligent, and he ran down Jefferson, and I thought he was hiding. If he was really smart and if he really had been lucky, he could have gotten on a bus – like a Greyhound or something ... and he could just listen to radio broadcasts on a portable ... the whole thing [plot] would have unfolded.... He would have said, "Oh, my God. I've been set up." ... But, he didn't. So, he ends up in the theater *hiding*, and then the police come into the theater, and you know the rest. They turn on the lights ... and they bring him out of the theater [and Oswald's] yelling, "I didn't shoot anybody...."

JH: Now, it's kind of interesting though ... [Dallas Patrolman Maurice Neal "Nick" McDonald] went up to him [Oswald], Oswald said something like, "Well, it's all over" ... he stood up, and he punched the cop ... He [Oswald] tried to pull the gun out is what the cop said.

67   Wikipedia: J. D. Tippit.

DSL: Well, why wouldn't he? He [Oswald] thinks they're [police] going to kill him.

JH: I was going to say ... maybe he should have just said, "Hey, I'm innocent...."

DSL: Well, he practically did that ... He said ... "I am not resisting arrest." That's in *all* of the police reports.

JH: And then they brought him out[side], and there was ... I counted in the one photo like five or six cop cars.

DSL: Five or six – right....

JH: For a guy that snuck into a theater ... without paying for a fifty cent ticket....

DSL: That clique of officers ... some of them have to be witting.

JH: In other words ... they knew, "OK, we're going to try and kill him if we can."

DSL: Yeah, but ... I also think they had the impression that ... he's the communist assassin. In other words, they don't think in terms of – like Mark Lane – that he's innocent and he's being set up. No, no, no. They think that he's the guy that killed the president, and now they're going to arrest him and become heroes....

Friday, November 19, 2021

DSL: I couldn't be doing the work I'm doing today with Kennedy if I hadn't had that training [Cornell University engineering degree].

JH: I believe it. I told you yesterday that the book [*Best Evidence*] – it's ... the most technical book.

DSL: Right....

JH: You cannot just run on the treadmill and read it. You have to really concentrate, but that's why it's so good. It's not ... [written like] a novel like a lot of these other ones are....

DSL: Well, Jim, the reason it's good reflects my training ... I recognized that there was a quote "before and after" situation on the body. There were a hundred reasons why I got trained to do the before and after in math and in physics.... Before and after was a common theme in Control Theory. You have a black box. A signal goes in. A different signal comes out. Your job is to figure out what's inside the box....

JH: [As we finish watching the trailer to Oliver Stone's latest film, *JFK Revisited: Through the Looking Glass*[68]] Did you see the part where Dulles tries to shake his [JFK's] hand...?

DSL: Yeah, I noticed – I was going to bring it up. Isn't that something? I never saw that before....

JH: [As we finish watching a French TV interview of Oliver Stone pertaining to his latest film, *JFK Revisited: Through the Looking Glass*[69]] So, what do you think of that, sir?

DSL: Well, I liked it. It's summarizing the controversy as it existed about the bullets and the trajectories. Oh, how do you feel about it?

JH: I agree with pretty much everything he [Oliver Stone] said....

JH: [As we finish watching the Joe Rogan interview of Oliver Stone[70]] Alright, so, what do you think of that? I wanted to make sure that you saw that....

DSL: First of all, I really appreciated it ... [However] I'm curious to know how Oliver Stone, so obviously knowledgeable [about the JFK Assassination] ... [could] leave out my work [*Best Evidence* in his latest film *JFK Revisited*] ...?[71]

FRIDAY, DECEMBER 3, 2021

JH: I finished *Martin Eden*.[72]

DSL: Oh, yeah?

JH: I'm really glad I read it. I'm glad you suggested it. To think that Oswald – that's what made him do what he did [defect to USSR]. But, it's kind of interesting at the end [of the book]. Did you read the book?

DSL: I read it years ago. He [Martin Eden] commits suicide.

---

68   Wikipedia: *JFK Revisited: Through the Looking Glass*.
69   France 24 English. "Cannes 2021: Oliver Stone Revisits 'JFK.'" YouTube, 2021, 10:00 minutes. Retrieved 7/3/2023: https://www.youtube.com/watch?v=rYiaKlg8l6s&t=1s.
70   JRE Clips [#1511]. "Joe Discusses the JFK Assassination with Oliver Stone." YouTube, 2020. Note that they discuss Mr. Lifton's book, *Best Evidence*, 9:24 minutes (circa 05:12). Retrieved 7/3/2023: https://www.youtube.com/watch?v=nQuEUsvy8nM.
71   Mr. Lifton and I spoke many times and in much depth about this topic. This really bothered him – rightly so. You cannot talk about the Kennedy Assassination and leave out his work. That's like talking about the end of slavery in the American Civil War and leaving out Lincoln's Emancipation Proclamation. *Best Evidence* is that important. I will leave it at that.
72   Wikipedia: Jack London, *Martin Eden*. Mr. Lifton believes that Lee Harvey Oswald, after reading London's book *Martin Eden* (1909) – a tale about a young man from the lower class who autodidactically becomes a heralded writer and moves within the circles of the upper class – decided to become an American spy, travel to the Soviet Union, and then write about the experience. Mr. Lifton told me that Marina Oswald told him that Jack London was Oswald's favorite author.

Jim Hoffmann sits at the same table Jack London sat at as a boy (1886), March 29, 2023, 7:07PM, Heinold's First and Last Chance Saloon, Jack London Square, Oakland, California.

JH: Yeah, he commits suicide. I'm like – What?

DSL: That's right. (Laughs)

JH: He had everything going right. And then all of a sudden … I think he just felt like he … knew the truth [about how life works], and he couldn't handle the fact that other people didn't know the truth. This is my interpretation. And it just made him so depressed, he thought, "I can't even have a relationship with the world because my eyes are open now so I'm just going to kill myself… ."

DSL: Yeah.

JH: I mean – everything was starting to go right for him. He got all of this money from all of his books and stories. But, you know what made me think [it] was interesting was *Martin Eden* killed himself, right? What did Oswald do? He quote unquote *attempted suicide*.

DSL: Well, that's a fake suicide.

JH: I know! But, maybe he got the idea from Martin Eden to do that.

DSL: It's much better than that. He [Oswald] got the whole idea [to defect] from *Martin Eden* – living your life as an adventure *so you can write about it*. The whole Russian trip and being able to write a book. (Laughs)

JH: But, I'm saying: what if when they [Russian official] said, "Hey, you have to go back" – and so he thought, "Well, what can I do? Oh, yeah, Martin Eden committed suicide. Well, I'll fake my suicide."

DSL: That's when he arrived. Yes. That's a fake suicide.

JH: That's only a fake [suicide]. I believe that. I'm saying, maybe he got the idea for a fake suicide from *Martin Eden* who obviously really did–

DSL: The whole thing was planned. Once when he was in the Marines–

JH: You think he planned to commit a fake suicide–

DSL: Well, the question is, he must have thought about the option … "Can he [Oswald] pull off a fake defection?" Suppose they–

JH: When you say "they" – do you mean like the CIA?

DSL: No, no, no, the KGB.

JH: The KGB – oh.

DSL: He [Oswald] goes over there and then suppose they'd say, "No."

JH: Right.

DSL: "You can't stay. I don't care what you're going to do." Yeah … his fake suicide was an act of last resort. Remember, he spent two years learning Russian – doing a whole bunch of stuff. There was a woman who befriended Khrushchev. She took a personal interest in the [Oswald] case and said, "Let him in. Let him in. He's an idealist you know." (Laughs)

JH : Really?

DSL: Yeah.

JH: Was she like a CIA plant? (Laughs)

DSL: No, no, no. She was friends with Khrushchev.

JH: Yeah. I'm joking but, I mean it's like–

DSL: She was his [Khrushchev's] girlfriend. She took pity on Oswald. That was one of the reasons they said, "OK, you can stay, but not in Moscow. We're sending you to Minsk." He's [Oswald] laughing it up. He can live in Minsk? Are you kidding me? [For] this guy it's a dream come true. (Laughs) [Note to the reader: for about 20 minutes or so, I waited for Mr. Lifton to close literally 50 or so open windows on his Macbook Air. Thus the following lull in the conversation. While doing research for his book *Final Charade* – which sadly has not been published yet though I understand from a family member that it might be – he would open one window after another and eventually his computer would start to slow down. I explained this to Mr. Lifton, that all the open windows took up a lot of memory, and so there were several times we had to go through this process. His computer would act up, I would wait for him on Zoom to close the plethora of open windows, and then he'd have to restart the computer, etc. As an aside, my friend, when I broached the subject with him about the possibility of Mr. Lifton's manuscript being "lost to history" if he were to pass away before publication, strongly encouraged me to ask Mr. Lifton if he had a copy of his manuscript in a safe place *in the case of such a thing*. He told me he did. I also asked Mr. Lifton many times if I could help him to prepare the manuscript for publication – even self-publish it if need be. He declined. I told Mr. Lifton many times that when his work would be published, it would be the final word on the JFK Assassination (i.e. How the plot was *supposed* to unfold.). He appreciated that.] You know Mark Twain … [said], "The more I know people, the more I love my dog." (Laughs)

JH: (Laughs) I love his, "There are lies, damn lies, and statistics." I say there are lies, damn lies, statistics, and alternative facts.

DSL: Here's another one [from Mark Twain]: "I deal with temptation by yielding." (Laughs)

JH: (Laughs)

JH: So you got to meet that guy, huh [Howard Schultz, former Chairman and CEO of Starbucks – who supported DSL's research on *Final Charade* at one point]?

DSL: Oh, many times! Many times.

JH: Down in LA somewhere?

DSL: Well, I'd get a call in the morning: "Howard's going to be coming down. Can you see him?" Yeah, of course I can see him.

Friday, December 10, 2021

DSL: The people who planned this crime really were very smart. (Laughs)

JH: Yes, yes.

DSL: I mean … the people who planned this crime not only killed the president but … presented to the public a false understanding of the events, and so … it seemed to be an accident.

JH: Right – a false narrative, yeah.

DSL: Yeah.

JH: A quirk of fate.

DSL : That's the way it was planned. The guy took a trip to Dallas and encountered this crazy man who shot him with a twelve-dollar rifle. That's crazy.

JH: I think that ... you mentioned this many times: it [the assassination] was like a screenplay. They wrote a script.

DSL: Oh, yeah, yeah-

JH: I believe that really makes a lot of sense to me – the way it was set up. It was set up-

DSL: Not only was it a murder, but it presented a false story of how he died.

JH: Yeah. Everyone had a place. There were actors.

DSL: Well, yeah, right. Once you penetrated the Secret Service and White House Detail with some "bad actors" ... the key person is chief of security – who was [U.S. Secret Service Senior Agent] Roy Kellerman sitting in the front right seat.[73]

JH: So, you think he was like the big one that was involved?

DSL: Oh, yeah! I mean, the driver [William Greer] is obviously a critical person. He's just as bad. But, Kellerman's up there with the concept ... He's the director.

JH: Do you think there were only a couple of Secret Service men that were really involved – the rest just didn't know what was going on?

DSL: Um, I think it was a "mixed bag." I think that ... on the Kennedy Detail, it was penetrated and Roy Kellerman was the breakthrough. Once Kellerman said "Yes!" – Kennedy was a dead man walking.

JH: Do you ... you said "penetrated." Do you think they brought in operatives into the Secret Service...?

DSL: Yeah, yeah. Yeah, well, this starts when Kennedy gets the nomination.... They must have pitched Kellerman back when Kennedy got the nomination [July 15, 1960]. Kellerman was Chief of Security under Eisenhower. In other words, he was there already.

73   Wikipedia: Roy Kellerman.

JH: What do you think they told him? … They can't just say, "Hey, we're going to bump him off." "OK, that sounds good."

DSL: Oh, no, no, no, no. What they do is, they give him the pitch that, "He's selling out the country to Russia. He's misguided. He has Addison's Disease, and he's going to be a dead man anyway … The country's been deceived. They hid the medical evidence about the medical condition, and it's affecting his judgment.[74] We're in the nuclear era now. We can't … [mess] around with this simply because his father is one of the richest men in the country." You know, his father in 1960 was like the equivalent … of Bill Gates in wealth.

JH: Yeah, yeah, yeah….

DSL: So, that's the kind of pitch it would have been….

JH: No, I understand … A lot of people say, "Well, who [was involved]?" We don't really know who. But you're saying, without a doubt, your evidence shows Kellerman for sure was one of them?

DSL: Oh … you cannot do this [assassinate him] if Kennedy's got iron-clad security. So, Kellerman's the chief of the detail, and then you've got to go one step up to … [Director] of the Secret Service, James Joseph] Rowley.[75]

JH: Didn't you interview Kellerman before?

DSL: Yes. I once got him on the phone in '65, and I asked him a question – I didn't know as much as I know now. I thought he wasn't in the car at the time. I had a primitive understanding – much more primitive than I grew to understand. The driver of the car was not [William] Greer.[76] But, Kellerman, yes, he was in the front right seat. With my primitive understanding, I asked him a question … "Well, you know your picture doesn't

74   Wikipedia: Addison's Disease.
75   Wikipedia: James Joseph Rowley.
76   Wikipedia: William Greer. This is a very controversial statement which is the basis for Mr. Lifton's "Godzilla" Theory. This ties into the fact that the limo was moving a lot slower than depicted in the Zapruder Film. In fact, there is some eyewitness and photographic evidence that it came to a stop. Remember that after the headshot, Secret Service Agent Clint Hill officially ran and jumped onto the back of the "moving limo," meaning it could not have been moving too fast at that point. Another wrinkle to this is the fact that JFK's limo driver, SSA Tom Shipman, died under strange circumstances at a Camp David dinner, October 14, 1963. Interestingly, it seems that whereas Shipman was a fan of JFK, Greer was not. Check out this post on Pinterest – what the CIA would dub "conspiratorial": Paterson, Aaron. "Agent Tom Shipman, JFK's Limo Driver Mysteriously Died in His Sleep at…." Pinterest, Date Unknown. Retrieved 7/4/2023: https://www.pinterest.com/pin/history--6262886973961008/. I showed this post to Mr. Lifton, and we discussed it. He was intrigued by it – to say the least. See also: Vince Palamara. "The Real Death of a Secret Service Agent the Month Before the Kennedy Assassination 10/14/1963." YouTube, 2023, 07:51. Retrieved 8/19/2023: https://www.youtube.com/watch?v=fWbllrlH_kU.

look like you.' I really thought (Laughs) I was on to something. I was not, OK? (Laughs) And he says – this is before I bought a recorder: "Mr. Lifton, I take a pretty poor picture." (Laughs)

JH: Now, you said Greer wasn't the driver, but Greer is officially known as the driver. Correct?

DSL: Yeah, but there's a driver that got shot.

JH: Right.

DSL: [Governor] Connally[77] shot the [original] driver.

JH: Wow. Because the driver shot Kennedy, right?

DSL: Oh, yeah. Connally's hearing all these rumors: … they're going to change the trip; they are going to have a motorcade; they're not going to have a motorcade. He knew something was up. He knew it was very serious. He tried to persuade Kennedy not to come.

JH: Really?

DSL: Kennedy insists on coming to Dallas, and Connally – basically his attitude is, "Well, I'll do the best I can." I can't imagine the conversations with Nellie [Connally] … I think what happened is … Oswald thinks he's involved in a covert operation to fake a lethal … [assassination] … So, they can go and blame it on Castro.… The reason I think something like this [Connally shooting the driver] happened is Oswald was very egotistical in a way and proud of himself.… There's a point where he actually tries to see the governor the month before, and he was up in the [Connally's] office. And Larry King-

JH: I read something about that, yeah.

DSL: And Larry King shunted him aside, and they postponed it or whatever. And that's what happened. That's how Governor Connally got tipped off. Because I think at some point, Oswald communicated to Connally, "Listen, in the upcoming operation we're gonna have–" to which Connally must have been thinking, "What the Hell is this guy talking about?" Cause he was the same – remember Oswald wrote Connally a letter when he was in Russia. Do you remember this?

JH: No. He wrote Connally?

DSL: Yes … the famous letter in the Warren Report.[78] When he's trying to get back to the United States.

77   Wikipedia: John Connally, Nellie Connally.
78   Oswald wrote (dated January 30, 1961) then Secretary of the Navy John Connally about

JH: Why Connally? Why would he write Connally?

DSL: He was the ... Secretary of the Navy.

JH: Oh, Secretary of the Navy.

DSL : That's correct. Yeah. That's all discussed openly in the Warren Report.... What I think happened is ... Oswald approaches Connally in 1963 and says, "Hey, Governor, this is really going to be some thing we're both involved in. You know, we're going to create this false (Laughs) assassination...."

JH: And of course, Connally's probably going, "No."

DSL: Yeah, Connally's going, "What the Hell is going on here?" He was close to Johnson. I think it's the kind of thing where Connally would say something to Johnson, and Johnson would [just] shrug. "I don't know what ... [this matter] is," he [Connally] would tell his wife [Nellie]. "We've got to be careful, though. I'll be much relieved once he's through Texas..." You may not know this, but when he [JFK] was in ... El Paso, there was an incident – and ... it was on the ... police radio. And there were two ... plain clothes men in a car.... A local constable, which I guess is like a deputy sheriff or something, hears these two guys [plain clothes men] talking, and what he hears is that one of them says to the other: "I don't think he's [JFK] going to make it through this city."

JH: Wow.

DSL: And ... so he [constable] reports that to the [El Paso] Police.... He copied down the license plate.... They shot a report to the police chief of El Paso.... [So] they were looking for this car. In other words, there were "rumblings" [talk of assassination]. So, there you have a situation where somebody is a low level [official] that gets wind of some piece of noise [but] it's not the signal, you know what I mean? They're alerted to something, but it was in the wrong city, and it's part of the actual public record – that we're looking for this car...

JH: Let me get back.... You said Connally was aware – I'm confused by the whole El Paso thing....

DSL: El Paso is not Connally.... But Dallas, Connally knows something's up. El Paso was, he was in El Paso in August or something? He went to the army base there or?[79]

his "belated dishonorable [sic] discharge." Note the misspelling of the American word "dishonorable" with the English spelling of the same word: "dishonourable."

[79]   Long, Trish. "Past Presidential Visits: John F. Kennedy in 1963." ElPasoTimes.com, Febru-

JH: My father-in-law told me that there was talk about killing him [JFK] in a motorcade in Chicago-

DSL: Oh, yeah. There's a whole bunch of stuff about that ... I personally don't think there was much to that. I wouldn't be surprised if there was a Chicago scenario, but I think Dallas was the big green light – because I don't think they had the police on board in Chicago. I don't remember if they had the secret service on board in Chicago, you know what I mean?

JH: Right, right, right. Yeah.

DSL: There are places where you can't do this.... They couldn't do this, for example, in Massachusetts. He's too beloved.... There's too much political support. You have to "poison the waters" to kill him in that [way] – it was easy to "poison the waters" in Texas. This is a Roman Catholic. He's beholden to Rome, you know – the Pope; anti-Catholic stuff.

JH: I was looking up – Who was the Black Secret Service agent?

DSL: Abraham Bolden.[80]

JH: Bolden, that's right. He was the one that wrote a book-

DSL: Kennedy put him on [the Presidential Protective Division].... Kennedy was very forward looking [and placed Bolden as the first African American in that position] ... [as] an indication to the Black community [that] Kennedy was open to [change].

JH: He [Bolden] felt like there was something odd–

DSL : He was hearing talk among some of the agents – I can tell you right now. I think I know who some of these guys were. There was anti-Kennedy sentiment on the White House Detail; very dangerous.

JH: Yeah, I mean if your guards....

DSL: It's a good indication ... [that something is seriously wrong] if your body guards ... [don't like you]....

JH: As soon as he got the nomination, they – whoever *they* were – set the thing [assassination plot] in motion. They had a plan prior to Kennedy even running.... They – meaning the military or people in power...

DSL: It's not the military necessarily, but it's a visceral click that's being paid off and recruited by and being lied to about.... You know, "We've got

ary 6, 2019. Retrieved 7/4/2023: https://www.elpasotimes.com/story/archives/2019/02/06/el-pa-so-past-presidential-visits-john-f-kennedy-1963/2796976002/#. Note that LBJ, John Connally, and Senator Ralph Yarborough were all present on that visit, Wednesday-Thursday, June 5-6, 1963.
80   Wikipedia: Abraham Bolden.

the information. He's going to do this with Russia. He's giving them all the wheat." Remember the Wheat Deal?[81]

JH: But, did you not say ... this plan was formulated in the late '50s to knock off the president [whoever he was] ... ?

DSL: I think ... Kennedy indicates that he's going to run ... when he recovers from the ... operation.[82] Because he was really in serious trouble medically, but he survived. ... He announces he's going to run ... I'm just saying, they don't have the plans for Dallas worked out that early...

JH: It wasn't just Kennedy. Could it have been Mickey Mouse? ... They're going to get rid of him, and they're going to get Johnson in there....

DSL: The point is, Johnson's gonna become president, but Johnson's got to get on the ticket.... Remember, he [JFK] didn't want Johnson on the ticket.... He wanted Senator Symington of Missouri.[83] And he was a good friend of his. He had been Secretary of the Air Force. And he was an Ivy League-type gentleman. ... Remember, they blackmailed Kennedy to get Johnson on the ticket, and once he's in the line of succession ... a whole list of possibilities opens up. That's the key. You could have an assassination of Kennedy, but it doesn't have much power if ... succession isn't covered. And remember there was tremendous puzzlement, "What the Hell is Johnson wanting to be on the ticket for–"

JH: Right....

DSL: "Because he's already Senate Majority Leader." And when you know the American political system – that's crazy. Why does the Senate Majority Leader want to become the veep? The veep doesn't have any power. *Unless lighting strikes.*

JH: When you look at stuff like that ... politics is dirty business. So, what is he [LBJ] thinking...?

DSL: Well ... Kennedy was aware of the possibility. He was forced to take Johnson on the ticket, and he said to Jackie or Kenny O'Donnell, "Johnson as a president would be a disaster, and so let's make sure there's no

81   JFKLibrary.org. "USSR: Wheat Negotiations, 1963." Retrieved 7/4/2023: https://www.jfklibrary.org/asset-viewer/archives/JFKPOF/126a/JFKPOF-126a-008. See also: Author Unknown. "Nation: The Great Wheat Deal." Time magazine, October 18, 1963. Retrieved 7/4/2023: https://content.time.com/time/subscriber/article/0,33009,873744-1,00.html.

82   By chance, prior to transcribing this conversation, I had just finished reading Bruce Lee's book, *JFK: Boyhood to the White House*, Crest Book, 1962, 152 pages. [Formerly known as *Boy's Life of John Kennedy*, Bold Face Books, 1961]. After his life-saving back operation in October of 1954, Lee states: "As Jack took his place in the Senate again [May 1955], only one thought could have been deep in his mind ... a try for the Presidency of the United States." (Page 113)

83   Wikipedia: Stuart Symington.

disaster."[84] Kennedy was very aware of the fate – the line of succession, and the cards he had been ... [dealt] – the poker hand he held ... [but] he thought he could beat the odds.... [However] remember what he said: "If they're gonna get me, they'll even get me in church." Did you know that?

JH: No, I didn't know that. No.

DSL: Well, that's in Evelyn Lincoln's book.[85]

JH: I ... read that he had said, "If they want to shoot me with a rifle from a building there's nothing I can do about it."

DSL: Well, that's that morning!

JH: Oh, wow.

DSL: November 22.

JH: Talk about ... being prescient....

DSL: I think he – yes, actually he didn't just say a remark, he pantomimed the idea that he was shot by a man in a crowd with a pistol, you know.... He was aware of the odds. He was very fatalistic about it. Look. Let me tell you how bad it was. Bobby Kennedy wanted to take the Protective Unit of the Secret Service, OK – what they call the White House Detail. Remember, the Secret Service has field offices all around the United States, and they chase counterfeiters. One of their big functions is to protect the currency. But, Bobby wanted to take the Protective Unit and put it under the ... DOJ.[86] There was actually a vote. He tried to get legislation passed in February of '63, and it was blocked by *Strom Thurmond*. He [Bobby] knew something was up.... One of their attitudes was, "Jack – don't go to Dallas. Don't do this. Don't do that." And Kennedy said "No" to all of that stuff.[87]

---

84   Wikipedia: Kenneth O'Donnell. See also: Klein, Rick. "Jacqueline Kennedy Reveals That JFK Feared an LBJ Presidency." ABCNews.Go.com, September 8, 2011. Retrieved 7/4/2023: https://abcnews.go.com/Politics/Jacqueline_Kennedy/jacqueline-kennedy-reveals-jfk-feared-lbj-presidency/story?id=1447793.

85   Wikipedia: Evelyn Lincoln. See also: Lincoln, Evelyn. *My Twelve Years with John F. Kennedy*. NYC: David McKay Company, Inc., 1965, 371 pages.

86   Vince Palamara. "David Lifton: Lecture at Bismarck State College 11/17/13." YouTube, 2013, 57:46 minutes. Retrieved 10/12/2023: https://www.youtube.com/watch?v=zgL38AA8Ewc. In one of his most important presentations, Mr. Lifton lays out the evidence supporting what Mr. Lifton dubbed the "Embryo Government Theory." LBJ began to immediately create a toehold in JFK's administration through the appointment of various individuals throughout same including the creation – and this is key – *his own Secret Service contingency answerable* only to LBJ. (Circa 14:37)

87   This issue of Bobby Kennedy trying to create his brother's own security force speaks volumes, and I found this interesting discussion about this exact topic: America's Untold Stories. "Mark Groubert Goes to Dallas w/ Special Guest Viva Frei." YouTube, 2022, 1:41:23 Minutes (circa 11:59). Retrieved 7/14/2023: https://www.youtube.com/watch?v=eMBc-O4_wOc.

JH: You had said to me, and I had heard this before, that they ... played on his [Kennedy's] ego.... Like Johnson would say, "Oh, you probably shouldn't go [to Dallas]." And Kennedy was like, "No, no ... Why wouldn't I go...?"

DSL: Yeah, I'm not going ... [is] to be a coward. His attitude towards fate [was obvious]. Remember his famous poem, "I Have a Rendezvous with Death" ... If I'm not mistaken, he wanted Jacqueline to read it to him at night before he went to bed.[88]

JH: Do you believe ... there's ... a picture that [allegedly] shows George H. W. Bush leaning against the book depository building-

DSL: That's not true....

JH: You don't believe that Bush had something to do with it.

DSL: No, I don't believe that ... Bush was an honorable person, and when he heard a rumor about trouble for Kennedy ... he phones it in or something...

JH: George H. W. Bush?

DSL: Yeah. He's in Houston, and he picks up something. He hears something. Yes. That's in the historical record. He didn't have the details, but there was a threat of some sort.

JH: Wow...

DSL: Look. You do understand. Connally was armed. That's against the law. He's not supposed to have a gun while he's riding in ... Kennedy's presence.[89]

JH: You had said that ... I have to find the ... picture of Connally coming out of the plane-

DSL: That's right! There are some great pictures. One of them is with him walking down the ramp. His head is downcast [with] his hands on Mrs. Connally. But, the best one is under the wing of the aircraft, before they get in the motorcade.[90] He is absolutely – you can *look at Connally's face,*

---

88   Seeger, Alan. *Poems* ("I Have a Rendezvous with Death"). NYC: Charles Scribner's Sons, 1916, 174 pages. Retrieved 7/4/2023: https://www.poetryfoundation.org/poems/45077/i-have-a-rendezvous-with-death.

89   I'm not sure where this thought came from. I think Mr. Lifton is making the point, with indirect reference to Bush's warning, that some leaders were aware of threats and "on edge" – thus Bush calling in a threat and Connally carrying a gun.

90   Mr. Lifton pointed out to me that there is an image of Governor Connally exiting the plane at Love Field with a look of serious concern on his face. He knows full well that there was a plot afoot; thus he's armed according to Mr. Lifton. For the image, see: Yesterday's America. "A President's Final Days in Texas." YesterdaysAmerica.com, Date Unknown. Retrieved 7/4/2023: https://

and he's frightened. Right there in his face … there's nothing subtle about it.… Here's what I think happened: He insisted that there be no motorcade. He was lied to and falsely assured that there would be no motorcade. So, he [initially] felt that this terrible thing that he was worried about was not gonna happen; [no motorcade]. He's coming down [from the plane], and he sees the cars lined up for a motorcade.… At that moment, he realizes he's been lied to.

JH: Wow.

DSL: Something terrible is going on. You didn't know about the note … the "no motorcade" business?

JH: No.

DSL: Yeah, that's in the record.

JH: So, he asked that there not be a motorcade … ?

DSL: No, no. Oh, he insisted. This is in [the] days before. When Kennedy arrived at Love Field, he wanted to go by helicopter directly to speak at the Trade Mart. And then … he was falsely assured as I recall the story – that would be the arrangement.… In an alternate universe, if he had said, "Jack, come over here. Let me speak to you for a minute. I got wind of dah, dah, dah, dah, dah." And Kennedy says, "Well, what am I supposed to do?" He says, "Well, you're going to suddenly come down with a very serious infection in your tummy … [and] we have to get you to the hospital." Remember, they don't know what's planned.… Furthermore … this is *my personal opinion*: They had a special agent who gave them back assurances, "Listen, I tapped into the anti-Castro underground here. There's nothing planned." And that special agent – get this – was LHO. In other words, Oswald thinks he's hot sh*t, and he doesn't understand that he's being set up. So, he "puts his ear to the ground" and reports back that it's OK. The fact that he's being set up has been concealed from him. So, he doesn't understand what's in store for him.

JH: So, do you think he … let his … handler know…

DSL: His handler's gotta be corrupt.

JH: What I'm saying is, he … is telling his handler, "Hey, these guys are trying to kill the president." [And Oswald was told] "Good job, Lee! We broke up the ring. Everything's cool. Go back to work." And then while that was happening, they were killing the president.…

DSL: Yeah. Sort of, but I think what's going on is, Oswald was able to issue false assurances that nothing's afoot; a lot of smoke but no fire.

JH: But when you say that he issued "false assurances" – who did he issue ... [them] to...?

DSL: I think he tells his handler ... What I used to say when I was researching – this was years ago – Oswald had two handlers[91]: a "good handler" ... [e.g. Bobby Kennedy's assistant] and the other one I called the "rogue handler" ... [who] leads Oswald to do certain things that don't make any sense, specifically, the trip to Mexico City [September 1963] ... I believe that when Oswald went to Mexico City,[92] the genuine – the "good guy handler" – loses track of him. See, I think they [Anti-Castro Cubans = good guys] said to him [late September] ..., "OK.... Your wife's having a baby ... Her due date is mid-October. Go back to Texas and have a nice life. We'll be back in touch with you later." But, he did his job. The evidence that something crazy is going on is that he [Oswald] makes this trip down to Mexico City. Remember, he's trying to go to Cuba.... He goes to the [Cuban] Embassy and says he wants a [transit] visa ... to go to Havana enroute to Moscow ... [Pro-Castro Cubans = rogue handler] told him, "OK, we have another job for you.... We're going to send you back to Russia" ... And he goes to the embassy, and that's when he has that big conversation with ... the KGB agent [Valery Kostikov].... He had two handlers.[93]

JH: I never heard that before...

DSL: That's my hypothesis. That ... [Oswald] had a rogue handler.

JH: What ... evidence is there that ... [Oswald] had a "good handler" though?

DSL: Well, I used to be more fluent in this. The evidence that he had a good handler–

---

91   I admit, this "two handler" theory gets a bit murky. I do not hold Mr. Lifton accountable for a lack of clarity, rather myself. Frankly, being truly the smartest man I ever met, I had trouble following his explanation with this at times. Unfortunately, where I could have asked clarifying questions, I did not, or they were substandard. Therefore, I apologize to the reader for any lack of clarity herewith.

92   See Mary Ferrell Foundation. "Oswald in Mexico City." MaryFerrell.org. Retrieved 7/4/2023: https://www.maryferrell.org/pages/Oswald_in_Mexico_City.html.

93   This theory lends itself to the idea that there were actually *two Oswalds*. Now, to say the least – this sounds kooky. I must state emphatically that I do not remember discussing this theory with Mr. Lifton. My guess is that he would dismiss it as ridiculous, but I could be wrong. I have studied this idea to a degree, and there is quite a bit of corroborating evidence to support it. For more information, see the books: Armstrong, John. *Harvey and Lee*. Quasar Books, 2003, 983 pages; Fleming, Glenn B. *The Two Faces of Lee Harvey Oswald*. Empire Publications, 2003, 343 pages.

JH: I get the rogue handler. That makes sense, but … what [circumstantial] evidence … what events made you think, "Oh, he must have had a good handler…."

DSL: I'm trying to remember. I'm sorry. My age is interfering.… The way you connect the dots there – what he [Oswald] was doing. OK. He's in New Orleans handing out those [pro-Castro] pamphlets. That's the good handler. In other words, he's got an assignment to "smoke out" any activity in New Orleans, right? So, he's handing out the pamphlets, and he's going to the [pro-Castro] meetings…

JH: You consider that … counterintelligence?

DSL: Well, whatever his function was.

JH: He's trying to figure out – someone came up [to him and said], "Hey, Lee, I want to fight for Castro…."

DSL: Right … There was two kinds of evidence there. There was a fork in the road. In New Orleans, he was handing out [pro-Castro] leaflets [i.e. pamphlets] and therefore attracting the anti-Castro community against him, right? Remember, Castro wasn't terribly popular in '63.… When Oswald was handing out the leaflets … it was not his own design. He's got a handler. Remember they got him on the radio twice: August … [17, 1963 – alone, and August 21, 1963] – opposite Carlos Bringuier?[94] … It was a debate. He [Oswald] … did very well.[95]

JH: That was set up by the good handler?

DSL: That debate … he would not have done without a clearance from the person running him.

JH: The good handler.

DSL: Yeah, absolutely…

JH: Would you say … do you think he fired at General Walker?

DSL: Yes.

JH: Was that the good handler or the bad [i.e rogue] handler [assignment]?

94   Wikipedia: Carlos Bringuier. For his August 17 interview, see: WYES. "Lee Harvey Oswald in New Orleans: Tricentennial Moment." YouTube, 2018, 2:20 minutes. Retrieved 7/5/2023: https://www.youtube.com/watch?v=q8KSAw42Rls.
95   Interestingly, PBS' *Frontline* notes that the debate "humiliated him." See: Rockwood, Bill. "Glimpses of a Life." PBS.org, 2013. Retrieved 7/5//2023: https://www.pbs.org/wgbh/frontline/article/glimpses-of-a-life/#:~:text=Two%20Radio%20Appearances%20in%20New%20Orleans%2C%20August%201963&text=In%20this%2035%2Dminute%20interview,days%20later%2C%20is%20more%20famous.

DSL: They created a situation … it was a deliberate missed shot. … After he got back from Russia in June of 1962, he's basically just working as a factory worker. Then, he's … [in Dallas] working at that shop [Leslie Welding Company]. … Then they shift him over to … the printing company [Jaggars-Chiles-Stovall] – which was great. … He could manufacture his own photography … which created the appearance of course [of Oswald] holding the rifle and everything. … That he's some sort of a pro-Castro, you know, a dangerous person on the loose. …

JH: So, when he [Oswald] went and purposely missed General Walker, was he there because the bad handler had him go do that or the good handler … ?

DSL: Hmm. (Sighs)

JH: See, I'm thinking the bad handler, but I don't know.

DSL: No, no. I … think the good handler knows about the Walker shot. I'm trying to remember. There's a great picture of Walker smiling and holding a cup of coffee that night when he gets shot at.

JH: So, you think Walker knew that was going to happen … ?

DSL: I think there was – yeah, I've always been suspicious that Walker was part of that set up – but he didn't know Kennedy was gonna be killed. … I know somebody who knew Walker at the time. Walker was kind of an old feeble man.

JH: Maybe, they [good handler] were just trying to generate sympathy for him … ?

DSL: Yeah. yeah … Here's what I think. I think Oswald was alone that night. A missed shot was fired. … The key to the whole Walker thing was not the firing of the shot, although that happened, but that Oswald comes *running into the apartment* where they lived – with Marina. … He turns on the radio, and she says, "What's going on?" She doesn't speak any English. … He says, "I'm looking because I was on a mission here. I want to see what happens as a consequence of Walker." She says, "What happened with Walker?" He says, "Well, I shot at Walker." He's role playing in front of his wife. It's dangerous, but he's doing it. He's impeaching his own character in the eyes of his wife.

JH: Why would he do that, do you think … ?

DSL : It's very important because if they [good handlers] don't do something like that – let me ask you a question? You do know that Lee Oswald loved President Kennedy?

JH: Yes.

DSL: Do you know that he made that love clear on numerous occasions? He was going through magazines and taking out pictures of Kennedy and pasting them up or something where they lived...

JH: I didn't know that.

DSL: There's no secret to Marina how much Lee adored Kennedy ... [as noted] when I interviewed her. And we put this on the national program *Hard Copy*.... He didn't just like President Kennedy. She corrected me: Lee *adored* Kennedy.[96]

JH: Wow. But why lie to his wife about Walker. What's the connection? I'm missing something.

DSL: Oh, he's gotta impeach himself because she'd [Marina] become a character witness on his behalf. Because once the event-

JH: She would be able to say, "He's crazy. He admitted to me [that] he shot at Walker." That sort of thing....

DSL: Correct. They have to do that. If that's not done, she becomes a witness that says, "He loved President Kennedy. He wouldn't shoot at him." Because of Walker, this terrible seed is planted in her mind that she's married to a crazy man. She's [Marina] terrified when he has this rifle ... and he's pretending to practice with it out on the porch at night ... dry firing it.... Remember he autographed a picture of himself with the rifle...? ... Here's what he wrote on the back of the picture of himself with the rifle: "Hunter of Fascists, Ha, Ha, Ha?" In other words, like it's a private joke.[97]

JH: Is that the one he gave to de Mohrenschildt...?

DSL: That's correct ... de Mohrenschildt knew how Lee adored Kennedy.... It was really unfortunate.... He was out of the country at the time of the assassination.

JH: Really? Do you think on purpose...?

---

96   Sherlock G. "Marina Oswald Talks (Part 1)." YouTube, 2013 (Air Date: November 19, 1990), 9:31 minutes. Retrieved 7/8/2023: https://www.youtube.com/watch?v=j4cdNJooptw; Sherlock G. "Marina Oswald Talks (Part 2)." YouTube, 2013 (Air Date: November 19, 1990), 5:26 minutes. Retrieved 7/8/2023: https://www.youtube.com/watch?v=yR4YyaAZF54; Sherlock G. "Marina Oswald Talks (Part 3)." YouTube, 2013 (Air Date: November 19, 1990), 4:14 minutes. Retrieved 7/8/2023: https://www.youtube.com/watch?v=gXTjj0Do7Yk.

97   See the tense interview Marina Oswald has with NBC's Tom Brokaw: David Von Pein's JFK Channel. "1993 Interview with Marina Oswald Porter." YouTube, 2013, 10:38 minutes. Retrieved 7/13/2023: https://www.youtube.com/watch?v=El_xm3rHrx4. Frankly, Marina made mincemeat out of Brokaw.

DSL: I think somebody – he was friends with Herman Brown [Brown & Root Construction] ... the war contractors who were connected with Johnson[98] ... I don't know what Herman Brown said [to de Mohrenschildt] ... Herman Brown ... was connected with ... [the assassination], but I think in an innocent capacity.

JH: I understand ... but did you not say that de Mohrenschildt was friends with Herman Brown?

DSL: He was ... :

JH: And that you thought that maybe Herman Brown suggested to de Mohrenschildt, "Hey, you better disappear for a couple of weeks ...."

DSL: Well, no, de Mohrenschildt had ... legitimate business dealings down in [Haiti] ...

JH: It just so happened that ... he was out of the country when Kennedy was killed ...?

DSL: I don't think it's happenstance.... I think they had to make damn sure that de Mohrenschildt.... We don't want to have a situation where de Mohrenschildt can testify, "Hey, wait a second. I was with Oswald last week, and he adored Kennedy" (Laughs), you know. His wife ... Jean de Mohrenschildt could testify to the same facts that Lee adored Kennedy.

JH: Real quick – at the Tippit Shooting ... what happened? Were there two shooters ...?

DSL: (Sighs) ... I used to know this stuff inside out. Basically what happened is, Oswald's supposed to be shot in the building.... Remember, it's like a screenplay. Kennedy rounds the corner, he's shot by the professional assassins, and the question I think is important is: Where is Oswald at the time of the Dealey Plaza shooting? OK. Now, I think I know where he was *supposed to be*. He was supposed to be upstairs in the fifth or sixth floor of the Depository. And I used to believe that – that he was really upstairs. I don't anymore. He's outside in Dealey Plaza over near the pergola behind Zapruder.

JH: Why do you say that though ...?

---

98   I found this interesting webpage with an accompanying song while researching Herman Brown: Gillete, Steve. "Two Men In The Building." AboutheSong.com, 1998. Retrieved 7/5/2023: https://aboutthesong.com/Blog/twomeninthebuilding. This reminds me of Bob Dylan's groundbreaking song, "Murder Most Foul" (2020), which Mr. Lifton heard and appreciated – because Dylan mentions pre-autopsy surgery in the lyrics (Verse 3), the thesis of *Best Evidence: Disguise and Deception in the Assassination of John F. Kennedy.*

DSL: Because of the enlargements I've made of photographs. There's someone in the pergola, and there's a resemblance to Oswald. So, that's what I think is going on.... He loved Kennedy and he wants to be there. He doesn't understand that he's being set up. So, the person who pokes the gun or some piece of wood or whatever it was out the [sixth floor] window ... that's not Oswald. That guy is part of the acting ... he's a role player.

JH: Do you think that the guy at the sixth floor window was actually not shooting at all or....

DSL: No, I'm 90% sure he was firing blanks.... It's a staged shooting [at the sixth floor].

JH: Do you have any idea of who it might have been...?

DSL: No. He was one of the professionals in this thing, and he's firing blanks. And by the way if it was Oswald, and I'm not saying it was ... it's a non-lethal operation. They're giving him some bullsh*t story, and Jack is aware of it, it's approved by Bobby Kennedy ... I believe blanks were fired from up there. That's what happened.

JH: So, he [Oswald] goes down there [Dealey Plaza] ... to see the president. He's down there, he sees the shooting, how does he end up back on the second floor [in the lunchroom]...?

DSL: OK. What I think happens is he's ... about forty feet behind Zapruder. He's right there connected with the [Grassy Knoll] gunmen. He [Oswald] thinks they're staging an incident. It's non-lethal.... They [gunmen] look at him and say, "Get your a** back to the lunchroom." ... So, he runs over to the building, over to the loading dock, gets his tush up to the second floor in the lunchroom. [Oswald was told], "We will meet you in the lunchroom." He understands that he's going to be falsely arrested by a Dallas patrolman and brought down to the police station ... where he can spout off his line about Castro. That's what *he thinks* is going to happen. [Oswald].... Doesn't know that it's a setup where *he is going to be killed*.... Here's the difference between David Lifton and popular perception of this. Popular perception is that he's upstairs, and he runs down the stairs.

JH: Right....

DSL: He ends up at the second floor lunchroom. For many years, I believed that was going on. I do not any longer believe it because they didn't need Oswald upstairs; to create the charade upstairs.... In their ideal world ... they would love it if Oswald would stick a rifle out of the window and fire blanks. But, I don't think he did. I think there's too much evidence that he was down in the lunchroom.... So, I think there's some operative up there firing blanks. Now, the only person who says it was Oswald [in the window] was Howard Brennan.[99] So, we have a fork in the road here ... either Oswald's in the window or he's not in the window. If he's in the window, then you go down one path. If he's not in the window, somebody else sticks a gun or something out the window ... [This] simulates the assassination ... so [Tom] Dillard and people in the motorcade go, "Look up there! There's a gun...!"

JH: Yeah....

DSL: Oswald, meanwhile, is downstairs. The question is ... "Did Oswald get downstairs because he was upstairs and ran down all those stairs?" It's possible. "Or, was Oswald in the lunchroom , and did he arrive in the lunchroom from some other location?" It's my recent reanalysis of the Moorman photograph that shows someone's in the pergola who ... looks like Oswald. I tend to favor that path. If that's true, then Oswald was like a bystander to the assassination ... but he didn't know that what he had just witnessed was a lethal event. So, he gets his a** over there [to the lunchroom as ordered], the cop runs in, Oswald's got the Coke in his hand, Truly – the superintendent of the building ... says, "He works here." ... Officer Baker takes the gun away from Oswald's ... [stomach] ... Truly and Baker then continue up the stairway.... After ... [they reach] the sniper's nest ... they go up to the roof on the elevator ... and Truly testifies that Officer Baker says to him.... "We must be careful. This man can blow your head off."

JH: Wow....

DSL: Did you know that?.... That's in the Warren Commission testimony of Roy Truly. So, by understanding that [statement], we understand the state of mind of Officer Baker – who's been given some cock and bull story [earlier] about ... "Castro's trying to kill Kennedy, and if that should happen anywhere in the motorcade, you've gotta go in and catch the assassin...."

JH: So ... at the point where Baker and Truly continue on their journey, what does Oswald do at that point? [At this point, Mr. Lifton goes

---

through Oswald's movements after he leaves the building, all of which he has already discussed above. However, I asked him to clarify some facts starting with the Tippit Shooting.

DSL: They're setting Oswald up to shoot the officer. Remember, the officer asks for his [Oswald's] ID. Tippit's not involved. He's just following the radio instructions. "Be on the lookout for a man five foot ten, one hundred sixty five pounds." That's the broadcast they put out.... Contrary to what the official version is, I believe there's a car – because I found a news article about this published on 11/22, *Dallas Morning News* – I believe that Tippit was shot from a car. Yes.

JH: But ... the story is that Oswald shot him facing him across the car, and you're saying a car drove by and shot him....

DSL: Yes, he [driver in car] shot him [Tippit], and Oswald runs away. Oswald draws a gun, and he fires back at the [second] car [not Tippit's]. That's witnessed.... Then, he [Oswald] turns and runs ... I left this out. Someone in that [second] car got hit. Now, how do I know that? Radio transmissions indicated [this]....[100]

JH: I want to jump back to [JFK's limo] ... You said Governor Connally shot the Secret Service Agent [i.e. the driver]. The car comes to a stop.

DSL: Connally shot the Secret Service Agent.

JH: Connally shot the Secret Service Agent who was driving [and] who turned around and shot Kennedy.

DSL: I believe so, yes.

JH: And then, someone from the follow up car ran and jumped in, and took over the driver-

DSL: That's Secret Service Agent ... [Name purposely withheld].

JH: And then the car went under the ... [Triple Underpass], and you said you interviewed a couple [of] witnesses who saw ... that the car came to a stop, and that Jackie tried to climb out of the car.

DSL: Yes ... that's witnessed...

JH: Why did she try to climb out of the car...?

---

100   Mr. Lifton's theory on the Tippit shooting – with two gunmen and a second vehicle – is incredible. Yet, there is plenty of evidence to support his theory. Admittedly, the entire crime never made sense to me. There is an excellent discussion on the Tippit Shooting available on YouTube where Mr. Lifton's research from *Best Evidence* is interwoven; frankly amazing. Check out: America's Untold Stories. "JFK Assassination Aftermath – Who Killed J. D. Tippit?" YouTube, 2021, 1:00:24 minutes. Retrieved 7/7/2023: https://www.youtube.com/live/oky-UZ1kGwo?feature=share.

DSL: Because there had been shooting in the car. She [Jackie] felt she was in jeopardy. We know that from Dealey Plaza she was out on the trunk of the car.

JH: Yeah ... right, right, right. Didn't she say something like, "They're going to kill me...?"

DSL: She told the nurse [Mary Gallagher[101]] ... when she was getting out of her bloody clothes that night.... "I was afraid they were going to shoot me, too." T-o-o. She knows what happened, however confusing it may have been – because when she got to Bethesda, she's up on the 17th floor, in that presidential suite, and Bobby's up there, and [Robert] Mc-Namara's up there.[102] I think they said to her, "Tell us what happened." She told them what happened. One of the things I'm pissed off about Bobby Kennedy is that nobody said, "Get a stenographer in here. Get a tape recorder in here immediately...."

WEDNESDAY, DECEMBER 15, 2021

DSL: Have you been to San Antonio?

JH: I have. I've driven through there. It's beautiful....

DSL: I know. It really is very beautiful.... They tried to get President Kennedy to visit San Antonio. It was "Plan B" [assassination site]. There was a big parade route discussion – an argument – about whether it will or will not pass through Alamo Plaza. And it really sounded so much like the news stories that preceded ... you know, which way will the parade route go ... in Dallas? So, the headline story – and I used to have files on this ... one of them is called the Express-News ... the other was called [the] San Antonio Light.... The headline of [one stated].... "The Parade.... A Route or a Rout?" (Laughs).... It made me very suspicious. Oh, it's worse than that....

JH: Yeah....

DSL: [Mr. Lifton then reviewed the story of the constable overhearing the two plainclothes men in the car – as recounted above – indicate a threat to President Kennedy. His explanation of this event continued.] "He'll never make it through this city." So, the constable phoned in this thing as a threat, and he got the license plate. It [his report] was on the police radio on Thursday afternoon [November 21, 1963].... Oh, they traced the license plate ... a Secret Service car. How do you like that?

101   Wikipedia: My Life with Jacqueline Kennedy.
102   Wikipedia: Robert McNamara.

JH: Oh, wow.

DSL: So ... that story was in the San Antonio paper on Thursday afternoon, and it was published before the assassination in Dallas. And so, it became a footnote to the Dallas story the next day. I have a file on this.

JH: *Wow.*

DSL: It really was a "wow" thing.

JH: So, you think that they originally were going to kill him there....

DSL: I just think ... it's a piece of information that was overheard – who knows whether those guys [in the car] were informed properly or not – it was never supposed to be on the police radio.... [This] became a news story after the shooting in Dallas the next day.... Obviously, the focus [by then] was on Dealey Plaza, Oswald, [etc.].

JH: Well, it's proof to me-

DSL: It became a little asterisk.

JH: After reading your book, it's hard to imagine the Secret Service not being involved....

DSL: Oh, yeah! They [conspirators] penetrated the White House Detail.... [Three] agents on the White House Detail who were not involved were the "Jackie Agents": Clint Hill, Paul Landis, and there was one other who jumped into the car, opened the door, and all that. So, three of those guys [White House Detail] were OK.... The problem is that the [key] person who was involved was Roy Kellerman, the Chief of the Secret Service Dallas Detail.... Once you've got Kellerman involved, Kennedy's a "dead man walking."[103]

JH: Did you ever directly ask Kellerman on the phone or in person ... "Did you do this? Were you involved....?"

DSL: Yeah, I had that weird conversation with him in 1965.... I knew the driver had to be involved. I was bluffing Kellerman to try to get him to talk, you know. This was back in my very, very early days – before [knowledge of] "surgery" before any of that stuff ... I was challenging whether he was in the car because I knew the driver couldn't be Greer. And I think

---

103   Wikipedia: Roy Kellerman. Note Reference #1 ("LBJ 'Shield' Gets Special Capital Post," *The Spokesman-Review, Spokane*, Washington, January 9, 1965.) for this Wikipedia article regarding Rufus Youngblood and Roy Kellerman. Both he and Kellerman were promoted in 1965 by LBJ – who apparently had a lot of trust in their abilities as presidential protectors. Youngblood I could see, but Kellerman?

you know that – that I found the picture of who really was the driver.[104] He was the driver who was in Ft. Worth, and ... in ... North Dakota ... I was remarking on the fact that his picture didn't look like him ... and he said, "Mr. Lifton, I take a pretty poor picture." (Laughing) He's like a character out of a John Wayne movie....

JH: (Laughs) Well, it's like ... when Allen Dulles was being interviewed, and he's smoking his pipe ... "Did you have something to do with this?" ... and he just lights his pipe and ignores him [the interviewer].

DSL: I don't remember that interview, but you do know that I met Dulles?

JH: Yeah – didn't you debate him at UCLA...?

DSL: Yeah – we had quite a ... [conversation] ... My naive days, and I was "Mr. Eagle Scout" who had bought the 26 volumes [Warren Report]. It was December 1965....

JH: When you ... talked to him.

DSL: UCLA and Hedrick Hall or something. There were about fifty students there. I had arranged with the student organizer.... I was naive then. How could Dulles sign this report when the head's going the wrong way ... you know, the head snap?[105] I arrived, and there ... [were] about fifty students there. And I was seated in the front row with my little file folder with the photographs prepared by Ray Marcus – a little exhibit showing Kennedy's head going backwards. I was one of the first people to question Dulles at that meeting. It's all described in my Chapter 2 [*Best Evidence*] ... he was very pissed off that somebody would start to argue with him.

JH: Really? You could sense he was mad...?

DSL: Oh, yeah ... I wrote a memorandum right away as soon as it happened.... I ran to my typewriter. There were no PCs then. This is 1965, and I typed up a 13-page report to the file.... I distributed it to the people I knew at the time: Sylvia Meagher and Vincent Salandria ... David Talbot, in his book *The Devil's Chessboard*, uses my memo as the basis for that

104   Unfortunately, I never got to see the picture Mr. Lifton had of this driver.
105   Mr. Lifton got Nobel prize-winning physicist Dr. Richard Feynman to examine Zapruder frames 312-313 which depict the backwards head snap. (See Chapter 2 of *Best Evidence*, "Richard Feynman and the Head Snap," pages 48-49 of the Carroll & Graf edition) Instead, Feynman pointed out that Kennedy's head moves "forward by a small, but perceptible, amount" between 312-313, a piece of data Mr. Lifton did not notice before. Interestingly, though indirectly related to this discussion, a filmmaker recently found another strange *forward* movement by Kennedy's head in the Zapruder Film – at frames 204-205. See: GrassyKnollFilms. "Zapruder Film Secret Revealed." YouTube, 2013, 7:46 minutes. Retrieved 7/19/2023: https://www.youtube.com/watch?v=Xd_FW-0Z9bR4.

chapter 2 or something.[106] He goes through it *line-by-line* and he reports it pretty much verbatim.

JH: Wow!

DSL: Yeah, it was really nice.

JH: Now, did he [Talbot] … ask you for permission to do that or did he just do it?

DSL: Who – Talbot?

JH: Yeah….

DSL: No, I think … Salandria was in touch with Talbot or something. Salandria must have sent him my memo…. He may have written me and said, "Can I use this?" But I said, "Of course." There was no problem. But all these people … were prepared to jump on me [i.e. work with me] because I had this relationship with [Wesley] Liebeler[107] … [This] was the smartest thing in the world to do because who else knew somebody on the Warren Commission and could talk to him anytime I wanted?

Friday, December 17, 2021

JH: I just saw your interview with Brent Holland.[108]

DSL: Yeah.

JH: You were on fire, man!

DSL: Good!

JH: I was … like "Wow!" he's really talking about a lot of the details [in his upcoming book, *Final Charade*], but you did … stop at a certain point….

DSL: Oh, I'm very good at being my own security officer….

JH: You touched on the fake ambulance, Oswald getting a ride, Oswald going to Russia … for the experience [to write about]. I don't think you mentioned Jack London…

DSL: No, I was very careful.

JH: Yeah. You mentioned meeting with Marina – and Rachel [Oswald's youngest daughter]…. You talked about how she [Marina] came to you, and you explained to her-

106   Talbot, David. *The Devil's Chessboard: Allen Dulles, the CIA, and the Rise of America's Secret Government*. NYC: HarperCollins, 2015, 720 pages.
107   Wikipedia: Wesley Liebeler.
108   NightFrightShow. "JFK: 3 New Witnesses Never Heard Before (David Lifton)." YouTube, 2017, 53:47 minutes. Retrieved 7/7/2023: https://youtu.be/1tffl08ins0.

DSL: It was like deprogramming her....

JH: And you talked about the trains, and the idea that the assassins were put in the train cars and they were gassed.... Brent Holland specifically asked you, "Was he firing blanks?" ... and you said, "No. I believe he was somewhere outside, and then he ran into the westside of the building...."

DSL: Well, Jim, somebody was firing blanks. My new understanding is that it wasn't Oswald....

JH: You went into the processing of the Zapruder Film and ... how they were able to edit the Zapruder Film...?[109]

DSL: Optical printer.

JH: I don't remember us talking about this. You talked about how the FBI sent out a note to all....

DSL: That's right – to collect all [of] the films [of the assassination].

JH: You did touch on the intubation of the body when he [JFK] was really dead-

DSL: I touched on the fake intubation.

JH: Yeah, the fake intubation, and the idea that if he's dead, why bring him in the OR [operating room]? Pretend he's alive-

DSL: You gotta pretend he's alive to get him up to the OR.

MONDAY, DECEMBER 27, 2021

JH: I sent you the interview of James Jenkins....[110]

DSL: Yeah ... First of all, you have a copy of my book somewhere? ... Open up the book to Chapter 27 ["The Recollections of James Curtis Jenkins et al."].... What happened was ... I had called him up ... roughly around September [1980] ... and I went to visit him in Texas ... I got money from Macmillan to do this multi-city trip and get these things [interviews of key witnesses] on camera.... And to my considerable ... [consternation] ... he was still frightened. Too many years had passed to remember all of the details. It seemed to me, he still hadn't gotten over the trauma of November 22, '63, when he was one of the two techs – along

109   Vince Palamara. "High Quality Z-Film (David Lifton Version) With Slow-Motion Included." YouTube, 2022, 8:45 minutes. Retrieved 10/13/2023: https://www.youtube.com/watch?v=hzgUp-8BaOKs. This is perhaps the best version of the Z Film out there today.
110   Valuetainment. "JFK Assassination – Untold Stories of the Autopsy." YouTube, 2018, 1:06:36 minutes. Retrieved 7/7/2023: https://youtu.be/2U7dXPA_juM.

with [Paul] O'Connor – in the autopsy room.[111] ... [Now] Paul O'Connor was absolutely the "John Wayne" of my film.[112] He was absolutely a straight shooter...

JH: My point was that you had said ... that Dr. Humes had to stitch up some of the throat wound to make it look less-

DSL: Somebody had – we don't know who....

JH: OK. Either way, it fit with what you were saying – someone stitched ... [the throat] together. That's odd....

DSL: Yeah, yeah, what they had was a hole in the throat which was WGYE: widely gaping irregular edges. That is *not* a normal thing to have. And Humes put ... those four words – "widely gaping irregular edges" – in the autopsy report.... And then you go to the [Warren Commission] testimony, and he said, "seven to eight centimeters across" – as opposed to the autopsy report which was six-and-a-half. Seven to eight centimeters is like three inches. That's crazy.... And then the other person that came to the rescue you might say of this hypothesis was the radiologist [Jerrol F. Custer[113]].... He said the ... [throat] had been stitched.... The question was [now].... "Who gave that order?" My conclusion was that for any stitching to have occurred – and if Humes had done it which I think he did – it was all on the ... basis of higher authority. That he had to do this. You know, "Fix this! Do this!" Whatever. It's like Admiral Galloway or somebody telling them "what have you ...."[114]

JH: And you can't say, "Well, why?" "That's not for you to decide. We're ordering you to do this," [so says the military]. Jenkins made the point that these guys [Humes and Boswell] were at the end of their careers. You're not gonna risk your career. [Looking over *Best Evidence*] You did a great job documenting everything....

---

111   Wikipedia: John F. Kennedy Assassination Conspiracy Theories. Though I reference this webpage page as a basic point of reference, I must clarify the title and first line. It should state "John F. Kennedy Conspiracy Facts" and "The assassination of President John F. Kennedy on November 22, 1963 spawned numerous conspiracy theories *which turned out to be true.*" See also Wikipedia: John F. Kennedy Autopsy.

112   *Best Evidence Research Video. Best Evidence: The Research Video.* YouTube, 2014, 36:28 minutes. Retrieved 7/7/2023: https://youtu.be/oAWFvcrp-ao. Originally recorded in October of 1980 and published by Rhino Video in 1989.

113   Ibid.

114   The more I think about this man's position in this historical event, "between a rock and a hard place," the more I think he was truly a hero. It appears to me that Humes had to not only be truthful, but hold back the obvious: JFK's body had been tampered with *by the military leadership above him* to conceal what really happened to the president in Dallas. See Chapter 18 of *Best Evidence*, "The Pre-Autopsy Autopsy," page 473 of the Carroll & Graf edition.

DSL: I know! (Laughs) I know … and the reason is … because the basic model that I was working off of was something I learned in physics.… When you have the physics of a collision … two little things hit each other – and you have *before and after*. That's why I was … [researching the] "before and after" on the body. I was reasoning by analogy. And by analogy – that's what it looked like: before and after. And Jenkins was one of these … [witnesses] that fit that model … That's what it [*Best Evidence*] was all about.…

JH: We were talking about [the fact that] you believe … the … [Moorman] photo – you can see Oswald … standing on the pergola or near it.

DSL: I believe the image in the pergola is very likely Oswald. I believe it is. I can't prove it.…

JH: And then, you believe … he was ordered back up to the second floor lunchroom, and that's why he wasn't all "winded" … following his role … pretending to be a part of an assassination – a fake assassination of the president.

DSL: Correct. He was involved in pretense. He was supposed to go up – first of all, he was not upstairs on the sixth floor.[115]

JH: I never believed that.…

DSL: But somebody stuck a rifle or a piece of wood or something out that window. I think when I talked to you last time, I said … whoever did that was staff [an extra in the script]. Some staff guy. (Laughs) So, he sticks something out [the window] , and now they're creating a charade, right? If you're in the motorcade like … [Bob Jackson or Mel Couch[116]], you look up and say, "Oh, my God! There's the gun…"

JH: One of the witnesses described it as looking like a [metal] pipe….[117]

DSL: It could have been a rifle. I don't know. Did I tell you the joke about the pipe…? So, I was going to Liebeler's class.… He wanted me to go

---

115   Perhaps the most important question in the JFK Assassination is, "Where was Oswald during the shooting?" Could he have shot from the sixth floor, hidden the rifle, and then dashed down the stairwell to meet Marrion Baker and Roy Truly in the second floor lunchroom – calm, cool, and collected? Victoria Adams was in the stairwell and did not see Oswald. See: Ernest, Barry. *The Girl on the Stairs: My Search for a Missing Witness to the Assassination of John. F. Kennedy.* Create Space, 2011, 422 pages. Note that Mr. Lifton wrote the foreword for the 2013 edition.

116   Wikipedia: Robert H. Jackson. See the Warren Commission Testimony of Tom C. Dillard. See also: Granberry, Michael. "Those Who Rode By Kennedy Remember." Deseret.com, November 21, 2003. Retrieved 7/8/23: https://www.deseret.com/2003/11/22/19797259/those-who-rode-by-kennedy-remember.

117   Witness Amos Lee Euins. Author Unknown. "3 Witnesses Saw Assassin Fire; One Gave Description of Oswald." NewYorkTimes.com, November 24, 1964. Retrieved 7/8/2023: https://www.nytimes.com/1964/11/24/archives/3-witnesses-saw-assassin-fire-one-gave-description-of-oswald.html.

to his seminar, and there were about 15-20 students seated around a big conference room table. Each one had to do a separate paper on some aspect of the Kennedy Assassination. There's a woman ... and ... she did a whole paper on what each witness said was sticking out of the window ... Remember this is mostly an all male class ... but there were two or three women in it. And she says, "Well ... they saw this ... [and] six inches of pipe is better than nothing." And Liebeler (Laughs), and says, "Yes, Miss Jones, six inches of pipe is probably better than nothing" – and there was this muffled laughter.

JH: (Laughs)

DSL: That's what happened (Laughs) in the class.

JH: Today, you'd probably get in trouble for saying something like that....

DSL: Yeah, you would ... I believe ... that it's very likely Oswald was down at or near the pergola.... I do not think they [conspirators] wanted him there. Somehow, he got over there. He's picked up on the Moorman Photograph. This image. Now, it's not perfect, but I think that's him. And so therefore ... as soon as the murder occurred, the handler – whoever is with him near the pergola – says, "Now, get the Hell over to the lunchroom." Because now ... [they're] going to do what I call the false arrest if this was a screenplay.... But, Truly reassures him [Baker], "No, no, he [Oswald] works here." ... Truly and Baker ... [then] Truly testified to the Warren Commission that Baker said – this is Baker revealing his state of mind ... "We must be careful. This man can blow your head off." What that shows you is the story Baker must have been given about there being some kind of a terrible assassin lurking in the building and if anything happens, you've got to be very careful because *this man can blow your head off.*

JH: So, you think he [Baker] was told ... "There might be an assassination attempt, be aware, and if you ... ever are in contact or you're chasing one of them...."

DSL: "Be careful...."

JH: He wasn't told ... "We're going to kill the president–"

DSL: No, no, no, no, no.

JH: Nothing like that....

DSL: No. But, he's told something which permits Baker to have a little bit of foreknowledge to believe that.... When you go to the original FBI reports,

Baker comes running up the stairs, and then he's watching Oswald [with suspicion] in the lunchroom.... And I think that's what happened....

JH: OK. Two quick questions: Did you ever walk from the pergola ... to the lunchroom?

DSL: Yes.

JH: How long did it take you – just normally walking?

DSL: Oh.... The minimum would be fifty seconds or forty-eight seconds, and the maximum would be one minute and eighteen seconds or something....

JH: Alright, now I would imagine if he was told, "Hey, Oswald, you need to get up to the second floor lunchroom now!"

DSL: That would be part of the plan....

JH: The other question because you answered the first one ... he was probably running up there....

DSL: No. Jim – I think it's just a trot.... From the beginning, he understands that he's gonna have a false arrest ... I think [that] he thinks he's gonna be very honored to play this role. They're faking an attempt on Kennedy's life because that's gonna permit all kinds of things to happen. They're gonna find out who the bad guys are. They're [bad guys] gonna attempt to come out of hiding and take over the government. Some cock and bull story he [Oswald] believes. And so he knows that his job is to go through this fake arrest and then spout the Castro line. Go on.

JH: Now, my second question was Marrion Baker ... said – and he had to argue with the [Warren] Commission about this – it took him about 90 seconds to get to the second floor....

DSL: Well, the Commission did a reconstruction and they "bracketed it." The smallest amount of time would have been about 50 [seconds], and the largest would be about 80 or 90 seconds....

JH: They said something to the effect, "You put down the motorcycle and then it took you 90 seconds–" He said, "No, no, it took me a *total* of 90 seconds. Once I saw the birds flying [off of the TSBD roof], hit the gas, I was in there [lunchroom] in no more than 90 seconds." Something like that ... [So] it sounds to me like there's no conflict of time. [Baker] would not get there before Oswald? Oswald would have plenty of time to get up to the second floor before Baker came up...?[118]

---

118   Friday, March 20, 1964, Baker was asked to recreate his movement from the motorcycle

DSL: I'd have to look at the data again, but yeah ... I'm just concerned about the more macroscopic picture....

JH: OK, Oswald made his way downstairs....

DSL: We *don't know* where Oswald was after the Baker encounter, but he's somewhere. Either, he's got a handler there[119] who's told him to "hide in this room" or whatever ... [Mr. Lifton reiterated his theory of Oswald's movement after he left the TSBD and was driven in a circuitous manner along Continental Avenue (about one-half mile north of Elm Street) and back to Elm Street east of the TSBD, according to Mr. Lifton: "one or two blocks on either side of Akard"[120]] I don't know whether it was his ... [sixth] sense ... [that] something's wrong – he got on the bus with his first landlady, [Mary] Bledsoe. And then he got the heck out of the bus and took a taxicab – which he never takes. That's like you buying caviar....

JH: [So, Oswald felt frightened?]

DSL: Remember, he gets on the bus. The bus is heading back *towards the building*, and as soon as he gets off the bus, police come on the bus and start searching it. So, in other words, he was one step ahead of the police ... [Then] he goes back to his [rooming] house – goes one block beyond, I guess to check the territory. Says [to the taxi driver], "Ok, let me out here." Then, he goes back into his rooming house and grabs the pistol and he grabs a jacket – a light jacket – which he tucks so the pistol can't be seen.

JH: You think he was at Tippit's car – and he shot at Tippit ...?

DSL: No, no ... I think he was there [Tippit Shooting] and witnessed what happened – which really was an attempt to murder him. He's prob-

to the 2nd floor lunchroom. He states: "The first run would be a minute and 30 seconds, and then we did it over, and we did it in a minute and 15 seconds." Warren Commission. "Volume III: Marrion L. Baker." History-Matters.com, page 252. Retrieved 7/13/2023: https://www.history-matters.com/archive/jfk/wc/wcvols/wh3/pdf/WH3_Baker.pdf. Curiously, the Commission had Baker help to recreate the alleged movement of Oswald *from the Sniper's Nest on the sixth floor to the lunchroom* (Ibid, page 253). Naturally, the Warren Commission was determined to prove the notion that there was no conspiracy. To quote from their investigation: "A series of time tests made by investigators and by Roy S. Truly and Patrolman M. L. Baker at the request of the Commission, show that it was possible for Oswald to have placed the rifle behind a box and descended to the lunchroom on the second floor before Patrolman Baker and Truly got up there." National Archives. "Warren Commission Report Appendix 12: Speculation and Rumors." *JFK Assassination Records*, page 648. Retrieved 7/13/2023: https://www.archives.gov/research/jfk/warren-commission-report/appendix-12.html.
119   See: Armstrong, John. *Harvey and Lee*. Quasar Books, 2003, 983 pages. He believes Oswald's handler at the TSBD is Manager Willam H. Shelley.
120   See this street map dating from 1962. You can see Elm Street does intersect with Murphy Drive some seven blocks east of Elm and two blocks west of Akard Street. Retrieved 7/14/2023: http://dallasfreeways.com/dfwfreeways/old-highway-maps/1962_enco_dfw_downtown_dallas_detail_med.jpg.

ably confused … A car comes by – and I believe it's from the car – that the shots [were] fired that killed Tippit. Oswald *fires back* across the hood of the car and then turns around and runs up that street [Patton Avenue] and ducks into the Texas Theater. Remember, when he's inside his rooming house getting his gun, Mrs. [Earlene] Roberts hears "toot toot" on a car horn, and she sees a police car….

JH: So, whoever dropped him off told the police – they must have….

DSL: Whoever dropped him off is part of the plot in a low-level position…. Remember, there were no cell phones back then. So, I'm not sure how the communication would work…

JH: Yeah, well, maybe they had a radio or something…?

DSL: Yeah, and if they had a walkie-talkie it would have been pretty bulky…. In the Warren Commission Report, you'll find that whole business of Mrs. Bledsoe on the bus, and she sees Oswald get on … and [stated], "He looks like a maniac."[121] Well, yeah, he's scared by that time….

JH: I want to ask you … [at] what moment does he realize, "Oh, my God … they lied to me…?"

DSL: I think he's calmed down pretty quickly because I think the real moment of truth is on Saturday night at the press conference….

JH: So, you think he really didn't realize, "Holy cow – I'm the patsy!" until when he got arrested…?

DSL: Well, let's think about this…. At the time of the Tippit Shooting … he's asked to pass his wallet through the [police car] window…. [Captain W. R.] Westbrook[122] … the officer is going through the wallet…. But, Oswald had two "moments of truth": one was at the Tippit Murder … [but] he must have been calmed down because when he was arrested, he was

121   Warren Commission Report. "Testimony of Mary E. Bledsoe." History-Matters.com, page 409. Retrieved 7/14/2023: https://www.history-matters.com/archive/jfk/wc/wcvols/wh6/pdf/WH6_Bledsoe.pdf. See also: The Portal to Texas History. "Affidavit in Any Fact by Mary E. Bledsoe." TexasHistory.UNT.edu. Retrieved 7/14/2023: https://texashistory.unt.edu/ark:/67531/metapth339150/.

122   The role of Capt. Westbrook is rather suspicious to say the least. See: Warren Commission. "Volume VII: Capt. W. R. Westbrook." AARCLibrary.org. Retrieved 7/14/2023: https://www.aarclibrary.org/publib/jfk/wc/wcvols/wh7/pdf/WH7_Westbrook.pdf. Interestingly, Westbrook states in his Warren Commission testimony that he walked to the TSBD from Dallas City Hall, 106 S. Harwood Street – some 9 blocks east of Elm and Murphy and some 14 blocks east of the TSBD – after sitting "around a while" (Ibid, page 110). Not accounting for the possible time variances involved, was Westbrook Oswald's handler – present to "coax him along" to where he needed to go? There is some evidence that he was present *during* the Tippit Shooting, although he claims he was at the TSBD when this occurred (Ibid, page 111). For a more logical, truthful, and gripping narrative than the Warren Commission Report, see: Armstrong, John. *Harvey and Lee.* Quasar Books, 2003, 983 pages. For a sampling, see: Armstrong, John. "Westbrook and Croy." HarveyandLee.net. Retrieved 7/14/2023: https://harveyandlee.net/WandC/Westbrook_and_Croy.html.

calmed down enough to trust him with a news conference … remember on … [Saturday, November 23]. And they already had a day-and-a-half to work on him, and tell him, "Yeah, it was an unexpected [and] terrible development that took place. President Kennedy was shot, but we'll get you out of this – and don't worry." That's what I think … The first one [moment of truth] was at the Tippit thing, and then the second … [was] on … [Friday] night, and that's when he exclaimed, "I'm just a patsy!"[123]

JH: Yeah, hmm.

DSL: And that's when he also told [H. Louis] Nichols [President of Dallas Bar Association][124] … in Dallas, he said, "If I can find someone who believes as I believe, and stands up for what I believe in … I might let him represent me." He knows by … [Saturday] night that something's terribly wrong. He's got to. The question is, "How could they bullsh*t their way out of this and keep his trust?" Because, you see, when he's on camera … let's just go along with me on this. We know what happened Friday night. He exclaims, "I'm just a patsy!" – right? Suppose he said, "I'm just a patsy. I'm involved in a covert operation with Robert Kennedy." Boom! That blows the whole thing. But he never said that. He never took the next step. He maintained his confidence in his handler. And so, on Saturday afternoon on camera, we actually see him saying as he's being hustled down the hallway, "I don't know what dispatches you people have been reading, but I've committed no act of violence." Do you remember that one?

JH: Yeah.

DSL: That's a really important one…

JH: Have you ever thought who his handler might have been?

DSL: Yeah.

JH: Do … who do you think it might – or do you have no idea?

DSL : No, no, no, I have plenty of ideas. I think – I can't prove it's this person, but it's either this person or whoever was acting as his admin.

JH: I always thought it was David Atlee Phillips.[125]

---

123   This was on Friday, November 22, 1963, 7:55 PM (CST). See: David Von Pein's JFK Channel. "Lee Harvey Oswald Declares 'I'm Just a Patsy (November 22, 1963)." YouTube, 2022, 00:55 seconds. Retrieved 7/14/2023: https://www.youtube.com/watch?v=NR7JJHqD7_c. The "press conference" was Saturday, November 23, 1963, 12:10 AM (CST) – the so-called "Midnight Press Conference." See: CNN. "Lee Harvey Oswald Speaks to the Press." YouTube, 2013, 1:08 minutes. Retrieved 7/14/2023: https://www.youtube.com/watch?v=jY8fRTLtgzA.

124   Wikipedia: H. Louis Nichols.

125   Wikipedia: David Atlee Phillips.

DSL: No. It was James Angleton.[126]

JH: Wow. But he's a high level person though!

DSL: That's right, no, this is a high level plot!

JH: Yeah, but ... wouldn't Angleton have a lower level being the intermediary?

DSL: Like I said, it's either Angleton or some kind of an executive assistant.

JH: Working for him....

DSL: Yeah, but I think it's Angleton. The reason I think it's Angleton is Oswald met the person – whoever it was – in April of 1959, before he went off on that trip to Europe. That person he met with, really fits Angleton to a "T": He was an older man, and he was wearing clothing that was completely improper for southern California. (Laughs) So, this guy flies in at the airport to meet Oswald who's the designated patsy. Now, whether Angleton.... How do I say this? Whether Angleton knew about a Kennedy plot is another issue. I don't know if he did. You could argue it either way because in 1959, when Oswald ... [got] back from Japan, who the Hell would believe it if you told Oswald that "we're working on a plot to kill President Kennedy two years from now?" I mean, it just sounds like it's out of a novel or something.

JH: Well, 1959, Kennedy hadn't even become president yet....

DSL: Correct ... That's what I want to point out to you.... But to a person like Lyndon Johnson and Allen Dulles, they're planning ahead. When I say that, they don't know about the Depository and all those details. I'm saying that in 1959....

JH: They were already planning to kill whoever got in there – unless it was Lyndon Johnson.

DSL: No, no ... They're planning ... Johnson's got his job: he's got to get on the ticket. To synopsize the whole thing: "If you get on the ticket, we'll take care of the rest."

JH: In other words, if Mickey Mouse won in 1960 and Johnson was the vice president, they would have killed Mickey Mouse. It didn't matter who was president....

---

126   Wikipedia: James Jesus Angleton.

DSL: That's right.... This is a plan to make Lyndon Johnson president under the guise of it being an historical accident....

JH: I really believe you "hit it on the nail" when you said it was like a movie plot.... You just made the point [that] the Book Depository [had not been selected] yet. They sent out [location] scouts....

DSL: No, no, no, no. It's a little bit better than that. I'll tell you the words they [plotters] used: it was "site selection." The persons – when Dulles and whoever set out to create this plan, they had to decide where to do it. I'll give you an example. If I was lecturing to an audience, I'd say, "Let me give you an example of a place that would be no good – at all: Cambridge, Massachusetts – Because Kennedy was much beloved." Right? OK. And then ... [there are] probably places that are in between. But, the reason I am so certain that this was a Dallas plot – you know, at the top level because remember the Mayor of Dallas [Earle Cabell] was the brother of the Deputy Director of the CIA [Charles Cabell]?[127]

JH: Right....

DSL: There's a number of these indications [of impropriety]. So ... they had to conceive of this as a scenario. In other words, it's like ... yes, they're gonna kill President Kennedy. All that's technicalities. But they are going to [do] two things: yes, they're going to kill President Kennedy, but they are [also] gonna create the appearance that it's an historical quirk of fate. So, they had to use site selection.... It was very helpful to have a place where Kennedy was disliked – and people in general believed this horsesh*t that "he was selling out to the Russians" ... They [plotters] had to create a site selection where they could ... basically reverse engineer this and pretend this [assassination scenario] is a screenplay. OK. They had to go through this whole business of it being a screenplay, creating a false reality that ... it was a quirk of fate.

JH: Yeah....

DSL: And that's what I mean by that. So ... let me just give you another example. Another city on this five city tour [JFK in Texas: Houston, San Antonio, Ft. Worth, Dallas, and Austin] was San Antonio. Remember there was a guy in a car – and he was overheard by the constable saying, "He's not gonna make it through this city?" And in San Antonio, the reason it's such a parallel is that in San Antonio, there was also a park area ... Alamo Plaza.... [128]

JH: [Yes.]

DSL: And it turned out that the car was a Secret Service car that this threat was coming from ... this commentary.... [129]

JH: I'm looking up Alamo Plaza....

DSL: But you won't be able to find the story I'm telling you ... Kennedy's trip to San Antonio is a very interesting one. He comes ... in the afternoon, he goes out to Kelly Air Force Base ... [and] to Brooke [Army] Medical Center ... where the astronauts were being trained in that pressure ... [chamber]....

JH: OK.

DSL: The thing is ... have you ... taken courses in screenwriting?

JH: I've studied ... I taught myself....

DSL: I took ... [a course with] Robert McKee ... and his notes he turned into a book which is now called *Story*[130] ... It was a *fantastic* class. All kinds of people who want to become movie executives would attend that class *to overflowing*.... Here's the deal: everybody that comes to LA – just like in Texas, you wanna strike oil where you dig the hole in the ground – in Los Angeles, the "big strike" [is] when you come in with an idea, you make a treatment for a screenplay, and you get circulated, and suddenly somebody says, "Yep – we'll option that!" Boom. And then they option it for let's say $50,000 dollars... [So] the story that they're gonna tell behind Dealey Plaza is not so much a diagram of the shooting, you know, here's

128   A quick analysis of a standard map of Alamo Plaza shows a lot of cover for snipers including tall buildings positioned similarly like Dealey Plaza. However, a *map of the proposed motorcade route* intersects Broadway and E. Houston Street – about two blocks northwest of Alamo Plaza. (See: Inside the Gates. "November 21, 1963: President Kennedy in San Antonio." DRTLibrary. Wordpress.com, 2009. Retrieved 7/17/2023: https://drtlibrary.wordpress.com/2009/11/30/november-21-1963-president-kennedy-in-san-antonio/.) Was the route changed slightly at the last minute? Interestingly, the San Antonio motorcade format appears quite different from Dallas. Whereas in Dallas, JFK's limo was placed out in front with no "protective umbrella" like *close multiple forward and/or flanking motorcycle policemen and close lead car and follow-up car*, the San Antonio motorcade does appear to contain these elements. (See: Pein, David Von. "DVP's Kennedy Gallery." Kennedy-Photos. Blogspot.com. Retrieved 7/17/2023: http://kennedy-photos.blogspot.com/2013/02/page-3.html.)
129   In my humble opinion, and I believe Mr. Lifton would agree, the best source for understanding how the Secret Service failed JFK – intentionally or not – is Vincent Michael Palamara's *Survivor's Guilt: The Secret Service and the Failure to Protect President Kennedy*, Trine Day, 2013, 576 pages. His YouTube Channel (Vince Palamara) is an excellent source of JFK Assassination information as well.
130   Wikipedia: Robert McKee. See: McKee, Robert. *Story: Substance, Structure, and the Principles of Screenwriting.* HarperCollins: Regan Books, 1997, 466 pages.

the shooter, he's gonna be behind this bush or behind this fence. No. It's a *concept* of a *screenplay* because what happens in the first few hours is not so much where a man is hiding behind a bush, it's this whole story that's being presented to the American public and the world that this is an accident of fate. So, the moving parts here are Oswald ... who's being set up. Then you've gotta have some control over the motorcade, right? ... Who's involved in that? [Lyndon] Johnson is involved "up to his ears." You know, "Kennedy, you've got to come to Dallas" ... the real reason is to arrange a motorcade, "but you have to come to Dallas for the luncheon. ... The day before ... [Congressman] Al Thomas is having a dinner." So, Kennedy says, "OK" ... [but arranges] a five city trip ... [and] they [conspirators] booby trap Dealey Plaza....

JH: Yeah, yeah....

DSL: Now, he could have just driven thirty miles from Ft. Worth to Dallas. It's very interesting because they didn't do that. If they had done that, they would have come into Dealey Plaza the wrong way (Laughs).... They couldn't have had the story they had. They had to come into Dallas [i.e. Dealey Plaza] from the airport [Love Field, a distance of some 6 miles]. And so, he [JFK] took an eight minute flight on a jet. Can you believe this?.... That's ridiculous. You take off and you land. But that's the way they were able to have an airport arrival.

JH: Hmm. Why ... did they do it that way? Why bother? In order to get him on that [specific] parade route...?

DSL: Yeah, yeah, yeah, yeah ... if this is a screenplay, the whole thing is to get [Kennedy to] arrive at the airport, go to the event, go back to the airport, go to the next city ... In each city [Houston, San Antonio, Ft. Worth, Dallas, Austin], there were two motorcades [planned], but in San Antonio – because of the Kelly Air Force Base – there were three. So, basically, he was killed in the ... [eighth] motorcade inbound. If they didn't do it that way....

JH: They needed to create the excitement of the motorcade ... [and] the crowds. The crowds create the opportunity to kill him.

DSL: Yeah, but it's really another thing. The whole event has got to look like a quirk of fate.

JH: Right, and so if you advertise it ... verses he drives down a road and he goes right to give the speech....

DSL: No, no, no, the Main Street motorcade was a huge factor.... The people who were involved in this ... was in a way a genius ... a genius in covert ops. To me, it goes back to what happened in World War II when they floated that body up on the shore with a false ID. It was supposed to mislead – which it did, it misled the Germans – where they were going to have the invasion [Sicily 1943].[131]

JH: Knowing that [screenplay concept for JFK Assassination], do you think they used like "Hollywood types" to help create the story, or was it ... military intelligence....?

DSL: I think someone with a *serious* background in screenplay writing ... to have this conception. I'm not saying it couldn't be two people – I don't know. This thing really reeks of someone familiar with screenwriting....

JH: So, I'll be honest, I never heard that before [JFK Assassination created as a screenplay] until you said it to me a couple of months ago.... It really struck me. Yeah, the more you look at it, there's *a lot* of detail that you'd see in a ... [treatment]....

DSL: At the conceptual level, somebody in their hands held a file that maybe had five pages in all – and it was a treatment. And then they had to flush it out.

JH: What proof is there?[132] For example, the picture of the FBI agent picking up the bullet in the grass [at Dealey Plaza].[133] They [conspirators] had to have these guys out there....

DSL: Yeah, but there may be a bullet in the grass ... I forget the man leaning over and getting it ... he's a ... plainclothes detective.... We know who he is.... [But] when the motorcade is heading down Main Street, there has to be a group of people ready to implement the scenario – stage hands or something. There has to be a few of them.

JH: Do you think there was someone shooting from the Grassy Knoll?

DSL: Yeah.

JH: And ... from the Texas School Book Depository?

DSL: No, no, no, no.

JH: Not at all...?

131   Wikipedia: Operation Mincemeat.
132   For lack of better terminology, these people could be dubbed the "stagehands" (low level – on the ground and visible) and the "directors" (high level – largely behind the scenes).
133   See: Kennedy Assassination. "Buddy Walthers: Sheriff's Deputy in Dealey Plaza – Mystery Death?" JFK-Assassination.net. Retrieved 7/17/2023: https://www.jfk-assassination.net/death13.htm.   97

DSL: Not at all because if you're going to have this "trajectory reversal scheme" based upon the body being messed with, *you can't have shots striking from the rear*. Because to get out those bullets, you'd have to enlarge the entry wound. If you enlarge the entry wound from the rear, it's going to look like an exit – which creates the appearance, because of the enlargement, that a shot came from the front. So, what makes *Best Evidence* work, and what makes it so radical, is it says from the shots only then it's trajectory reversal – to widen the entries to make 'em exits and to put some false entrance on the back to create the appearance of shots from behind.

JH: So, you believe there's no shooting from the rear at all?

DSL: That's correct ….[134]

JH: What about … James Tague … [or] Governor Connally's wounds …?

DSL: Connally – if I'm correct – is shot from the front because the X-rays show that. The ribs were bent inward … and the hole in the clothing. There's a small little hole. That's an entry [wound]…. Remember the guy … his name was Douglas … that Connally became friendly with…. They shared a flight together years later. And Connally said to him, "it was like being shot in the stomach" or something like that….

JH: Well, of course, you said that Connally pulled out his pistol–

DSL: I think so.

JH: And shot at the driver….[135]

DSL: I believe that when … Connally pulled out the gun, he is firing to kill the driver – because the driver has just shot Kennedy. Connally fires. The driver's dead. [Secret Service Agent XY] runs in from the follow-up car, Connally's back in his wife's lap. But people don't remember what the documents say that when they pulled into Parkland, he was able to *get out of the car* and start to walk. And then they put him on a stretcher…. You were asking the question about the Tague shot….

JH: James Tague.[136] He said that the shot, the cement [curb] by the Triple Underpass in the middle there [where] he was standing … and the shot ricocheted and pieces of the concrete … hit him in the cheek….

---

134   The concept of shooting *only* coming from the front is almost unfathomable (e.g. James Tague, Governor Connally), but I wanted to hear Mr. Lifton's thoughts on this.
135   "Godzilla" Theory.
136   Wikipedia: James Tague.

DSL: But if you look at the diagrams published by the Warren Commission – and they're pretty good – that shot could have easily come from the Grassy Knoll....

JH: You know, I never gave it much thought....

DSL: Remember – never ignore this that all [of] those doctors, thirteen doctors at Parkland, *no one sees an entry on the rear of the body*....

JH: Both Kennedy and Connally?

DSL: First of all, definitely not on Kennedy ... Then the question becomes Connally, and I don't know the answer to that in this conversation. I'd have to go [and check my research]....

JH: Do you think that that back wound on Kennedy ... "the back wound" Humes probed with his little finger – was just a fake wound...?

DSL: Fake wound. This is all spelled out in Chapter 14 [of *Best Evidence*] called "Trajectory Reversal: [Blueprint for Deception]" ... Remember what Humes said when he called up – please remember this. He called up the Dallas Doctor Perry... [He said] "Did you make any wounds in the back...?"[137]

JH: He [Humes] thought it [throat] was an exit wound, and it was actually a tracheotomy [over] ... an entrance wound....

DSL: Yes, that's true... But you've got to deal with three separate [sets of] data. You've got the Dallas data, you have Bethesda data, and then you have the autopsy photos and X-rays... Remember what ... [Nursing Supervisor Doris] Nelson told me. I'll never forget this in December '82 ... while on my book tour... First of all, she says in her report that, "He [Connally] received a shot in the chest." It's *in her report* written in the afternoon [November 22, 1963]... Then, when I spoke to her, and I have this on audio tape, she says, ... [regarding wounds she saw versus the Warren Commission] "Oh, they found another wound, did they?" (Laughs)

JH: (Laughs) So, she says he was shot in the chest....

DSL: She says . ... yes, quote, unquote: "He received a bullet in the chest." I'm pretty sure that's accurate to the syllable ... I wish I had more fluency.

JH: No. It's fine ... There are certain things ... I want to talk to you about a little more in detail like the autopsy, what happened, go through the process again. The body comes in on the plane, go through it, but that takes a whole hour, so.

DSL: Yeah….

JH: I keep this [these topics] in my head so when we talk, I want to ask you about it….

DSL: But don't put it in your head. *Make some notes.* Write down those notes, and we'll make that the structure of the conversation. No problem.

JH: I will. I wanna do that next time….

My Notes Circa January 2022

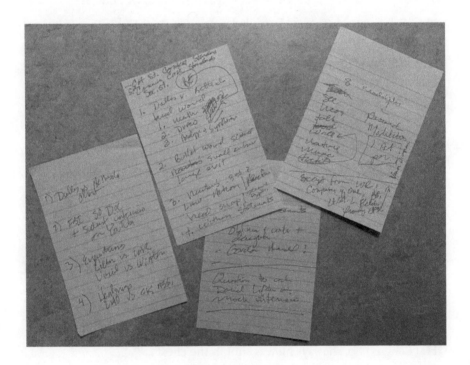

2022

FRIDAY, JANUARY 7, 2022

JH: Alright, well I've got a couple of questions for you. Number one – How many file cabinets do you have … in storage? I'm just curious.

DSL: Forty five.

JH: How many?

DSL: 4-5.

JH: Oh, my gosh….

DSL: Yeah….

JH: And … I wanted to ask you … it would be an honor – I would gladly help you try to get your manuscript together. I don't know where you're at in the process, but if you need me to help you, I will do it….

DSL: Oh, I appreciate it, I'm just writing. You know….

JH: If you need me to start putting it into a Google Doc … and lining it up … I'd be happy to do that….

DSL: One of the reasons it slowed me down a little bit is that the hypotheses I'm working with changed … only because as I worked, I came up with new … [information] … But, I've got the whole thing in my head … I basically solved the structural problems, and I know where I'm going … Now … I just got to locomote over there….

JH: I have … [another] question for ya. I thought this would be interesting, and I want to ask you something … CE 399 [Magic Bullet] … To me, this screams as a setup. How did that bullet end up on that hospital bed? … Who do you think put it there…?[138]

---

138   SSA Paul Landis, who was riding in the Follow Up Car behind JFK in the motorcade, issued an explosive claim (September 2023) that he placed – as opposed to "planted" – the Magic Bullet on Kennedy's gurney after finding it on the limo seat. See McNeil, Liz and Chamlee, Virginia. "Former Secret Service Agent Makes Startling Claim About Bullet Found After Kennedy Assassination." People.com, September 12, 2023. Retrieved 10/22/23: https://people.com/paul-landis-jfk-assassination-claims-the-final-witness-7966788. To be clear, Mr. Lifton believed that Paul Landis was one of the "good guys" – and not one of the conspirators.

DSL: OK ... Either this is spelled out or it's certainly implied in my book *Best Evidence*.[139] Let's start at the beginning. You wanna know what I believe happened is that ... this plot to kill President Kennedy is what I call a "body centric" plot. By body centric, I mean, the body tells the story of the shooting ... It's not just a matter of where wounds are located, but this also includes the concept of planted ... [evidence] ... [and] so the concept of a false Sniper's Nest. So ... two things are happening at the same time: A) they're gonna kill President Kennedy; and B) manufacture a false story of how he died.[140]

JH: Right.

DSL: The murder of Kennedy is to make sure he's dead, but ... simultaneously ... change the story of how he died. That is, to falsify the autopsy conclusions about trajectory, and to create the false story that he was shot from the building by a sniper – a pre-designated patsy who's Lee Harvey Oswald. So, first of all ... the Sniper's Nest is put up there: the rifle and the three shells. And then you've got to deal with the body of Kennedy. So, as soon as he's ... murdered, the purpose is to get his wounds changed.[141] So, how do they do that? ... Here's where my understanding gets connected with my training in systems engineering. What they did – first of all: Connally was never supposed to be shot ... That was an accident.

JH: Right....

DSL: Not an accident of marksmanship, but it was just an unexpected event. Because *originally*, if you go back and look – and I did, Kennedy would be driving ... alone in the back seat. His wife didn't agree to go on that trip until late in the game – you know, the "eighth inning" or something. She [Jackie] said, "I don't want to go with you to Dallas." ... Connally was supposed to be sitting with the Johnsons – in his car – a few cars back [from JFK's limo]. He'd be alone in the back seat and make an easier target, but that's not the way it worked out. Jackie [suddenly] wanted to

139   See Chapter 4 of *Best Evidence*, "Was Bullet 399 a Plant?" and "What About the Two Fragments?," pages 90-94 of the Carroll & Graf edition.

140   Before the Magic Bullet was conceived, developed, and birthed, and in order to account for the throat wound, the conspirators came up with another cockamamie explanation that "the throat wound resulted from a fragment of the head shot." See Chapter 14 of *Best Evidence*, "Trajectory Reversal: Blueprint for Deception," page 347 of the Carroll & Graf edition.

141   The *New York Times*. "Gov. Connally Shot; Mrs. Kennedy Safe; President is Struck Down By a Rifle Shot From Building on Motorcade Route – Johnson, Riding Behind, is Unhurt." NYTimes. com, November 23, 1963. Retrieved 9/9/2023: https://www.nytimes.com/1963/11/23/gov-connally-shot-mrs-kennedy-safe-president-is-struck-down-by-a-rifle-shot-from-building-on-motorcade-route-johnson-riding-behi.html. Even this source indicates that, at least at the time, the throat wound "had the appearance of a bullet's entry."

go on the trip. Connally [and his wife] ... ended up escorting them to the limo, sitting on the jumpseat....

JH: CE 399 ... did they [conspirators] originally intend at some point to insert that into the evidence or was it a result of the fact that Connally got ... shot...?

DSL: No. It was part of the original plan. You've gotta understand what the original plan looked like. OK. I don't know that you and I have talked about it. We may have talked about it. You've got to understand ... Kennedy was supposed to be transferred to an ambulance. So, the ... [limo] pulls over, [and] he's transferred to an ambulance ... Now, [let's] make this like a professor questioning his student in class: Given the fact that he was shot by [an] expert marksman, when the car pulled over [hypothetically speaking], and he was transferred, do you think he was dead or alive?

JH: Oh, he was dead for sure....

DSL: Correct. But, [the original plan was] they're gonna alter him in an operating room under the guise of legitimate surgery to save his life – which ... medicine would call "clinical surgery." But, once ... [JFK's] dead, it's no longer clinical surgery [for] if you're going to the morgue, that's called "pathological surgery." That's the autopsy. So, there's the dividing line between "before death" and "after death" – and before death is called "antemortem" and after death is called "postmortem." So, the key to this plot in the beginning was to get him [JFK] upstairs to the surgery suite. So, to do that, they had to pretend *he was alive.* Now, what was the plan to do that? Do you understand what the plan was? Let me tell you.

JH: OK.

DSL: [After JFK is shot] pull over and transfer him to an ambulance. When they transferred him to the ambulance, *and this is all recorded in the radio transmissions I have* – because the dispatcher can't keep his mouth shut, and he thinks ... [JFK's] dead. He doesn't understand (Laughs) ... what happened. But anyway ... [they were supposed to] transfer him to an ambulance, and in order to create the appearance that he's quote unquote "still alive" – *they intubate him* [Emphasis added]. So, do you know what intubation is?

JH: Yes.

DSL: OK ... this is what was supposed to happen. It didn't work out. But, what was supposed to happen [was] they transfer ... JFK to an ambulance, intubate him, and now when he comes into the hospital – intubated – they've created a false appearance that he's alive, right?

JH: Right....

DSL: Now, they bring him up to the sixth floor, or the second floor, or whatever floor it was on, and they're now gonna take the bullets out and do wound alterations ... under the guise of "clinical surgery" to save his life. That was the plan. That's not how it happened, but that was the plan. Unfortunately for them [conspirators], the extra victim was shot – that is Connally. It complicated everything. So, when he's [JFK] brought to the hospital, and he pulls in, he has not been transferred to the ambulance, and he has not been intubated. And because of that, it becomes obvious that he's almost – if not already – DOA. So, they rush him into the emergency room, and they [conspirators] can't bypass the emergency room yet because he's not been intubated. So, then they do the tracheotomy, and then the whole thing falls apart because when they do the tracheotomy, it's clear that ... [JFK's] dead. They pronounce him dead. So, they can't do any operations over at Parkland under the guise of clinical surgery. Why? Because for clinical surgery, he has to go up to the OR, [but] because of the unexpected developments ... [JFK's] pronounced dead *in the ER*.

JH: Right.

DSL: So, that's the end of it [original plot]. Basically, Johnson says "Get the guy [JFK] out of here. Get him over to Air Force One." Then the whole problem becomes, "What is Johnson gonna do [now]?" and "How are they gonna get ready for a fake autopsy?"

JH: So, they [conspirators] knew at one point they're going to plant this bullet [CE 399] to tie it to the rifle...?

DSL: It's much worse than the bullet. There ... [are] two other fragments in the car ... in the front seat, remember?

JH: Yeah....

DSL: Those three fragments – imagine someone [i.e. a conspirator] carrying a pocketbook like Lady Bird?[142] So, they've got a bullet, and they've got some fragments. Now, the bullet was gonna be *matched* to the wound which they created in Kennedy's [back right] shoulder. OK? Once they created that wound, they ... have two options: they can put the bullet inside the wound, or they can put it on the stretcher and say, "Oh, during

142   Wikipedia: Lady Bird Johnson.

heart message it fell out." That [false assassination story] is more than just one bullet. The whole Sniper's Nest is false. So, you've [also] got the two fragments in the front seat. They're just as phony as the bullet. So, you've got the elements like an erector set creating the false story of how Kennedy died.

JH: Who do you – I've read accounts that implicate Jack Ruby as the guy that dropped the CE 399 [onto the stretcher] ....[143]

DSL: No, no, no, no. No, no, no. It's gonna be a Secret Service agent. Jack Ruby doesn't enter the story at all until the failure to kill Oswald presents the serious problem that this guy knows the whole plot, but he's supposed to die on 11/22 – one minute after Kennedy dies. So, they've got a live guy who's told, "Don't worry, Lee. We'll get you out of this ... There was a problem down in the plaza ... The agent shot the president ... You just hang tight." You know what I mean? So, they've got 48 hours or whatever it took to get Ruby ... involved so he'll interrupt what they call the transfer [of Oswald] from the city to the county jail. And that part of the story plays out on Sunday [November 24 at 11:21 AM CST] ....

JH: You know, it makes more sense that the Secret Service agent – they're all over the place – they could easily-

DSL: They have to be ... There's a group of them that are bad guys, and this clique, this clique of agents are the ones that are involved – I'm sure – in any kind of bullet planting.[144]

JH: And ... this clique would have been the ones that hijacked the body, I'm sure, right, from the coroner... ?

DSL: I don't consider it a hijacking. They had custody of the body by [federal] law, but I see what you mean ... they get the body away from the city authorities ... The Texas authorities would want to perform an autopsy – which would have been fine if the original plan [i.e. ambulance transfer, intubation, clinical surgery of wounds] had been executed properly ... Why? He [JFK] would have "died in surgery upstairs [at Parkland]"-

JH: Quote unquote.... (Laughs)

DSL: Not only quote unquote – that's the story published in one or two of the papers the next morning. So, I know what was supposed to happen, but *did not*. It [this "cover story"] was accidentally published, and one of

---

143   Wikipedia: Jack Ruby.
144   Again, to be clear, with reference to SSA Paul Landis' recent admission of placing (as opposed to "planting") the Magic Bullet, Mr. Lifton believed that Landis was one of the "good guys" – and not one of the conspirators.

my main discoveries was the discovery of the [newspaper] story that he died in surgery.

JH: Why do you think that happened? Did ... somehow ... whoever it was – released this story, this false story, ahead of time or sent the wrong one out? ... How did these stories get published which said, "President Kennedy died in surgery" – which is totally false...?

DSL: No, no, no, no, no, no. No, no, I have the answer. The planning for the assassination of President Kennedy involved several aspects. One, of course, is you have to have the patsy. The second is you've gotta have shooters. OK? Now, another one is they arranged [a false story]. When you do a coup in Guatemala or wherever you are – remember how the local papers will be involved pushing false stories? ... That's exactly the same scenario [with JFK]....

JH: So, they used their assets in the media?

DSL: Hold it, hold it. Let me finish. Let me finish. The asset they're using now is a newspaper publisher. So, I'll give you a test ... Who is the newspaper publisher they [conspirators] are using in Dallas?

JH: Is it the *Dallas Morning News* or something?

DSL: Exactly! That's the guy that hated Kennedy.[145] Dealey Plaza is named after him. Ed Dealey, Jr. is the son. But, Ed Dealey [Sr.] is the Kennedy hater who's standing up in the White House and yelling at Kennedy, "What this country needs is a man on a white horse, and all you've got is Caroline on a tricycle!" That was the Spring of '63. Yeah, it's the *Dallas Morning News*. So, if you wanna know what the conspiracy [leadership] is thinking, you go to the *Dallas Morning News* ... How did David Lifton get the original scenario? I ... had the insights to understand some of this stuff [elements of conspiracy] as a concept. And, so, what did I do? I ordered the *Dallas Morning News* on interlibrary loan. So, now I have it [during my student days] coming into the UCLA Library.

JH: Wow....

DSL: And there it is. Right there in the God d*mned microfilm ... the *Dallas Morning News* publishes the scenario in the first edition after Kennedy's shot ... They published an extra [edition] that afternoon. And the *Dallas Times Herald*, which I don't think is involved in the plot, also pub-

---

145   The infamous "Welcome Mr. Kennedy" advertisement was published in this paper. See: Wisconsin Historical Society. "Welcome Mr. Kennedy." WisconsinHsitory.org. Retrieved 7/19/2023: https://www.wisconsinhistory.org/Records/Image/IM97353.

lished their extra. And then … by Saturday morning, you've got it [false story] laid out in print. What does the *Dallas Morning News* say? "Kennedy died at one o'clock. They tried to save his life. He was in a surgery suite on the second … floor." … That's all in the *Dallas Morning News*. That's how I learned what was supposed to happen but did not … I have those printouts [news stories on microfilm]!

JH: Wow.

DSL: Go on. I want to hear your questions….

JH: That's … the one that I wanted to ask specifically….

DSL: Wait a second … There's one more part. Hold on. The other source of information is not on microfilm of news [stories] that … [is] important. It's the *Dallas Police Department radio transmissions*.

JH: Right, right, right. You've said that.

DSL: The murder occurs – the dispatcher doesn't have [mind reading abilities] … All he can do is deal with the facts as he knows them. He's in on the plot, but he doesn't have the right [i.e. current] information. So, as the car's speeding to the hospital, it never occurs to him, "Watch what you say. He's not dead yet." … So, he starts giving radio transmissions: "Car so-and-so, cut the traffic at such-and-such. Car B, cut the traffic at this cut-off," [etc.] … And somebody [breaks into the traffic], "What's the problem? What is all this … [about]?" "Signal 19. Signal 19. the shooting of the president." So, in other words, the dispatcher gives away his state of knowledge by arranging for all these freeway exits or streets to be cut off … And that's why they're having … the business of … clearing away for the ambulance taking *the president to the hospital*. So, that's what I learned from the radio dispatches – what was supposed to happen *but did not*. I was wearing a headset in 1974 or whatever, listening to this stuff and saying, "Oh, my gosh … this guy [dispatcher] is not in the loop. He doesn't understand what's happening. He's giving away the plot." … That's how I learned [this] … [and] it's coming out of the mouth of the Dallas Police Department dispatcher.[146]

146   The DPD Dispatcher was Murray Jackson, and I'm not sure what to make of the notion that he was involved – perhaps unknowingly. It makes sense that the dispatcher is involved given the need to get JFK into the OR with an ambulance to make it appear he is still alive. Either way, see: Parks, Scott K. "Dallas to Honor Man Whose Report Led Police to Lee Harvey Oswald on 47th Anniversary of JFK Assassination." PalmBeachPost.com, November 21, 2010. Retrieved 10/22/23: https://www.palmbeachpost.com/story/news/2010/11/22/dallas-to-honor-man-whose/7285741007/. See also: Myers, Dale K. "Murray J. Jackson, Former Dallas Police Dispatcher Dies at 77." JFKFiles. Blogspot.com, June 13, 2012. Retrieved 10/22/23: http://jfkfiles.blogspot.com/2012/06/murray-j-jackson-former-dallas-police.html.

CONVERSATIONS WITH DAVID S. LIFTON

JH: How did you get access to the [Dallas Police Department] dictabelt or....

DSL: The tape ... it all starts with Mary Ferrell in Dallas.[147] She was an elderly, scholarly lady who got this stuff from someone she knew at the police department. And then she shared it with a number of [researchers] ... Remember there were all the stories about the audio tests and whether it showed three or four shots? The acoustics. The result was that ... a couple of people had these tapes who were friends with Mary, and one of them was my friend ... I want you to hear this ... Mary had a son who was sixteen. Fred Newcomb had a daughter ... Anyway, Fred Newcomb's daughter and Mary's son hit it off ... [Thus] Fred Newcomb had access to these [Dallas Police Department dictabelt] tapes pretty early as I recall. Now, Fred died a few years ago, but I'm very close with his son, Tyler. Tyler Newcomb and I are good buddies.

JH: You know, it's interesting, I'm thinking like, Mary Ferrell goes to the Dallas Police Department [contact] ... [and says], "It's an historical record. Can I have it?" "Sure...."

DSL: No, no, no, no, no, no, no. Mary is kind of known [at the time] as the grande dame of the Dallas area researchers. By the way, she is not highly reliable. When I say that, she ... [could] be very dishonest. I'll tell you this story, OK?.... Here's my characterization of some of these Dallas people. JFK lands in Dallas, he comes down the ramp with Jackie, and they say, "Good luck, Jack! See ya at the Trade Mart." You know? Knowing full well he's going to get his head blown off. OK? That kind of local hypocrisy ... How do I know that? First of all, I've had all kinds of experience with these people. Second of all, let's go to January 1981 when my book was published – that's forty something years ago.... My book is published and Mary says (mimicking her voice), "Well, David, when you come through Dallas, you've gotta stop at our house. We'll have a big party for ya." ... Now, the reason is that Mary wanted to get copies of my interviews for the *Best Evidence* video which I was using, remember? On-

JH: Yes, yes....

DSL: My book tour. Paul O'Connor, and this one, and that one. And of course, Mary wanted to throw me this big party, right? But, she didn't have the video which she lusted after ... So, I go over to Mary's house. I was staying by my publisher's [Macmillan] expense account at a very nice hotel in Dallas. Her husband Buck ... picks me up, and he seems to be a nice guy ... I mean, there's a hundred people in Mary's house. The place is like a joyous New Year's Eve ... And then, (mimicking Mary's voice) "David's here! OK, now you're going to give your little talk here and show us our video." ... So, I say, "Sure, Mary" I came with my little three quarter or one inch video cassette [Beta or VHS].... So, I have my video tape in my hand [waiting to speak] ... and of course, I'm going to show it to the group.... And then I decide [that] I better be careful here. So, I stalled or did something – and I want you to know what happened next. Before I started my talk, I said [to Mary], "Let me just check this out [VCR or Beta recorder]." And I noticed when I was giving the cassette to her, to put it into the video recorder-

JH: Uh, huh....

DSL: I was very careful, and I noticed there was a cable going out from the back of the video recorder and I knew something was going on. And I followed it [cable] closely with my eyes halfway around the room where there was a pile of coats. So, I lifted the coats ... one at a time, and there was a *second* video recorder – set on record with the wheel[s] turning. So, she [Mary Ferrell] was going to create her own God d*mn bootleg and distribute it all over the world or [to] who the Hell knows ... right? So ... I pressed "off" ... disabled the machine by taking the cable out of the back, and said very casually, "I'm sorry. No duplicates can be made of this without my publisher's permission." Nobody else had this stuff.

JH: Yeah....

DSL: So that's the story of Mary Ferrel ... She says, ... "Well, my God! Now, how did that happen?" (Laughs) This is in her home, in her living room.... Now that's what happened. Now you go on with your question....

JH: Yeah, so you ... got to listen to these tapes. Did you make your own transcripts....?

DSL: Oh, my God, yes! I listened to the tapes, and the transcripts were published in the twenty six volumes [Warren Commission] in *three different formats*: First comes the kind of crude format when an officer ... testified ... Dallas Police Department ... [exhibit] ... then came the Secret Service exhibit ... and then the third one ... the staff lawyers on the Warren Commission were getting fed up with all this confusion about the radio transmissions. And they said, "Will you please have the FBI create a[n] absolutely accurate transcript of these tapes, and you've got like a week to do it?' Because it was already August [of] '64. They had stenographers working on it in the Dallas Field Office ... So, you've got three separate transcripts: the [Dallas] city transcript, the Secret Service transcript, and the Warren Commission authorized transcript, and I had all three transcripts. I photocopied them and put them in a notebook.

JH: So, you didn't make your own, you got the ones from the Warren Report....

DSL: Oh, no. It gets better than that because then when I got the tapes [from Mary Ferrell], I went over those transcripts with a fine tooth comb, and I used colored pens. And anytime I heard something that was different from the transcript because of a secretarial incompetence or whatever, using a red pen I would write in what those words were. So, I had a pretty complete transcript.

JH: Do you think it's possible that they [conspirators] purposely left stuff out or not really?

DSL: There ... were one or two cases where there was that possibility of it being changed....

JH: So.... The FBI I'm assuming had the best transcripts...?

DSL: No, no, no, no, no. There was a retired Dallas officer, his name was Bowles, and Bowles got the tapes from the Dallas Police. He actually *had the actual* tapes that were in the tape audio machine at police headquarters, and he made a separate recording – and those were called the Bowles Recordings ... They came out years later, and there were people who spent hours on this stuff making transcripts. So, I had the Bowles Transcripts.

JH: When they [researchers] made these transcripts, they had no idea that the evidence that was in these transcripts – they just thought it was just chatter....?

DSL: No, no, no. They had the evidence, but they didn't know how to interpret it ... They didn't understand that there was a plan to alter the president's body and bring him to the hospital [as if still alive]. They just assumed everything was legit ... I'm not saying no one in Dallas [Police Department] was involved in the set up. That's not true. What I'm saying [is] you can't [clearly] tell from the transcript who it was ... here and there there were "giveaways." OK, for example ... this one is really good....

JH: Yeah.

DSL: So he gets on the radio ... and says, ... "Description of the suspect is a white male, about five foot ten, hundred sixty five pounds," dah, dah, dah, dah, dah.[148] Well, when you go back to the actual radio [transmission] ... police headquarters gets that and says [in APB], "All units, listen, all units, the suspect is ... hundred sixty five, five foot ten, slender build," dah, dah, dah, dah, dah, dah. He's [dispatcher] added "slender build." OK, but he wasn't told slender build [by motorcycle cop]. So, that's the scenario. You understand? They're working off a script – and that guy gives away the fact that there's a manufactured (Laughs) script....

JH: Wow.

DSL: Of course, the first guys didn't say it. That's in *Best Evidence,* Chapter 24 – the whole ... thing about "slender build...."

JH: Right. So the guy who sent out the APB added the "slender build?"

DSL: Yes! He added that.

JH: He added that characteristic – and it's like, "How did he know that?"

DSL: Well, it's not "How he knows it?" – it's "Where did that come from...?"

JH: Where did that come from – unless he's part of the plot or something.

DSL: You see, unless there's a scenario and the first guy [motorcycle cop] left it out and the second guy [dispatcher] plugged it in. That's in Chapter 24-

JH: Of *Best Evidence.* Of ... all the evidence that you have, what would you say would be like your number one top piece of evidence? [That] this was a body centric plot that they – this is proof no question that it was a plot to kill the president ... To me, I'm thinking ... you have the eyewitnesses ... Paul O'Connor....

DSL: No, no, no, you're jumping around. No, no. The answer to your question is to go to my story; how it started. The answer to your question is two FBI ... were assigned to watch the autopsy, and they made notes based on what the doctors ... were saying. And they wrote it was apparent ... when the sheets were unwrapped, and they saw the body [of JFK], it

---

148   See Chapter 14 of *Best Evidence,* "Trajectory Reversal: Blueprint for Deception," pages 368-369 of the Carroll & Graf edition. Mr. Lifton points out that the original TSBD source of the suspect's description for the APB is Dallas Police Department "Inspector Herbert J. Sawyer" [sic]. See also: History Matters. "J. Herbert Sawyer." History-Matters.com, pages 321-322. Retrieved 8/2/2023: https://history-matters.com/archive/jfk/wc/wcvols/wh6/pdf/WH6_Sawyer.pdf.

was apparent there had been "surgery of the head area, namely, in the top of the skull."[149]

JH: That makes – that's the number one piece of evidence....

DSL: That, to me, that's number two [piece of evidence] because when I first looked at the Zapruder film frames, the head goes back [head snap] – so that's Newton's laws. So, I knew he had been struck from the front, but the autopsy said [that] he had been struck twice from behind. So, then, when I got the Sibert and O'Neill Report – remember I wrote "The Case

for Three Assassins."[150]

149   Assassination Archives and Research Center. "MD 44 – Sibert and O'Neill Report on the Autopsy (11/26/63--'Gemberling Version')." AARCLibrary.org, 6 pages including cover sheet, (Page 3). Retrieved 7/21/2023: https://www.aarclibrary.org/publib/jfk/arrb/master_med_set/md44/html/Image0.htm.

150   Lifton, David and Welsh, David. "The Case For Three Assassins." Ramparts, January 1967. Retrieved 7/19/2023: http://jfk.hood.edu/Collection/Weisberg%20Subject%20Index%20Files/R%20Disk/Ramparts/Item%2005.pdf. For a direct link to a PDF version of "The Case for Three Assassins" (January 1967), one is found in the References section of his Wikipedia page: David Lifton.

JH: I've got it right here (Points to frame on wall)....
PDF signed by Mr. Lifton, Tuesday, July 6, 2021

DSL: Great! OK. Where was I? It was July 1966, and I'm in San Francisco [at] *Ramparts* magazine which is the story of how I got that assignment ["The Case for Three Assassins"].[151] But what happened was, one of the financial backers of *Ramparts* magazine was Stanley Scheinbaum.[152] He was a very well-known man ... a lovely-like grandfatherly man; very ideological. He live[d] in the Santa Barbara area, and he married a woman who was very, very wealthy ... Stanley came to my apartment in '65. He was interviewing the Warren Report researchers. First, it was ... Los Angeles [based] Ray Marcus ... and Ray Marcus says, "Well, make sure you speak to David Lifton." ... Ray basically – either his mother or father were communists. OK?

JH: Uh, huh....

DSL: So, this was the "Old Left." He had been completely upset with the Alger Hiss Case and then came the Rosenberg Case, so now came the Kennedy Assassination.[153] OK, so he's keeping scrapbooks and all the rest ... Scheinbaum comes to my apartment ... and there I am trying to ... complete the courses I had to complete for UCLA. I had taken an incomplete, and then a *second* incomplete, and then a *third* incomplete, and then a *fourth* incomplete. And then the question was [from Dean Elliot in Late September 1966], you know, "You can't do this anymore. You've got to now make up these incompletes or drop your idea of becoming an engineer in the space program."[154] ... [But] first came the stint at *Ramparts* magazine in December of '66. So, Stanley [Scheinbaum] in the Spring of '66.... He says, "Well ... do you wanna write for us? You can write this up in an article, David." ... I [already] had a rough draft of a document I called, "The Citizen and the Critic: Dialogue in Defense of Conspiracy." He liked it, but he said, "You've gotta write this up as an essay." He said, "Why don't you come up to *Ramparts* magazine" ... basically "We'll give you an office in San Francisco and a person to work with, Dave Welsh, who's on our staff. And you [can] write this stuff all up." So, that's how "The Case for Three Assassins" got written in San Francisco at *Ramparts* offices, 301 Broadway ... and was completed by July 19 [1966] after a month-long residence at a hotel in San Francisco – which they paid for.

151   Wikipedia: Ramparts (Magazine).
152   Wikipedia: Stanley Scheinbaum.
153   Wikipedia: Alger Hiss and Julius and Ethel Rosenberg.
154   See Chapter 5 of *Best Evidence*, "The Sibert and O'Neill Report and the Emerging Controversy," pages 97-98 of the Carroll & Graf edition.

So, it gets written, and I said, "OK, thank you very much. Here it is." And they said, "We'll call you if we want to use it, and you and Dave Welsh can be on the telephone and make up additional … final edit[s] …."

JH: Yeah.

DSL: So, now, I flew on a plane back to L.A., and I had four incompletes … I tackled the first one and passed the exam … I was finished with Thermal Dynamics. So, now I had three left, and … the UCLA [Daily] *Bruin* [student newspaper] wanted to publish it ["The Case for Three Assassins"].[155] … So, I was working on the second one [incomplete] when I found *surgery of the head area* … I knew there was a conflict between Newton's Laws and the impact of the [head] shot. It came from the front according to physics, but it came from the back according to the Navy autopsy. The question is, "How do you reconcile those two?" And then, the idea that the president's wounds have been altered – is what blew me away. When I found the passage [about] the surgery of the head area. I said, "Holy sh*t!" And by that time, I knew Professor Liebeler. I bought it to him, and I think I was blessed because who else has a professor in the Warren Commission who not only knew me well enough to trust me, but was [also] blown away by my discovery and said, "This has got to go in a memorandum to Earl Warren."[156] And that's when the Liebeler Memo was written which is Chapter 9 of my book *Best Evidence*.…[157]

JH: Right, right….

DSL: Once I got onto this, I realized that if I wanted to get *accurate information* of what was supposed to happen, then I better get the news stories published in Dallas – which meant ordering the *Dallas Morning News* and the *Dallas Times Herald* on microfilm [through the UCLA LIbrary]; which I did. And then, I ordered [newspapers for] each city he [JFK] was in, for I knew there was another set of Texas witnesses. So, there were five cities, and he was killed in the fourth, right?[158]

JH: Yeah….

DSL: He was killed in Dallas. So, I ordered the first one which was what – San Antonio. Two papers: the … [*San Antonio Express-*] *News* and the *San Antonio Light*. So, I got them. Then came [the newspapers in] …

---

155   Which they did on Thursday, January 5, 1967.
156   Wikipedia: Earl Warren.
157   See Chapter 9 of *Best Evidence*, "October 24, 1966 – A Confrontation with Liebeler," pages 207-231 of the Carroll & Graf edition.
158   JFK never made it to Austin – and the LBJ Ranch, the fifth and final city on his itinerary.

Houston ... Ft. Worth ... Dallas ... Austin was going to be a dinner – a big huge dinner.

JH: What I read [was that] he was going to "hang out" with LBJ....

DSL: No, no, no. I wouldn't say hang out. He was going to stay at the ranch one night. [Mr. Lifton then proceeded to review the San Antonio "threat" again where the constable overheard the two secret service agents in the car talking, and he added an additional concept] ... So, there's a total of ten motocades [minus the 3rd one in San Antonio] ... That's the deal: inbound, outbound. Ft. Worth airport arrival inbound/outbound. So, Kennedy basically was like a duck in a shooting gallery ... because ... they ... had ten chances [to get him] ... I'm not saying it would have been the same autopsy, obviously it wouldn't have been ... If you get outside Dallas County, you're in a different county with a different medical examiner. Basically, that's the deal ... same motorcade....

JH: Wow....

DSL: [Back to the San Antonio threat] So, then the question became, "Well, what the Hell is going on here?" ... What was going on here was somebody [Secret Service agents in San Antonio] had knowledge of what they thought was gonna be – what I call a "San Antonio Scenario." OK? So, then I found another news story pertaining to San Antonio. What's really amazing is that, get this: When the assassination occurred on November 22nd, they were recalling in the [San Antonio] newsrooms this incident that had occurred on the 21st in the afternoon ... about the San Antonio remark.... The reason it was important, and you could only find this in the San Antonio newspapers, *which I had ordered on microfilm* ... was that in fact, there was ... a wider scenario.... In the news stories, I discovered there was a guy named John Glenn who would have been the patsy ... Get this: he was an Air Force intelligence officer who was in Indiana, and who started ... a Fair Play for Cuba Committee.[159] OK? So, you've got this U.S. Air Force officer who's in counterintelligence who had testified a week or two in Washington before the assassination about – his name was John Glenn! It has nothing to do with the astronaut.

JH: Right.

DSL: He was connected with the Bloomington-

JH: Fair Play for Cuba Committee.

---

159   Wikipedia: Fair Play for Cuba Committee. I waiver on the spelling of the surname. Obviously, my first thought was John Glenn the astronaut.

DSL: Yeah, right! Bloomington, Indiana – OK, here's the deal. In Dallas, there's another city involved – New Orleans where Oswald did his thing [pro-Castro leaflets, TV and radio interviews, etc.], right? If this had been a San Antonio assassination that got the green light, there was no New Orleans, there was Bloomington, Indiana, you know with this whole thing with this Fair Play for Cuba Committee.

JH: Wow….

DSL: And this guy named John Glenn. So, so, get this. I figured, "Well, I'm going to try and find this guy John Glenn." OK. I found him. He happened to be living in Venice, California. So, I met with him at the UCLA Student Union. It was like talking to a … Lee Harvey Oswald … It was very weird. About that time, do you know the writer Robert Sam Anson?[160]

JH: Yes….

DSL: OK. So, Anson and I got to know one another. We were friends. He comes out to California to do a big story for *New Times* magazine … about the assassination … I told him the story [about John Glenn] and he said, "Oh, we have to follow this up." So, he and I … went back to John Glenn's apartment and met with him and talked with him … Anson was fascinated with this. I don't know if he used it in any of his stories … for *New Times*, but it was an interesting sideline that indicated a San Antonio alternate scenario for the Kennedy Assassination, complete with all this nut stuff I've been telling you about. He [Anson] was fascinated by it. He thought there was something to it, and I think there was, too. We were talking … [about] the story of a scenario that didn't happen, and I always thought that if Kennedy had [to visit] … Dallas, the ideal thing would have been to have the San Antonio Scenario first … San Antonio was the *first city-*

JH: First city, yeah….

DSL: Yeah, but you want the thing [assassination attempt] closer in time because, you know, you don't call off Dallas when you have Lee Harvey Oswald set up … because of weather. And if San Antonio comes before Dallas, you've blown it … When it starts to rain, you don't have your "Plan B." San Antonio would have to come *after* Dallas. But anyway, that's what had happened. You get into this whole business of multi-cities and alternate scenarios, and it's very interesting.

  160   Wikipedia: Robert Sam Anson.

JH: I'm fascinated by that. So, they [conspirators] – do you think they had more than like Oswald and this guy John Glenn? Do you think they had other patsies in other cities...?

DSL: Umm, I don't know. I think that there was at least one alternate city ... The easiest alternate city would have been Ft. Worth because it's just a 20 minute drive or a thirty minute drive from Dallas. So, you might have a situation where it's raining in Dallas, but it's clear in Ft. Worth. You could then get the same patsy. You start theorizing about this. You could use the same patsy, and say, "He took a bus" or "He was driven." So, Ft. Worth and Dallas should be considered one multiplex. Just because you switch from Dallas to Ft. Worth doesn't mean you have to switch ... [around] your plot. If you go to the others, if you go to Austin or ... [Houston], it [the plot] would be different. But anyway ... it turned out the weather was fine in Dallas.... All of that is interesting....

JH: Wow.... Did you broach the subject with John Glenn and say, "Hey, you might have been Oswald. You might have...."

DSL: Yes. We pushed it, but we didn't reveal to him immediately what we were driving at. We asked him things like, "Did anybody try to control where you were ... on 11/21?"

JH: What did he say?

DSL: Well, as far as he knew, no. He didn't know of anybody attempting to tell him to work here or not. Do you know what I mean?

JH: What does that – what's your ... take on that? What's your conclusion?

DSL: Well, we concluded that if he [John Glenn] was involved – then the plan wasn't executed. If there was a San Antonio Scenario ... it never got executed. I mean, I, I – that's the best I can do ... There was too much evidence to indicate there was ... a San Antonio Scenario, but it looked like it hadn't been executed.

JH: But I mean, how could he not have been controlled? I'm trying to figure that out.

DSL: No. That's what I'm saying ... I'm just hypothesizing. Maybe there was a San Antonio Scenario where it was a friend of his [John Glenn's] or something who ended up being the designated patsy. OK. There's no question there's a John Glenn. There's no question that there was a Fair Play for Cuba Committee ... John Glenn testified *before a congressional committee* on November 18th … I pulled the hearings [transcripts] … I don't have any reason to believe that John Glenn was *the specific patsy* in the San Antonio Scenario. But, there's too much evidence that there wasn't something afoot….

JH: Maybe a year or so before, he might have been considered, but by that time, they [conspirators] knew it was going to go down in Dallas….

DSL: Yeah, that's one idea, but I think the other idea is … it was "systems go" for Dallas … Circumstantial evidence of the San Antonio Scenario was never flushed out … It was like the skeleton without the bones.

JH: But, it's like you said, Dallas was perfect. They had the cops, they had the sheriff….

DSL: Yeah.

JH: They had the mayor….

DSL: Oh, yes. Dallas was perfect. It's absolute that Dallas was perfect, yeah.

JH: You described how you met Marina Oswald, and how you became really good friends with her and you had to quote unquote "deprogram her" from thinking that her husband was guilty to realizing he probably had nothing to do with it.

DSL: Correct….

JH: And also including his daughter. Is it Rachel that you had to deprogram, too…?

DSL: Rachel didn't take that much … it's been so many years ago … Rachel was relieved to realize that I was saying that her father was innocent. See, we held a whole party for her. She was not just pleased. It wasn't academic with her. It was right in her gut. She wanted her dad to be innocent, and then along comes this evidence that it might very well be the case.

JH: Do you think … that Oswald will ever be cleared?…. A lot of people already believe it, but do you think like publicly the government will say, "Yeah, he had nothing to do with it," or do you think that will never happen?

DSL: Well, what you're asking is … Will the government ever issue a White Paper? … I don't know. You know, there's another force operating besides me, and *Best Evidence*, and *Final Charade*, and that's Oliver Stone.

You know, he's just come out with this new movie. I was just reading about it, and, you know, he assiduously *leaves me out.*[161] Can you believe this...?

JH: No. Why do you think he [Stone did this]?

DSL: I don't know ... He does not like me. Now, I don't know whether it's the "like" or he doesn't believe the body was altered ... He may really think this whole thing of altering the body is ridiculous. All you've got to do is falsify the autopsy – so you have some dirty doctors. Why mess with the corpse? And that may be also what's going on. I took the corpse very seriously, and the Liebeler Memorandum ... recognizes how serious it is. Now ... that's the proper way to proceed. You start with the body in a murder. Not with the document [autopsy] that's been falsified, you start *with the body.*

JH: Yeah ... I really believe that the body ... is not in his tomb. It's gone. They got rid of it. What do you think?

DSL: Oh, no. Kennedy's body is in his tomb.

JH: My view is that's the final piece of evidence. If they ever exhume his body, they'll be able to study it and know that it doesn't match....

DSL: No, no. If they ever exhume his body, it will have craniotomy evidence that there was a hole in the back of his head. Sure, that's true. But, I don't think there's anybody else's body in there.... There's no need to [get rid of it]. The purpose of the Warren Commission and the FBI [investigation] – it's over....

JH: But, you think that they falsified the body that well where a normal person....

DSL: No, no. The body is the body that's described in the autopsy report, and when you go to the pictures and X-rays – that's the way the body looked after midnight when they "doctored it up" for those photographs. But, there's no need to not put the body in the tomb. There's no need to do that. Even if they admit that there's a patch at the back of the head, a simpler hypothesis if you wanted to go down that path ... there's always somebody [from the government] who would produce a memorandum that would say, "We altered the wounds for national security reasons to avoid a nuclear war with Russia ... [and thus] create[d] the appearance that Oswald did it alone.' You don't need to not *bury the body.* The body can be there. The body's *been altered.* And there's an X-ray and photo record of what it looks like at the National Archives. That's ... [when] all the

161   Wikipedia: JFK Revisited: Through the Looking Glass [Released July 12, 2021].

119

examinations were done by the experts … You don't need to do that. The body can be buried just as it was when the photos and X-rays were taken. Remember what they did: as soon as they were finished with the photos and X-rays after midnight, they called in the embalmers. They embalmed the body, fixed him up, put him in the coffin, Jackie and Bobby got a peek, and then that's the end of it. They buried that body.

JH: Do you remember that day? The burial? What you were doing…?

DSL: Umm, no, because I wasn't interested in the assassination that much. It was all very sad, and I remember I was at [the house of] my cousin Janice.

SATURDAY, JANUARY 15, 2022

JH: Your parents, I would assume, when they were younger lived in the city [New York] at one point…?

DSL: Umm, no. What happened was … my father was born in Russia … He was the youngest son of five. So, the five brothers came over here in 1909, something like that – within a year or two of 1909 … They settled in Brooklyn … and then his next older brother Irving and Al [Lifton's father Alexander] decided together to start a business. Each one of them was productive in another area: Nat was in real estate, Morris was in plumbing, and Irving and Al set up a little electrical supply … [store] selling cable – you know, *wholesale*.

JH: What was your dad's name…?

DSL: Al – Alexander. So, they set up … a store in Brooklyn selling cable at the wholesale level that goes into houses … and then they added lighting fixtures … People would come in and decide what fixture they wanted to hang in their dining room or something … They had three little showrooms there. They had fixtures hanging there.

JH: And you said [in earlier conversation] that that business is still operating?

DSL: Yeah … OK. I didn't want anything to do with electrical lighting. I was turned on by the moon program and all that, and I didn't want to go into my father's business. That was just out of the question that I studied all of [that] physics and math to go into uh selling electrical lighting fixtures for ladies in Queens? I mean, you know, forget it. I didn't want to do it … I was turned on by Project Apollo….[162]

162   Wikipedia: Apollo Program.

JH: Yeah, yeah ….

DSL: So, Irving and Al went into the … electrical supplies, and their mother who[m] they adored – she was a lovely woman – took sick … They owned the real estate above the store, so they had one of those [rooms] converted into a rather lovely apartment for her … They had a full time nurse … And I would go up there and hold her hand … and she would always say, uh – but, she spoke Yiddish. You know, "I feel besser." She meant better, … and I would hold her hand and visit – it was very sad. Umm … I had to deal with her death at a relatively early age, thirteen or fourteen. I remember that ….

JH: Wow. That'd put it around … '52-'53, around there ….

DSL: Yeah. That's correct … So, they put Grandma … there's a Jewish word for grandma: "bubbe." I never called her grandma. But anyways, she was upstairs, and I guess he [Al] said "Hello!" to her everyday. I'm not sure, but he was very attached – as was Irving. I mean, the two of them took care of Grandma or Bubbe … until she died. Oh – now, my grandmother on my mother's side was … [tough] … and she lived with us … The whole family bought a very large plot … at the cemetery to handle all five Lifton Brothers, and their children, and their childrens' children ….

JH: Oh, wow.

DSL: It's a very interesting story. You know about the Rosenberg Case?[163]

JH: Yes ….

DSL: OK, well, the Rosenbergs were buried in the same cemetery – one hundred feet from my family plot.[164] (Laughs) Ethel and Julius Rosenberg – they were electrocuted and lowered into the earth … We had to go out there for some ceremony for the family, and I got interested in where the Rosenbergs were … I found them. They were a very short walking distance; in other words, *my grave* is already picked out …. (Laughs)

JH: Quick answer to this: Do you believe they [Rosenbergs] were guilty or were they framed, or?

DSL: No, no, no, no, no. I know a lot about it because I knew the Rosenberg's oldest son.[165]

JH: Really … ?

163   Wikipedia: Julius and Ethel Rosenberg.
164   Wellwood Cemetery, West Babylon, New York. See: Find a Grave. "Ethel Greenglass Rosenberg." Retrieved 7/31/2023: https://www.findagrave.com/memorial/901/ethel-rosenberg.
165   Wikipedia: Michael Meeropol.

DSL: Oh, yeah. My family. We took him out to dinner and all the rest. I read a lot about it [Rosenberg Case]. If you're asking, "Did they enable the Russians to get the atomic bomb?" That's ridiculous. That's laughable. However, if you ask whether they were willing accomplices and made the effort ... I think, as I understand it, the answer is yes. But, it was really not the husband [Julius], it was Ethel – whose real goal in life was to be an opera singer....

JH: How did your family know them though...?

DSL: What happened was, you know who Pat Valentino is? ... He and I drove cross-country in a truck when I moved ... Anyway, Pat's sister was Linda Valentino. Linda, who's very smart ... never finished college ... she's very well-read ... but anyway she was active in the Rosenberg Case[166] ... So ... because of Linda, I met the Rosenberg's son ..., and we had dinner ... I actually got to know him. My mother and dad took him to dinner with me ... in New York [City].... In terms of going back to the '40s, Ethel was more of the activist.... By the way, they never, ever, ever, ever would have sentenced them to death under the known facts as we know them today.

JH: Yeah, I was gonna ask you that....

DSL: And ... the sad thing was, when she [Ethel] was set up for electro-cution, she would sing operas late at night in the death house [Sing Sing Prison, Ossining, NY]. Her voice would resonate, and she sang her favor-ite operas. It's described in a book written about all of this that I read, and I kept breaking out into tears. It was so sad because she knew that she had not – she knew that she was not guilty as charged.... She was electrocuted *and her husband* was electrocuted, and that's because of the *crazy atmo-sphere* of McCarthy[167] in-

JH: Right.

DSL: 1952 and the behavior of the prosecutor Roy Cohn....[168]

JH: Really? ... So, [do] you think they [Rosenbergs] were like "stepping stones" for ... people like Nixon and...?

---

166   Wikipedia: National Committee to Secure Justice in the Rosenberg Case. Note that when Linda Valentino got involved in the Rosenberg Case and the extent of her involvement is unknown, however Mr. Lifton believed this issue was very important to her.
167   Wikipedia: Joseph McCarthy and McCarthyism.
168   Wikipedia: Roy Cohn.

DSL: Well, the way I understand it is, there were three major cases in the aftermath of the Cold War. The first was the Hiss Case.[169] That's a big deal. Then came the Rosenberg Case. This is what Ray Marcus used to tell us ... And then came the Oswald Case ... The Russians did not get the atomic bomb because of the ... [Rosenbergs]. That's – that's ridiculous ... She [Ethel] wouldn't be able to ... write a simple equation for ... quantum mechanics ... There was a British guy named Klaus Fuchs who-[170]

JH: Right, Klaus Fuchs....

DSL: And he worked at Los Alamos, and he played a key role ... Who's the one[171] that turned them [Rosenbergs] in and made the false charge – and then later he said, "Well, I had to say these things to protect my own self and the fact that my ... [wife] would ... [be implicated]?" ... Once you know the complexity of building a bomb, and the physics behind it, the notion that the Rosenbergs [wrote this down] – she [Ethel] wouldn't even know how to write, "F=ma." ... It was a prosecution based upon false archetypes, you know? The idea that there was some secret, and the communists couldn't figure it out, and a Jewish lady who wanted to be an opera singer turns [over the secret] ... (Laughs) It was absurd....

JH: I can tell you though, being a history teacher, I can remember – even recently – the textbooks having pictures of the Rosenbergs. You know, they were under arrest, going to trial, whatever ... and they were selling secrets to the Russians. But, then when I started doing my own research ... I learned ... that might not have been the case, and now you're telling me *that's really not the case*. I mean, they were selling secrets perhaps, but they....

DSL: No, no, no. First of all, the book that really got to me emotionally was a book that came out a year or two or three years ago written about Ethel Rosenberg. It is a biography written by a ... *very good* researcher and writer from Britain.... It's *really* good, and ... it'll make you cry. It's so beautifully written and so carefully researched.[172]

JH: So, I had another question. Your *dad* was born in Russia. Was your *mom* born in the United States....?

169   Wikipedia: Alger Hiss.
170   Wikipedia: Klaus Fuchs.
171   Wikipedia: David Greenglass.
172   See: Sebba, Anne. *Ethel Rosenberg: An American Tragedy.* St. Martin's Press, 2021, 320 pages.

DSL: Yes. My father came over here about age five or eight or something, and my mother was five years younger than him ... I forget how he met her, but I think it has to do with Atlantic City [New Jersey] and seeing her on the beach or something.... My sister would [know]. I should remember this stuff, and I don't remember the story of how he met her. But he met her, and they each had a common background.... She was born in the U.S. and was a teacher – well, licensed to be a teacher. My father ... he never went ... [to] high school. He and Irwin went into business immediately.... But, my father knew immediately that he wanted to marry her.... There's a real disparity. My dad had no formal education past the 8th grade. My mother had gone through the equivalent of teacher's training....

JH: And your mom's from New York or New Jersey...?

DSL: New Jersey. Newark, [New Jersey] ... area.

JH: And is she Jewish, too – your mom....?

DSL: Yeah. Well ... she was the youngest of eight, and my father was the youngest of five. But, she wasn't a religious Jew. I mean ... my mother was unusual in the fact that ... when other people were starving during the [Great] Depression, she already was an executive at the equivalent of Macy's in New Jersey. And she had hiring and firing authority which is very unusual for a person that was that young. She [Mom] was very organized and intelligent ... and all the rest of it....

JH: Well, I can see where you get your organization [skills] from then....

DSL: My father was also ... self-educated. My father was an autodidact compared to my mother.... I don't know how someone [Al Lifton] could think I could be trained in physics and math and be interested in the Apollo Program, would want to go into LB Electric Supply? I mean ... my imagination was on fire with the idea of going to the Moon and the [Apollo] Program.... And then once I got to California ... there was this whole business of the girls were beautiful ... and UCLA Campus....

JH: Do you remember the moment when you had to go to your dad and say, "Dad, I don't want to ... follow you in the store business."

DSL: I think that once I was on fire with the Kennedy Case – I suppose it must have been a puzzle to him ... [and] when I got the agent [Peter Shepherd] and made the discoveries I did ... [that was it].... By then [mid-1970s], I was writing the book at home and meeting with people.

JH: This had to have been way earlier – like mid-60s when you finally said, "Hey"....

DSL: I graduated [from] Cornell ... It was a four year ordinary liberal arts program. I would have been in the Class of '61 but engineering physics was a five year program. So, I was Class of '62 and because I had gone to Europe the Summer before in '61 – remember the wild a** trip I had–

JH: Yeah, the airplane crash and everything.

DSL: The airplane on the way home, and also the business of the Berlin Wall having gone up [recently].[173] You know, I was in Berlin two weeks after the wall went up?

JH: I don't remember you saying that. OK....

DSL: Oh, yeah. Oh, yeah. I should be able to go to the CIA under the Freedom of Information Act and get the picture of my Volkswagen going through Checkpoint Charlie. They photographed everybody.[174] ... And the Russian tanks were there the week before. They were parked on a side street when I went through.

JH: Wow. That's '61 – two weeks after the wall went up. That had to be tense....

DSL: Oh, yeah ... Let me tell ya. I was in the world's hotspots – twice. I mean, it's really weird. In 1958, as a sophomore at Cornell ... I ended up going to Miami . . ., [and] I was in my hotel room at the Nautilus Hotel – right there near Miami Beach.... My door was closed and out in the hall-way I hear a voice of this guy saying, "Hey, anybody wanna go with me to Havana tomorrow?" So, I said, "Yeah! I wanna go." I open the door. I don't remember his name. So, the next morning we're on a Cubana airliner ... We landed in Havana. This is the week before Castro took over. It was very exciting.... We get into the taxi cab ... [as] we had reservations for a hotel room at the famous Nacional Hotel[175] ... I always paved the way for the revolutions. (Laughs) I sent my parents – they didn't know I did this ... a postcard ... I remember the wording, "I am in Havana. The food is good, and the rebels are friendly...."

JH: So, you went there [Havana] ... in ... '59, and then you were at ... [the Berlin Wall in] August of '61.

---

173   Wikipedia: Berlin Wall. It was hastily erected on August 13, 1961, which would put Mr. Lifton's presence there around August 27 of that same month.
174   Wikipedia: Freedom of Information Act (United States) and Checkpoint Charlie.
175   Wikipedia: Cubana de Aviación and Hotel Nacional de Cuba.

DSL: I'm like ... Forrest Gump (Laughs) ... I had no care....

JH: Well, if you think about [it], you were there in Havana two days or so before Castro took over. You were at the Berlin Wall – that was tense. And then you almost got on a plane that crashed, and you didn't – that's a lot of luck. That's good luck.[176]

DSL: That's right. There was a coin toss....

JH: Oh, my God....

DSL: My reason for going to Europe ... OK. I'm gonna go to Europe, and we want to get a Volkswagen. I'll buy it at the factory and save a lot of money. So, I took a student boat on the Holland America Line from Hoboken [New Jersey] as I recall or maybe New York City, and it landed in ... La Havre [France] I think ... I had to then take a train ... to the Volkswagen factory.... So, I picked up my car in Wolfsburg, and then I drove from Wolfsburg ... to Paris where I signed up for courses in French cause I already took four years in ... high school ... [but I wanted to] really learn how to speak ... the real French that the French would speak. So, I went to the Alliance Française. That's like going to UCLA Extension ... Of course, everyday you read the newspaper. I always did. The newspaper then that was available in Europe was not *The New York Times* but the *New York Herald Tribune* ... and I open the newspaper and it says the Germans are building this wall. And I said, "Holy sh*t! I gotta go there." You know, when you're young, you can do anything, right? You're not going to get hurt.

JH: Yeah....

DSL: So, there was this other guy, or maybe ... a woman from Cornell, I forget. I met this person, [and] I said, "OK. Let's go there." ... And then when I was through with Berlin, after the adventure I had there, I then drove the rest of the way ... to ... one of those three beautiful cities on the Mediterranean – the [French] Riviera ... and then all the way down to Rome. I parked my car in a storage place in Rome, my VW, and took a student flight to Israel. I was in Israel for ten days, and I took a bus trip to

---

176   Wikipedia: 1961 President Airlines Douglas DC-6 Crash. My late friend, Adolph Kuhn, Sr., who told me he survived 19 near misses as a U.S. Navy sailor on Ford Island during the Japanese attack on Pearl Harbor – including boarding the USS *Arizona* "to rescue injured sailors and Marines" *after it had been hit* – would argue that Mr. Lifton was protected by his guardian angels. See: BBC News. "How My 'Guardian Angel' Saved Me at Pearl Harbor." BBC.com, 2015, 04:55. Retrieved 8/1/2023: https://www.bbc.com/news/av/magazine-34935991. The story of Adolph Kuhn, a La Crosse, Kansas farm boy and WWII veteran, is widely available on YouTube as well as Amazon

(Adolph Kuhn: An American Journey, et al.).

the southern tip of Israel called Eilat, E-I-L-A-T.[177] And I swam in the Red Sea. I was all alone down there, as a matter of fact, and then this bus arrives with two hundred American students; all female ... I forget why, but they were there for a night.... And then [I] went back to Northern Israel, flew back on the charter ... to Rome, made provision to ship my car from a port like Marseilles ... back to the U.S. And then, I took a ... student flight which had one engine go out over the English Channel, and they had to land at Shannon [Airport, Ireland].... There were three planes ... and now two of them were being repaired because the engines were out, and we had to sleep on the floor [of the airport].... The first plane was repaired. There were two groups: the German farmers and the U.S. students. There was a coin toss ... and the other group won ... I went into the bathroom, and it was a rainy night ... I was ... getting myself cleaned up or maybe shaving at the mirror, and I heard this huge bang.

JH: Oh....

DSL: And that was the plane that crashed and everybody died.... It was like a truck having a collision right outside the bathroom.... I went out-[side], and they were pulling bodies out of the muck – out of the Shannon River.[178] ... Then ... flew into New York, and I had to get my a** up to Cornell to start classes. But, you can imagine when I came back, you know, to Cornell, there was an unreal quality about the whole thing because I had been exposed to all this different stuff.... Just imagine: the Berlin Wall, Israel, the air crash, dah, dah, dah, dah, dah, dah.... It was amazing to go and sit down to the classes ... like a normal student.... Also, that was the semester where ... I loved all the stuff about matrices ... differential equations.... The teacher was a Greek [professor]. I could hardly understand the ... [man]. First of all, he spoke too fast. Second of all, he had a serious accent. His name was Kasimatis ... and I couldn't keep up with him. I tried. My friend George Ryder, who became a famous physicist, would give me his notes so I could answer the problem sets, you know.

JH: Yeah.

DSL: He went too fast. I loved matrices. I learned all about them ... and it affected my thinking a lot about mathematics.... So, I caught up [one day] with Mr. Kasimatis cause he flunked me. He gave me a "D" or something in the course.... He was on the Cornell Campus walking by. I saw him and ran up to him … "Mr. Kasimatis!" I said, "You told us at the beginning [of the course]" … Did I ever tell you this story?

JH: Yeah, but tell it again.

DSL: "I promise you if you turn your homework in on time you will not … fail." … "I turned all my homework in on time!" Of course, it came from George Ryder, but that's another subject … [Mr. Kasimatis] remembers me. He says, "Mr. Lifton. The homework is meant to push a man over the border, not lift him out of the grave." (Laughs)

JH: Yeah…. (Laughs)

DSL: (Laughing throughout) I … even though I was in this terrible situation with the math, I could not get over the … the joke was so funny! He was not trying to intentionally be funny, but I had to laugh at my own predicament. "The homework is meant to push a man over the border, not lift him out of the grave." … Oh, and by the way, I took the course over again.

JH: With Kasimatis or?

DSL: No, no, no. This time, I went to Columbia. I took a summer school [course] … My father was p*ssed off. It was $550 dollars…. I also took a course in math at Brooklyn [Collegiate and Polytechnic Institute] … Arnon Mishkin, who was a good friend of mine, his *father* was a professor there.[179] … I like math, but please *go slower* number one. And number two … hire somebody who does not have a *Godd*mn thick accent*, you know what I mean? The guy was speaking rapidly, and he was Greek – and it was practically Greek to me. And I was sliding by with George Ryder's homework, and I never liked that. I really wanted to understand. So, then I took additional books out. Cornell had a math library, and I took out extra books. I always learned – like if you have a second textbook from a different POV [point of view]-

JH: Yeah….

DSL: It helps! It really helps to get a second author's teachings…. It really helps a lot….

JH: So, when you were in Israel, though, did you go anywhere prominent…?

DSL: Yeah, I went to the BáHa'í Faith Center up in Haifa.[180] And I went to Eilat at the Southern tip – Israel [290 miles] is only like the length of

179   Wikipedia: Arnon Mishkin.
180   Wikipedia: BáHa'í World Centre.

New Jersey [150 miles]. Oh, yes! There was something special in Israel ...
I met somebody in Paris named Ami ... from Israel. He said, "When you
come to Israel, I'll fix you up." ... He fixed me up with the Israeli Queen of
Beauty who had been in the Miss Israel and the Miss Universe contest[s]
the year before.[181]

JH: Whoa....

DSL: That was my date for the night, and I took her dancing at the Dan
[Tel Aviv] Hotel. I remember that, because ... Israeli women wanted to
meet Americans at the Dan Hotel so that they could come to America
and emigrate.... Yeah ... [Israel] was really good. It really was an amazing summer and then to come back. You know, I'll tell ya, when I came
back – I'm trying to remember another thing that happened. I went to
a dance one night ... in Paris ... and there was this really ... [strikingly
beautiful woman].... She agreed to meet me ... [Enroute] I ended up in
my Volkswagen, and I met this guy who was a survivor of the ... Warsaw
Ghetto. And we ended up in this really intense conversation ... he [even]
had personal experience with one of the camps ... I was transfixed by this
conversation, and when I went back to my hotel room, the manager says
to me, "These two very attractive women ... came by looking for you."
(Laughs) I never visited the camps the way a lot of people do ... I didn't
go to Auschwitz [or elsewhere]. I didn't go to this one that my [friend]
John Martinson went to. John Martinson would lead a group of teachers
every summer and go into Berlin and other places.

JH: I've been to Dachau....

DSL: Dachau is the place! Yeah....

JH: Every year at Chapman University they have the Holocaust Art and
Writing Contest[182], and our kids [i.e. students] would go. And about three
years ago [2019], we went and ... it's incredible. You get to meet these
people [Holocaust survivors]. To me, they're rock stars ... I'd rather
shake their hand[s] than Elvis or ... The Beatles....

DSL: Yeah. They have amazing stories. I used to listen to them on the
Internet....[183]

---

181   Wikipedia: Aliza Gur.
182   Wikipedia: Chapman University. I highly recommend this opportunity at Chapman University to educators and students. I was honored that year to have met and spoken to Dr. Jacob
Eisenbach, a survivor of Auschwitz. See: McCartney, Karen. *Where You Go, I Go: The Astonishing Life
of Dr. Jacob Eisenbach, Holocaust Survivor and 92-Year-Old Full-Time Dentist.* Self-Published, 2015,
248 pages.
183   See: USC Shoah Foundation: The Institute for Visual History and Education. SFI.USC.

JH: The whole point is, kids – let's say they write a poem about somebody [survivor], [or] they make a … short movie about somebody … They're [biographies of survivors] in this database [Chapman.edu] … The kids win awards . . ., [and then] you go to this tented area with five star food and all the survivors come and sit, and you can walk up and talk to them and get their autograph. And the last time … I was there, and it was in a crowded room, and I see this little man with a little cap on, and he's shuffling through. I said [to myself], "Oh, my God. That guy totally looks like a survivor of a camp." And I … muscled my way up to him because it was crowded, and I'm like, "Sir. Are you OK?" He goes … "I've got to go to the bathroom right now." He was … say, ninety years old. His name was Dr. … [Jacob] Eisenbach … And so I said, "Follow me." I'm pushing people out (Laughs) of the way, [and saying] "Get out of the way! Emergency!" So, I got him down there [washroom] … and then I [almost] left. He was in there a while. I almost left, but I thought, "No way! I'm not gonna blow this." So, I waited [outside], and then he came out. And I thought, he's gonna think I'm weird – like I'm a stalker (Laughs) or something.

DSL: Yeah…?

JH: And I said, "Sir. Do you know where you're going?" He goes, "No." I go, "I know where you need to go." So, then, I led him [Dr. Eisenbach] to the tent where they have the meal … for the kids to come up and get autographs. And so, he started talking and he's telling me his story … he was in Auschwitz … I said, "Man, I'm so glad I got to meet you." … The irony [was] his brother was at Auschwitz, and then after they got out, his brother survived, became a cop in Poland, and some anti-Semite killed him….

FRIDAY, JANUARY 21, 2022

JH: I found a little interview of Bill Greer.

DSL: Really…?

JH: And it's like two minutes – right before he died, and I thought we could watch it … It's from North Carolina, a TV station down there. I think it would be interesting to have you watch it because you interviewed him.

DSL: I actually went to his home and spent an hour there.

---

edu. Founded by Steven Spielberg in 1994 "to videotape and preserve interviews with survivors and other witnesses of the Holocaust" – this is, to my knowledge, the largest such collection in the world. True story: I interviewed for an "historian position" with the foundation back around 2005 – on the Universal Pictures lot in Hollywood inside Spielberg's bungalow. Three interviews but no job.

JH: In North Carolina, or somewhere else…?

DSL: Uhh, when he was in … [Rockville, Maryland].[184] The last thing he said to me when I was on his (Laughs), his doorstep? … Of course, I was more naive then. Maybe I told him a little too much. But anyway, I was trying to get him to talk to me when I'm sitting there with my Sony recorder … and he says, "I'll tell you one thing … [Secret Service] Chief Rowley would sure like to know what you're doing."[185] (Laughs)

JH: I'm sure they knew what you were doing – don't you think…?

DSL: I don't know….

JH: [After watching the video] What's your take on that…?

DSL: Well, I have a lot to say about that. Number one … Bill Greer was not driving the car.[186]

JH: Yeah, I remember you telling me that. He [Greer] took over *after* the first guy was killed, right…?

DSL: Umm, somebody else took over. It was Agent … [X] on the fol-low-up car.[187] But, now years later, Bill Greer claims that it was him. In other words … [X] never said, "I took over." Greer … tried to create the appearance of continuity. You know, he was always driving the car. No, … [X] took over. Now, how do I know that? Because … first of all, the inter-views that I did, and the picture that was altered to create the appearance that it was Greer [driving]. There's a whole story there. But, no, Greer was not driving the car at the end. *The man that was driving the car*, the one who was at Love Field, and the same guy that was driving it at Ft. Worth that morning – *that guy got shot* by Connally, and he's dead. He's brought into the hospital, and then they [Secret Service presumably] put him in a laundry basket … They got him … out of Parkland, and they got him over to Air Force One. And, they had removed six [i.e.] two rows of seats, and he's [dead limo driver] in that coffin they brought up on the other side of Air Force One … It's called "Lyndon's Luggage…." (Laughs)

JH: Oh, God … Definitely skeletons in that luggage. (Laughs)

184   Mr. Lifton interviewed Bill Greer in February of 1971. See Chapter 18 of *Best Evidence*, "The Pre-Autopsy Autopsy," page 448 of the Carroll & Graf edition.
185   Wikipedia: James Joseph Rowley. Though the specific video I shared with Mr. Lifton is no longer available online, I accessed something similar: Vince Palamara. "Secret Service Agent Bill Greer: Only Known Audio and Video!" YouTube, 2017, 27:14. Retrieved 8/7/2023: https://www.youtube.com/watch?v=QwY-CEtaZHQ.
186   This discussion relates back to the "Godzilla" Theory.
187   This Secret Service Agent is still alive, and therefore I use the letter "X" as a representa-tion of his identity. According to Mr. Lifton, he was not part of the plot - contrariwise, he was one of the "good guys" in the Secret Service.

DSL: Right. It's a whole other story, but yeah.

JH: That's interesting. I didn't realize that [Lyndon's Luggage] ... The initial driver you said you know who the guy is, there ... [are] hardly any pictures of him....

DSL: Well, no, there are pictures of him in Ft. Worth and the day before....

JH: Did you say [previous conversation] he was in Miami – and he was a driver...?

DSL: You're absolutely right. He's the one in Miami because ... when Kennedy steps off the plane, he's on one of those visits to visit his father [Joe, Sr.] who was in Palm Beach. Umm, he was standing upright, very erect and upright at the ... limousine that's waiting to drive him to his dad, yes.

JH: He [Greer] says, "I was torn up" or whatever – I find that not believable....

DSL: No, no, no. Oh, no, no. Any interviews that Greer gives after the fact – it's all fabricated and lies. In other words ... he's not the driver ... The reason we know that is because the driver got shot....

DSL: His state of mind is very interesting to theorize what happened ... I used to be able to answer a question like this very fluently years ago, and I'd have to ... try to remember ... Another person that knows very well about this area is ... Fred Newcomb's son ... [Roy] Kellerman's involved in the death of the guy who was really driving. I'll ask Tyler. I can prepare it in a hundred words and send it to you. I mean, I just don't remember. I'm getting old. I don't want ... to give you misinformation. But ... they had to account for the death of the driver, and I'm trying to remember how they did it....

JH: The Secret Service is like the military. You just shut up and do what you're told....

DSL: That's true ... but there's a question of whose body [driver] is buried and all this other stuff ... Fred [T. Newcomb], who died years ago, is the one who had the idea which I used to ridicule but I don't anymore ... I'll never forget this. This is back in [the] late '60s: "Oh, my God! The driver turned around and shot the president." I said, "What, are you crazy?" (Laughs) And then years later ... I said, "Oh, my God!" (Laughs) "There's validity to that."[188]

188   For more detailed information about the book, *Murder From Within: Lyndon Johnson's Plot Against President Kennedy*, visit the official website TylerNewcombFilms.com.

JH: But what made you change your mind that the driver shot Kennedy...?

DSL: Fair question ... There was a picture ... one of the Zapruder Frames when I realized that they in fact had altered the imagery of the Zapruder Film ... The Zapruder Film was purchased by *Life* [Magazine] and certain frames were published. But then, we [assassination researchers] ... got a hold of the original film and in fact – there's a whole story about that. I don't know if I ever told you about it. But, I wrote this up, and it's been distributed among different researchers. OK. What happened was ... Do you know who Haskell Wexler is?

JH: No, I don't....

DSL: OK. Haskell Wexler is a famous Hollywood producer who produced the film *Medium Cool* [1969][189] ... I forget how I got introduced to Howard Wexler, but maybe it was because of Fred [T. Newcomb]. Somehow, we got introduced to Haskell Wexler ... We wanted to look at the Zapruder Film under high magnification. OK? The question was, "How are we going to do it?" ... I came up with this idea that we were going to tell *Life* Magazine – the people in charge who actually had custody of the Zapruder Film in the *Life* vault – that there was this "eccentric zillionaire" who wanted to purchase it, but that in order to decide whether or not to go ahead with the purchase, he wanted to have it examined by competent experts. (Laughs)

JH: Yes ... and you happened to be one of the experts?

DSL: Me and Fred were the experts. (Laughs)

JH: (Laughs) And they fell for it....

DSL: They fell for it. A – they fell for it. B – one of the reasons they fell for it was that the person who ... had the film at Life was named [Richard Otts] Pollard, the Director of Photography, and his assistant wanted a trip to California or something like that ... So, we had the perfect reason and the perfect excuse for her to make this trip. The film needed a reliable courier. (Laughs) ... The film headed to the West Coast, and then ... they introduced us (Laughs) as the experts ... There was a *Life* office in Beverly Hills. They didn't know who we were. But, they knew me because Liebeler had gone to the same office to say, "I want the Zapruder Frames flown out here so my class can see them, and we can examine them." So, I had

---

two shots under a microscope: once when I was with Liebeler's class, and then when this other opportunity came up with Haskell Wexler.

JH: But, you literally used a microscope…?

DSL: Umm … no, no. I did a little bit better than that. What I did is … Let me go back in time a little bit … [Back then], you had rows and rows and rows of microfilm, 35 mm microfilm. And … if you wanted to look at *The New York Times* for November 22, you go up to the library … and you go up to the shelves of microfilm that were at the periodicals room, and you pull on the one for November 1963. You go into a room with rows and rows of microfilm readers.

JH: Yeah, I remember those….

DSL: And you put the thing on the roll. You go forward. OK. So, that's what happened … I remember that very clearly … E842.9. I remember that was the Dewey Decimal [Classification] number where the books on Kennedy were … The microfilms you had to go to a different floor of the [UCLA] library – the second floor; the microfilm [was in] the periodicals room … I ordered a microfilm reader – there was a place in LA you could rent them [from]. So, I rented a microfilm reader, and we brought it up to the *Life* Magazine office … The [Zapruder] Film was flown out in the custody of this woman [Pollard's assistant], and we put it up on the … [microfilm reader in order to] be able to look at it. Fred and I had different hypotheses. I hadn't told him my hypothesis. He was into the idea that there was shooting in the car. Now, subsequently he persuaded me that, yeah, there probably was shooting (Laughing) in the car, but I didn't believe him at the time. So, Fred … bought a very beautiful, expensive, high-powered 35 mm camera up there [*Life* Magazine office]. And then … when she [assistant] went out for a break, or when she wasn't looking – I forget how it worked. I think she went out [and] she said, "I'll be right back. I gotta go to the bathroom." He whips out his camera, and he starts taking pictures of these frames of the Zapruder Film.

JH: Wow….

DSL: "Put that camera away, Fred, she's gonna come back! We're gonna be accused of fraud!" … We almost got into a fist fight … "Put that God d*mn camera away!" You know? … She comes back into the room, and … it's like a Groucho Marx comedy. (Laughs) … I had two bites [as Libeler's student and as an "expert"] of the apple [viewing Zapruder Film]….

JH: The frames that you saw-

DSL: No, no. We had the *Life Magazine transparencies.*[190]

JH: OK. But, could you literally see whoever the guy was [original driver] turn around – could you see a gun in his hand...?

DSL: [No]. But what was most significant to me when I looked at those frames was that you could see that the head wound was fabricated. They had ... [screwed] around with the ... [head wound] ... That blew my mind. How did they do that? That's when ... I went up to the UCLA Film School which was in Melnitz Hall, and that's when I learned for the first time, "How do you alter a film?" I knew how you would alter a picture of Oswald with a rifle. You use what's called an enlarger ... You can mess around with the negative, but that's not how film works. With motion picture film, you use what? It's called an optical printer. Remember?

JH: You talked about that, yeah.

DSL: OK. So, I had to learn about the optical printers, and I learned about them at the Melnitz Film Library. I went there, and was asking [questions like], "How do they do this?" In other words, I did not know the name, I did not understand the technology of film editing and alteration. But once I learned about it, I was a very fast student and thought, "Ahh! That's what they did. They messed around with the Zapruder Film." ... I had to learn all about optical printers ... by reading journals and [other] stuff up in ... [that] library at UCLA.

JH: Could you ... in a couple of sentences explain ... how did they edit that [head shot on Zapruder Film]?

DSL: Oh, no, I'll tell you exactly how they did it. When you have an optical printer and you want to do frame alteration, there's a word for that. It's called "insert matte photography." ... That's how Robert Groden messed around with the film.[191] I learned the name of an optical place in New York

---

190   This is a bit confusing to me. I'm not sure if Mr. Lifton meant he only saw the transparencies in Liebeler's class and/or as an "expert." I would assume the entire Zapruder Film was there for that second opportunity during the "sting operation" so described with Pollard's assistant from New York City.

191   Wikipedia: Robert J. Groden. In my "quest for knowledge" after reading *Best Evidence*, I vowed to read every JFK Assassination book I could get my hands on whether pro-conspiracy or pro-government. I must say, Robert J. Groden's books are foundational, and his contribution to the JFK Assassination Research field via his enhancement of the Zapruder Film is unsurpassed. See: Livingstone, Harrison Edward and Groden, Robert J. *High Treason: The Assassination of JFK and the Case for Conspiracy.* Basic Books, 1998, 672 pages. I read the Berkley edition published in 1990. This important work was originally published in 1980. See also: Groden, Robert J. *The Killing of a President: The Complete Photographic Record of the Assassination, the Conspiracy, and the Cover Up.* Viking Penguin, 1993, 223 pages. The photographic evidence in the latter work is phenomenal.

... and we had to raise money for me to get access to the optical printer ... It cost like – what – $300 dollars an hour or some crazy number. So, my parents put up $2500 dollars, Fred Newcomb put up $2000. We raised a little kitty of $10,000 dollars, and I went in there and used the optical printer to make beautiful 35 mm knockoffs of the Zapruder Film.

JH: Really?

DSL: Yeah!

JH: Are those still in your files to this day?

DSL: Yeah. I have them all. Yes, they are. We sold ... [copies] to different researchers. A guy in Oregon – I forget his name. He bought ones for $2500 ... We had five or six customers who bought these things....

JH: Let me go back ... The picture of the [original] driver ... He's turning around ... So, you're telling me [that] you really can't see a gun, but it looks like it could be a gun....

DSL: Umm. That's probably a fair statement ... Fred's [Newcomb] position was that's the driver, he turns around, and he shoots the president. I wasn't sure you could see that....

JH: Well, and he uses his left hand....

DSL: Remember. The film's been altered. The car came to a halt. When he [driver before Greer] turns around, the velocity [of the limo] is no longer eleven miles an hour ... He had to turn around and shoot the president ... You gotta remember what happened here. They bring him [JFK] in front of the Depository, right? The first shot is fired ... Forget about missed shots. People have different theories about whether there was one or two missed shots. A shot is fired. It goes into Kennedy's throat. That's a missed shot. That doesn't hit him where it's supposed to hit him. [They're] ... trying to hit him in the head. OK? The question then becomes, "Since these guys are so smart with guns ... how come ... [the bullet] hit him in the throat?" The throat. Have we discussed how come it hit him in the throat?

JH: I don't ... know. I don't think so. If we did, I don't remember....

DSL: Well, let me refresh your recollection. When the car rounds the corner ... from Houston onto Elm, do you remember the witnesses who were on the sidewalk who said Kennedy was standing up...?

JH: Oh, yeah, the seat went up! Yeah....

DSL: Well, let's … clean up our English a little bit … [Let's] not use our passive voice. It's not like there's some magical force. Somebody pressed … the button to raise the seat.

JH: Oh, my God….

DSL: Because – how do you think the seat went up at that moment? Why would the seat go up? … You're finished with the downtown motorcade, right? They're about to go onto the entrance to the Stemmons Freeway … [The limo] makes a 135 degree turn. The car's going slow.

JH: Wow. That is crazy….

DSL: But, it's better than that. It's better than you know … When they're in front of the Grassy Knoll, in that area, he [SSA Kellerman] hits the button, and the seat goes up … Consider … [Kellerman] the director of the shooting … of the operation … But, there's another question: How come the seat can be raised that much? Did we ever discuss this?

JH: Yeah, that they [Secret Service] put some kind of contraption-

DSL: They didn't put it, they *installed it* after Kennedy won the election … They sent the car [to a workshop] and they installed the apparatus. I actually have the pictures of the installation. I got them under the Freedom of Information Act. So, they actually installed a 1/4 horsepower motor in the trunk [of the limo] … They arranged this thing so they could press the button in the front *and the seat would raise.* (Laughs)

JH: And the … official reason [for installing the raising seat] was so that he [JFK] could be seen by the crowd, but the … secret reason was….

DSL: No, no, no, no, no, no, no. There's no official reason … Oh, that would have been *the justification* … As far as I remember, there's no investigation by *anybody* – as to why the seat went up except that it did.

JH: I do remember you mentioning it like a month or two ago.

DSL: Well, not only do they do that, but they rehearse this thing … When Kennedy went earlier in the … [year] to that Air Force base in New Mexico, and I forget the name of it, it was kind of like a rehearsal of that apparatus – and they actually raised the seat.[192] And here's another thing … they used that same button to raise the seat when [Ethiopian] Emperor Haile

---

192   I believe he's referencing JFK's visit to White Sands Missile Range on June 5, 1963. See JFKLibrary.org. "Presidential Visit [JFK at White Sands], 5 June 1963." Retrieved 8/19/2023: https://www.jfklibrary.org/asset-viewer/archives/USG/USG-03-B/USG-03-B.

Selassie [visited] … He only was about four [feet] eleven [inches] … just about five feet … they used that to raise the seat there, too.[193]

JH: So, he [JFK] was shot in the throat. What did that have to do with the raising seat…?

DSL: Oh … It's very simple … the target is Kennedy's head. OK? The target is the forehead. That's the shot, right? And you're shooting him … I can show you where the shooter is who fired that [throat] shot. He's in the v-shaped tree with a crotch.

JH: Yes. On the Grassy Knoll…?

DSL: Not, no, no. On the opposite [side of the street] where [Phillip] Willis' daughter was standing, remember?[194] On the other side of the car. That is, using the language of the navy, on the port side [left] of the car, not the starboard side [right].

JH: But, by the tree near the overpass…?

DSL: No, no, no … As soon as the car makes the 135 degree turn … it's the tree on the left with the crotch in it … like a little "V."

JH: And that's in photographs – this tree?

DSL: Yes, yes, but it's better than this. The crotch is artificial. In other words, the tree doesn't grow with a crotch.[195]

JH: Oh, are you serious?

DSL: Yes … What I'm saying to you is they strapped this thing [the crotch] onto the tree.

JH: I see….

DSL: The tree goes straight up. It's a single [trunk] tree. It goes up and it blooms. In advance of the motorcade coming to Dallas, OK, they [con-

---

193   JFK.org. "JFK Events: ***1 October 1963, Dinner, Emperor Haile Selassie of Ethiopia [2 of 3 Folders]." Retrieved 8/19/2023: https://www.jfklibrary.org/asset-viewer/archives/JFK-WHSFSLF/025/JFKWHSFSLF-025-005. Further, I found Selassie's height incredulous. "According to the Internet," Selassie was anywhere from five feet two inches to as tall as five feet four inches according to an article in The New York Times, "Selassie of Ethiopia Dies at 83," dated August 28, 1975. Retrieved 8/19, 2023: https://www.nytimes.com/1975/08/28/archives/haile-selassie-of-ethiopia-dies-at-83-deposed-emperor-ruled-ancient.html. I suppose that is still quite short for an emperor.
194   Wikipedia: Phillip Willis and Rosemary Willis.
195   I'm not sure what Mr. Lifton meant by this statement. Obviously, trees can grow in a "V" shape – with a crotch. I believe he found evidence of a "doctored tree" (via a clear image of Willis 12). Did he mean there was a horizontal platform attached to the crotch, a seat of sorts – which created a triangle shape inside the tree limbs? I'll never know. I did not pursue further explanation of this evidence.

spirators] attached some kind of an attachment to the tree with ... Do you know what a turnbuckle is?

JH: I've heard of it ....

DSL: Turnbuckle. Sure ... So, they attach this thing [platform for a shooter] – this is in preparation *for the murder* ... This is preparing the damn scene ... The result is this tree had a little crotch in it, and in that crotch they had a shooter ... Listen, he's [shooter] not Wilt Chamberlain. He's not seven feet tall. The guy [shooter] is about five [feet] two or something ... I don't know, but there's somebody there. *You can see this guy's legs hanging from the crotch of the tree* in Willis Slide 12. You can actually see his legs ... I made these discoveries years ago. This is 1965.

JH: Why didn't anybody...?

DSL: No, no, you have to really get a good picture of Willis 12. I ordered original slides from [Phil] Willis and paid a pretty penny for them....

JH: [Since we are on Zoom, and I'm sharing my screen, I search for Willis 12 while Mr. Lifton elaborates....]

DSL: Willis 5 has a black arrow ... vertical showing Kennedy, and it corresponds to Zapruder Frame 202 ... Willis 6 is the crowd [after limo speeds away]....

JH: [I find Willis Slide 12] OK, here is the Slide 12, right here...?

DSL: Yep! ... I was so excited when I made the discovery ... [As we examine the various Willis Slides via Zoom] 5 is the famous one.

JH:[Display Willis 12 on screen] That's 12....

DSL: Where? Where?

JH: Right here....

DSL: Yeah, yeah, yeah....

JH: [Using cursor as a pointer] In the crotch right here?

DSL: Yes! Yes. You have to blow it up though and really study it....

JH: Huh. [I see nothing.] Alright, I'll look at it at another time.

DSL: Yeah ... OK, look ... you've got to get the highest quality to Willis 12 to see what's going on.....[196]

---

196   The Portal to Texas History. "Phil Willis Slide #26 (Willis 12) Side: 1 of 1." TexasHistory. UNT.edu. Retrieved 8/19/2023: https://texashistory.unt.edu/ark:/67531/metapth1352826/m1/1/. The tree in question is in the center, left of the image, on the viewer's side of the street opposite the squad car. As Mr. Lifton told me many times, and as described in this work, a photograph is not

JH: Right. Wow. That's crazy. Didn't you interview the Willis Family?

DSL: I sure did – on camera.

JH: Wow ... They didn't buy the whole Oswald [did it]....

DSL: No, no, no, no. Then they got all excited by it ... You know, he [Phillip Willis] was thinking in terms of money. "Oh, my God! My slides are more valuable." He was always in a competition with "that Jew Zapruder who got so much money (Laughs) for his film." Willis only got $5,000 dollars [and] Zapruder got like millions....

JH: So, they [conspirators] actually had a guy in the tree firing that shot into Kennedy's neck.

DSL: They had a little guy in the tree ... but you missed something that I said. He shot at Kennedy's-

JH: Head...!

DSL: But, but, but, but, [SSA] Kellerman at that moment had pressed the button, and the seat rose ten inches, and so the shot intended for Kennedy's head *struck him in the neck* [i.e. throat].

JH: Got, yeah....

DSL: OK ... We used to tell jokes. Sean Fetter[197] and I – when we first found the image ... We ... [used to say], "Well, the guy must be getting hungry up there." (Laughs) I mean, he couldn't climb down out of the tree. (Laughs) Sean used to make this joke about bringing him lunch later in the afternoon. "OK, what would you like, a ham-" (Laughs)

JH: (Laughs)

DSL: "A ham sandwich?"

JH: Oh, my God....

---

definitive proof of anything; think UFO or cryptid imagery. Frankly, I do not see anything in the crotch of said tree *with this particular Internet image,* though I could be wrong, and/or the image could be of poor quality. I will say that it appears that this image was taken many minutes after the assassination due to the fact that there are few people in the frame milling around, walking around, etc. I would assume an assassin would have fled by now, but without a doubt, Mr. Lifton saw *in his blown up copy,* what he believed to be "legs hanging from the crotch of the tree," and I believe him 100%.

197   I'm not sure of the relationship Mr. Lifton had had with Sean Fetter, but I did find this interesting article online. See the Illinois Wesleyan University news article: Fetter, Sean and Murkin, Scott. "Lifton Discusses Camouflage of the JFK Killing." *The Argus,* January 25, 1985. Retrieved 8/20/2023: https://collections.carli.illinois.edu. This is found in the Carli Digital Collections through the University of Illinois Urbana-Champaign. Interestingly, I attended Eastern Illinois University at the same time Mr. Lifton was interviewed for this story in 1985. It was in June of 1985 while attending summer school there when I first became aware of his research and book *Best Evidence.*

DSL: (Laughs) Then, he'd [Fetter] say, "They'd say [bystanders], 'What's that guy doing passing a ham sandwich up into the tree?'" ... Anyway.

JH: Wouldn't you think that somebody would say, "Hey, what's that guy doing up in the tree...?"

DSL: No, no, no, no, no, no. No. I'm telling you ... Whether it's the [Grassy] Knoll in the front, or that tree, the key to this whole thing is that the people who did this really knew the art of camouflage ... I've got books on camouflage ... This is Freshman Camouflage 101, I'm telling you ... The guys who did this, if you wanted to disguise them, they'd wear what I used to call a petal, P-E-T-A-L, a petal suit. These guys were very smart....

JH: Do you think ... they [conspirators] used elements of Hollywood – people that came in and maybe helped them [to] create this, stage this [assassination] scene...?

DSL: Yes. Absolutely. More importantly ... to me [is] they used standard techniques from guerilla warfare and camouflage ... But, the beautiful thing about Willis 12 is you can see the guy's legs hanging there. I'm telling you....

JH: My question to you [is], did Jackie or anybody, maybe Clint Hill, somebody say [in their testimony], "Yeah ... the seat was raised – or did Kellerman...?"

DSL: No, no, no, no. The answer to your question is "absolutely yes." There were ... *bystanders* who said he stood up ... and none of that makes sense unless you understand [the raising seat]. Oh, and then [Mr. and] Mrs. Connally ... [They] watched what was happening, and ... [were] right there in the jump seat ... Either she or John say in their testimony ... "Kellerman, the agent in the front seat, was punching some buttons on the dashboard. Now, I don't know what that was all about."[198] Now, come on, what's that? You know ... what is he [Kellerman doing], tuning in a music station? I mean, give me a break ... Kellerman knew that he was raising the seat. Kennedy would have experienced it, as "What the Hell is

---

198   In Governor Connally's Warren Commission Hearings testimony (Vol. IV), Arlen Specter asked him directly about the ability of the back seat to be raised and lowered. Connally stated, with relation to the jump seats he and Nellie occupied and why they were lower: "The back seat of that particular Lincoln limousine ... has an adjustable back seat." (Ibid, page 131) Note that Specter asks Connally if it was "elevated at the time" of the assassination. (Ibid) Governor Connally added that while in San Antonio, he rode in the back seat with JFK while it was elevated. (Ibid) Connally later stated, "I assumed he [Kellerman] was moving a button or something" as the car sped from Dealey Plaza. (Ibid, page 133)

going on?" in the last seconds of his life. Why is my seat being raised ... after we passed the crowds downtown? Why is this happening ... ?

JH: Do you think, I mean, Kennedy was ... a sharp guy, a really smart guy-

DSL: He's not only sharp ... he was very fatalistic, and he knew – remember what he said to his secretary Evelyn Lincoln. He knew he was pissing everybody off with the Test Ban [Treaty][199] ... and he said, "I don't care what happens. I know they're going to get me ... They'll have to get me in church," or something like that ....

JH: Umm, so, do you think that within those few moments he said, "Oh, my God. This is it. They got me ...."

DSL: Yes. I think he could have. Absolutely. He wouldn't have had more than five seconds of that moment when he realized his seat was being raised [at the wrong time]. But, who the Hell would ever think it [assassination] would happen in a motorcade with a mechanical aspect, an electro-mechanical aspect ... But you can ... actually see the seat raise [up]. You can see the Godd*mn seat raise. Fred Newcomb's son and I used to discuss this all the time, yes. The way Fred could show it, by the way, was that if you took the Moorman Photograph ... you could see the shoulder "x amount" of inches above the rear seat ... It changes. When he's [JFK] going through Dallas, he's like sunk down in the seat, but then when he comes out of that turn [Houston to Elm], it [seat] suddenly goes "zoop" and he's exposed more ....[200]

JH: I do remember ... [JFK] driving down ... [Main Street]. I think there are pictures literally with his arms like this on the side of the car, very low ....

DSL: But afterwards, after the seats raised, it's very high. You see it in his shoulder and how high his shoulder is with regard to the back seat.

JH: So, that should be noticeable ....

DSL: It was noticeable. And also with regard to the tree, they [conspirators] created that "V" crotch ... but back in 1964 or 5 when you look ... [at] the wonderful pictures taken from the Sixth Floor window of the so-called Sniper's Nest, you look down [and see that] they couldn't remove

---

199   Wikipedia: Partial Nuclear Test Ban Treaty.
200   If you compare the Moorman Photo with a photo of JFK in the limo prior to Dealey Plaza, it does appear that he sits lower in the seat prior to Elm Street. The following article notes that the seat could be raised as high as twelve inches: Cappola, Christine. "What happened to the Limo After the Kennedy Assassination?" TheCollector.com, September 26, 2022. Retrieved 8/20/2023:
https://www.thecollector.com/what-happened-to-the-limo-after-kennedy-assassination/.

the crotch in the tree so soon, Jim … Otherwise, we'd have pictures taken, "Oh, yeah, this was taken on November 23rd, but look over here – on November 29th it's different." So, they left it there … and they didn't remove that crotch thing … I don't think … until after the Warren Commission Report. Then suddenly, the tree was back to a normal tree … And when I saw that … when I saw what was going on – I'm trying to remember the exact chronology – people were making fun of me, and so I shut up about it after that … I had too much serious stuff going on with the alteration of the body and the Liebeler Memorandum.[201] So, I didn't want to get into that. People [would say], "Oh, look! He believes there's a man in a tree." So, you know, scr*w you….

JH: Yeah….

DSL: I remember also the business of smoke coming from the trees [Grassy Knoll]. Remember, those accounts? But, what the Hell is that all about? Those are the trees up in the Knoll. God knows what they were doing up there … Remember there was smoke coming-

JH: Yeah. Puffs of smoke….

DSL: Yeah, well that had to do … most likely with what they call the … machinery … the device used. The reason there was smoke was that there was a backhoe….[202]

JH: Right, you've talked about that, yeah … The construction equipment would mask the sound….

DSL: That's correct. Exactly … As soon as you turn on the backhoe, you and I have discussed this … it would "cough" … The point is, the puffs of smoke would come out … because … the engine was [running].

JH: I want to switch gears real quick … I want to share this picture [via Zoom] with you. I just want your honest opinion on this picture … This is uhh-

DSL: Oh, George Bush….

JH: I wasn't aware of this [image] until recently. This is a normal, accepted [picture] – this is him … and then this is a picture purported to be him outside-

DSL: That's an altered photograph.

JH: I was gonna ask you. It almost looks kind of fake, but-

---

201   This puts Mr. Lifton's "sniper in the tree" discovery circa Fall of 1966.
202   Wikipedia: Backhoe.

DSL: It is fake ... [It's] somebody messing around.

JH: So, you don't believe that [it's genuine].

DSL: No, I don't.

Saturday, January 29, 2022
The following was a Q&A Zoom sessions we held for some of Mr. Lifton's GoFundMe supporters...

PARTICIPANT ONE: I just have an obvious question. When will the book [*Final Charade*] finally come out? I've been waiting for it for what, eight years, ten years.

DSL: That's a good and fair question. The book that you originally were waiting for eight or ten years ago is no longer the same kind of book that I now have. Because ... I have had all kinds of new information concerning an area which I'll sum up in one word: cryptography. And because I'm adding that to *Final Charade*, [it] ... becomes a different kind of animal – much more sophisticated, and I think you'll be very happy with it.

PARTICIPANT ONE: I think originally ... *Final Charade* was gonna concentrate heavily on Oswald. Is that not correct...?

DSL: That is absolutely correct, and it still concentrates on Oswald – only now there's a new dimension to Oswald concerning his ability to deal with cryptography. In other words, coded messaging – and that's all I can say about it.

PARTICIPANT ONE: David was on some show or program. I don't remember. [It was] a few months ago ... He was making a big deal about ... some new witnesses [who saw] the limousine – before it got on the Stemmons Freeway – [and] had stopped for some reason ... I wasn't clear [on] the reason why that was so significant. Maybe you could expand on that a little bit....

DSL: Um, I'd like to. I developed that completely with that Canadian appearance on that show.[203] And I really would refer you to that show because he [Brent Holland] archives all that stuff. And I had notes in front of me [during the interview]. I did the best I could to answer it at that time ... Your question is: Why is it significant that the car made a stop?

203   NightFrightShow. "JFK David Lifton '*Final Charade*' New Witnesses & Theory Autopsy '*Best Evidence*' Brent Holland Show." YouTube, 2021, 01:40:17. Though not positive, I believe this is the episode referenced above by the Zoom participant. Either way, this a great interview with Brent Holland. In fact, in my humble opinion, Brent Holland is in the same class of truly interesting interviewers as Art Bell, George Noory, and Joe Rogan.

PARTICIPANT ONE: I guess I don't understand the significance of it.

DSL: OK, the significance of it, of the second car stop. In other words, there's one car stop in Dealey Plaza and about the point in the Zapruder Film which would be like [Frame] 313; somewhere in there between, let's say 280 and 320 … If there's a second stop, then the question is – to the Secret Service which they're not going to answer … "Why did the car stop a second time?" What was going on there? Were all these witnesses imagining a second stop or did something happen? … I'm telling you that something serious happened … The driver of the car [William Greer] that arrived at Parkland Hospital is not the same driver who's driving … from the airport [Love Field] and to Dealey Plaza. So, there was an event that happened. And, I'm willing to call your attention to the public reports which you should be aware of – and I think you probably are – that a Secret Service Agent was shot during the assassination. That [event] is not properly dealt with in the Warren Commission Report but has to be understood to understand the kind of answer you need to your question. Something really bad happened, and it involved the necessity to change the driver because the [limo] driver was shot … [unexpectedly].… That will be dealt with in *Final Charade*, and that's the best I can do.[204]

PARTICIPANT ONE: There were media reports of a Secret Service Agent being killed initially.

DSL: That's correct. Those media reports came out – first of all, let me deal with a concept. The earlier a recollection occurs, you know like if it's one minute later, two minutes later, five minutes later – it's usually much more reliable that something occurred five years later, OK? And I think that's reasonable. If we want to know the best evidence of what happened in Ford's Theater, we don't want to go to 1910 or 1920 when someone's seventy five or ninety five years old [rather] we want to go to witnesses who were right there [at that moment] … That's the same with the Kennedy Assassination … Going back to your question … I am saying to you that I place a lot of credence in the fact that someone else was shot, and this posed a very serious problem to explain what the heck was going on. Because if they [Warren Commission] didn't explain that, and if it was on the wire services [e.g. AP/UPI] that a Secret Service Agent was shot[205]

204   Again "Godzilla" Theory.
205   The evidence of this online is scant. I found this document but am not sure what to make of it. It's definitely intriguing. The name of the Secret Service Agent could be Robertson, or Chuck Robertson. As indicated in this work, I do not recall Mr. Lifton divulging to me the name of the limo driver who was shot in the car. See: JFK-Assassination.net. "Gems from the 26 Volumes: by Vince Palamara." Retrieved 8/27/2023: https://www.jfk-assassination.net/parnell/vp1.htm.: An in-   145

and it was not a misunderstanding or a bad journalistic report, Johnson could never have become president … It would be clear that there was something much bigger going on. So, they [wire services] simply issued a retraction about two hours later. And I think they [the media] said, "No, nobody else was shot." Well, that's wrong. Somebody else was shot, and it was very serious. They had to get his body out of Parkland Hospital, over to Love Field, over to Air Force One, and put him onto Air Force One … They [Secret Service] had removed three rows of seats to accommodate that coffin. They threw a tarpaulin over it and, believe it or not, it was called "Lyndon's luggage." (Laughs)

JH: Geez.

DSL: I'll have more on that in *Final Charade*, but that's what happened.

PARTICIPANT ONE: Have you resolved the timeline of when you suspect the body [JFK's] was transferred out of the ceremonial casket at Love Field?

DSL: Yeah. Essentially, I'll be presenting those details in *Final Charade*. I think you must keep in mind [that] no matter what I say in *Final Charade* or what anybody writes, this will always be a debatable proposition. But, I can tell you that that body [of JFK] was taken out of the coffin within five or ten minutes of the time that it was put onto Air Force One. So, the body was brought – you know, that ambulance arrives from Parkland – they *struggle* with that coffin, they get it up into the fuselage, and … events were occurring on the plane at that point where it was quickly offloaded – not the coffin, the body. It was offloaded on the opposite side of the plane through one of those half doors, you know that they use at the airports to load the … food onto the plane?

PARTICIPANT ONE: Yeah – galley door.

DSL: Galley door! And it [body] was brought off the galley door and put onto a forklift truck … [which] then drove a hundred twenty feet – whatever it is – and it was put into luggage in the forward luggage area … That's about as much as I can say without going back to the chapter I've written … [and] getting into further details. But, that was the essence of the deception, and furthermore, that [death of driver] was not supposed to happen. I have to emphasize this: it was not part of the plan to mess with the body [JFK's] or the transportation of the body over at Love Field.

teresting corroboration to "Godzilla" is the curious concern Mrs. William Greer had for her husband, limo driver William Greer. She "thought for several hours that her husband had perished that day!"

Ibid.

The [assassination] plan as originally conceived, and this is what's so critical to understand[ing] the Kennedy Assassination – is to set aside what happened and try to figure out what was supposed to happen but did not … I've done that in spades, and that's going to be in *Final Charade*. That [how plot was supposed to happen] deals with an entirely different kind of timeline than the one you brought up [removal of JFK's body from coffin] – *which is true* but was not something planned in advance.

JH: Any other questions…?

PARTICIPANT ONE: Yeah, I have another question.

DSL: Sure.

PARTICIPANT ONE: I teach a class at … [XYZ] on the JFK Assassination, and David, I think I spend a whole class just on your first book. And when I tell people about all this manipulation … they tell me I'm crazy, or they just say that … "If it wasn't on … [Mainstream Media], it didn't happen." Help me … What can I tell the students? … How do I tell them this is what happened and everything you've been hearing about for … [over] fifty years is not true? What can I do to convince them…?

DSL: My answer to that would be a question I have for you: Have you shown them the *"Best Evidence Research Video…?"*

PARTICIPANT ONE: I gave them a link to it, yes.

DSL: That video was made to address the very question you're raising. The book [*Best Evidence*] was finished and turned in – the manuscript – the contract was granted in … 1978 in December. And then, I had to finish it by a certain point and time. By the next July, I'm working on it and finishing it with what I thought was an August 31 [1979] deadline. And what happens? I find out in July [after] I get a hold of Dennis David and these other witnesses [that] … "Oh, my God. The coffin is empty."[206] I had to re-analyze the situation. You know, put in new timelines, change the ending of the book and all of that. So that's … what happened to me when I was writing the book … And then we [my publisher and I] decided that we'd better film some of this [eyewitness accounts of autopsy] … before … [the book's] published. Because, without the film[ed interviews], a person can say, "Well, I don't remember this." Or, they could go back on their story, and it would be a … media contest between David

---

206   Dennis David confirmed Mr. Lifton's extraordinary discovery that there were at least two caskets – a subterfuge designed to get JFK's body back into the original coffin. See Chapter 19 of *Best Evidence*, "Certain Preliminary Examinations," page 492 of the Carroll & Graf edition.

Lifton – who had telephone interviews – and the Warren Commission Report with all of its authority. So … they [publisher] authorized me to spend $12,000 dollars to film the key witnesses, the three or four key witnesses.[207] … I made up a budget … [and] I went back to the publisher [and said], "It's not going to be $12,000, it's going to cost $27,000 dollars." They said, "OK. Do it!" They gave me a "green light" … I went in the October period of 1980, and I filmed all of those key witnesses you've seen … I'll never forget editing it on Thanksgiving weekend [1980], and the book then was gonna be published the third week or second week of January 1981. So, that's what happened. We [publishers and I] were very aware, very aware of the issue of credibility … The whole idea that anybody would mess with the body of the president was so unbelievable that I could only tell you that I had problems … when I first came across this [concept] and said, "Oh, my God!" Then the question is, it's one thing to write text and write chapters – which I did … I'm sure you're familiar with my Chapter 25 ["The Lake County Informant" – Dennis David] … and all that [Chapters 26-29, Paul O'Connor, et al.]. But … we needed film, and I'll never forget Mr. Kaplan up at Macmillan [headquarters in New York City][208] … He was leaving for a new assignment in Europe, and he transferred the authority over to a fella named Lattuca … They both backed me up. We did the filmed interviews, and all I can say is, I held my breath when the book was released … The question was not the evidence. I knew I had the proper evidence … The basic idea *was so darn unbelievable* that *anybody* would plan in advance to mess with the body of President Kennedy … in order to change the story of how he died … If I hadn't studied the physics, and the math, and the systems engineering – my desk was filled with flow charts and this and that – I would not have been able to make the presentation we did. We made the presentation, published the book, and it was on the bestseller list within three weeks – and stayed there for three-and-a-half months.

PARTICIPANT ONE: Oh, yeah. That [book] was the one that got me interested in the JFK Assassination. That was when I started, yeah.

---

207 Phone interviews were conducted as follows: Dennis David (Chief of the Day/Bethesda; interviewed 7/1979), Paul O'Connor (Laboratory technician/Bethesda; interviewed 8/1979), Jerrol Custer (X-ray technician/Bethesda; interviewed 9/ and 10/1979), and Aubrey Rike (Funeral home assistant/Dallas; interviewed 3/1980).

208 Jeremiah Kaplan, President of Macmillan Publishing Company from 1965-1973 and 1977-1986. See: Pace, Eric. "Jeremiah Kaplan, Veteran Executive in Publishing, 67." NewYorkTimes.com, August 11, 1993. Retrieved 8/27/2023: https://www.nytimes.com/1993/08/11/obituaries/jeremiah-kaplan-veteran-executive-in-publishing-67.html. Unfortunately, I could find nothing about Lattuca online – assuming even that's the proper spelling.

DSL: Well, my agent at the time [who later] became a very good and important friend of mine, Peter Shepherd, he said [that] he was in touch with the editor of the [William] Manchester book, *Death of a President*.[209] ... Evan Thomas[210] said, "Peter, he's ... got to write this as a personal narrative." ... My original drafts were written more or less as a scientific paper. You know, as if I was presenting (Laughs) the Theory of Relativity or something.

PARTICIPANT ONE: (Laughs)

DSL: He [Shepherd] said, "That's not gonna fly ... You [have to] take the reader by the knot of his necktie and bring him over your shoulder and tell the story of how you found, what you found, and then really it's up to 'the gods' how the public's going to get it." I remember people saying [about my thesis], "Oh, my God! That's the answer." And there were some [book] reviews just like that. And then, there were other people who said, "I don't care if he's proved everything, and dotted every 'i' and crossed every 't' – this could not have ... happened in this country." And furthermore, the ... publisher that Evan Thomas introduced us to in the beginning [prior to contract with Macmillan] ... when we had the meeting where I explained everything to him, he was very polite. He [President of Harper and Row] listened to everything ... [and] said, "Young man, I don't care what evidence you have. That could not have happened in this country." Quote unquote. That's the kind of problem we were dealing with because it is fairly unbelievable. Let's face it: if that's true, we had a coup. No one wants to believe we had a coup.

JH: Yeah....

DSL: They like to argue about whether there's a second assassin, a third assassin. All that stuff is subordinate – much, much less important. So, the question is, "Was there an organized plan to not just murder the president but to falsify the facts about how he died, and do so within let's say the first hour after the president's murder?" ... That's what happened in this case, and that's why we ended up with one year of ... nothing much changing in the world and then, "Boom!" As soon as Johnson got inaugurated in '65 January, within three months we ... [insert] five hundred thousand troops in Vietnam, and the war gets escalated. And the rest is history.

---

209   Manchester, William. *The Death of a President: November 20-November 25, 1963*. Harper and Row, 1967, 781 pages. See also: Wikipedia: William Manchester and The Death of a President.
210   SFGate. "Evan Thomas II." SFGate.com, March 6, 1999. Retrieved 8/27/2023: https://www.sfgate.com/news/article/Evan-Thomas-II-2943468.php.

PARTICIPANT ONE: I've got a comment and a question … Doug Horne's book *Inside the AARB* [211]

DSL: Right.

PARTICIPANT ONE: Um, essentially vindicates David's original assumption, original findings about the body, and the … alteration of the medical evidence. But, Horne believes that Commander Humes did the alterations, and I wonder how you feel about his findings, David?

DSL: Well, I have a lot to say about that. (Laughs)

PARTICIPANT ONE: (Laughs)

DSL: First of all, I was flown out to Honolulu to give a talk at the private school that Barack Obama attended … Punahou … very fancy private school. [212] I think his grandparents or somebody paid for him to go there, and it's very important to his development and education. So, I was out there, and … I had a lecture engagement at Punahou. And at the end of the lecture, there was a Q&A period as there always is … This fellow comes down out of the audience and introduces himself as Doug Horne. He had just read my book … and was fascinated by it … We became friends … talking on the phone three, four, five times a week. Now, what became really serious and different was when Doug Horne [called me one day and] said … "Guess what? I've been appointed … to the ARRB [Assassination Records Review Board]." And I said, "Great! That's wonderful. Let's stay in touch." … Our conversations were so technical and detailed, and I said, "Doug, let's record our conversations." So we recorded – I recorded with his permission. And I have shoeboxes full of these tapes.

PARTICIPANT ONE: Oh.

DSL: So, to answer your question in detail, I'd have to go back to those shoeboxes, But, there came a point where he [Doug Horne] said, "Well, I've found something new … and you're not going to agree with my interpretation … [so] let's try to remain friends," blah, blah, blah.

JH: (Laughs)

DSL: Some years went by, and out comes his interpretation, and I couldn't believe some of the stuff he concluded – *which was that Humes did the surgery* … I don't buy any of that. But, first of all, it's not really surgery. What

---

they [conspirators] did was bash in Kennedy's head … If you're in the Bethesda morgue, and you are an eyewitness to this, Humes is shocked by what he sees. He is *astounded* by it. Nobody bashed in the president's head in front of Humes. So, what happened before that body arrived had to have happened after Love Field [Dallas, TX] and before the arrival at Bethesda [Bethesda, MD, circa five hours later] … That's what I believe happened, and Doug has a different view … when he did his five volumes. Now, look – he had a special opportunity that I didn't have. He and Jeremy Gunn, who was the … head of it [ARRB] … went all around the country, and they did a lot of different interviews.[213] But, it doesn't change the fact: He [Horne] had this theory that Humes was the bad guy. I don't buy it … and at that point when I realized his devotion to his theory – look, he's entitled to his view – I cut him off … I stopped telling him stuff that I'm talking about in this broadcast. So, he [Horne] did not have the benefit of any of that for his five volumes … I wish him luck in the five volumes. They were published years ago, and a lot of it is very useful. For example, he [Horne] and I agree that the Zapruder film was altered, and he did some very important interviewing for that.

JH: Any other questions for Mr. Lifton?

PARTICIPANT ONE: Yeah. I was going to ask about the Zapruder film. David, I was in the audience when you testified in front of the ARRB in Los Angeles, and I believe you donated to … [them] the best copy you had of the Zapruder Film … Does that [your copy] differ from what's in the [National] Archives … Can you explain why it was altered? Cuz, to me … if you alter that film, you have to alter all [of] the other films.

DSL: That's correct. You have to alter three other films.[214] Here's the basic question that is fundamental to any answer … Are you aware of the record of how many people said the car stopped? Momentarily.

PARTICIPANT ONE: Hmm.

213   Dr. T. Jeremy Gunn, former Executive Director of the ARRB, later a Professor of Law and Political Science at the International University of Rabat, Emory University School of Law. See: The Federalist Society. "Dr. T. Jeremy Gunn." FedSoc.org. Retrieved 9/2/2023: https://fedsoc.org/contributors/t-jeremy-gunn.
214   The known films of Dealey Plaza that day – though not necessarily of the moment of the assassination include: Tom Alyea, Mark Bell, Charles Bronson, Mal Couch, Jack Daniel, Elsie T. Dorman, Robert Hughes, John Martin, Ernest Mentesana, Marie Muchmore, Orville Nix, Tina Towner, Dave Wiegman, and of course Abraham Zapruder. See: Groden, Robert. *JFK: Assassination Files – The Case for Conspiracy* [DVD]. Delta Studio, 2003, 01:10:00. See also: KERA. "Sixth Floor Museum Acquires Third of 4 Known Home Movies From JFK's Dallas Assassination." KERANews.org, June 28, 2017. Retrieved 9/2/2023: https://www.keranews.org/texas-news/2017-06-28/sixth-floor-museum-acquires-third-of-4-known-home-movies-from-jfks-dallas-assassination.

DSL: And we're talking about at the *very least* sixteen to twenty people, but if you start to relax a little bit and say, "OK, not completely stopped but almost stopped" you get up to about fifty people. So, it was during this period, back around ... 1978 or so, as I recall ... I was working with a woman who is now passed away, Pat Lambert ... We would work together three or four times a week, and ... one of the goals we set is to do a *very careful* reevaluation of where all the witnesses thought the shots came from ... We started with Josiah Thompson's book *Six Seconds in Dallas* and the chart that he published in the back.[215] And ... it was during that period with Pat that we had to set up a new category – which I didn't understand in the beginning. I was confused. I said, "Pat, a lot of people thought the car stopped." I had no idea about this, so we set up a "car stop" file, and within a day or two, we had fifteen, twenty, whatever twenty five witnesses in the group. ... So, then the question became, "How the heck – if the car stopped – did they alter a film about it?" I didn't know how this technology worked. It's not that I didn't have the ability to understand it, but I was never exposed to it. Fortunately, I was out at UCLA, and they have a wonderful film school up there ... in a building called Melnitz Hall. So, I went up ... [there] and into the library ... looking for ... [information about] how films are altered ... Within like an hour, I said, "Oh, my God! There's a thing called an optical printer." I learned about optical printers, and the next thing I was very fluent in them. There's not that much to learn about how an optical printer works. And then came the business of raising money [to actually rent one]. I had to get myself to New York, and I actually operated ... an optical printer and learned all about it....

JH: [PARTICIPANT ONE steps off camera confusing Mr. Lifton.] I'm here.

DSL: Look, here's the thing about this plot in Dealey Plaza because that's when [using an optical printer] I learned more about it. You cannot do what was done in Dealey Plaza – which was being prepared not to just murder the president, but to [also] alter *two different records* of how he died: one is the medical record, the other is the film record. So, everybody is familiar – probably – with the concept of altering the body and messing with the wounds, but they're not probably as familiar with [film alteration] ... I wrote about it in an essay called "Pig on a Leash" – that they [conspirators] had to film the assassination just the way in a military

215   Wikipedia: Josiah Thompson. See also: Thompson, Josiah. *Six Seconds in Dallas: A Micro-Study of the Kennedy Assassination*. Random House, 1967, 323 pages.

operation you film the damage that's done when you make a bomb run. Or in a football … [game] you have to film the football play and then run it back to find out what the heck is going on. That's what happened in this case … Here's the progression of ideas … The film had to be altered because it's not a perfect crime. You [conspirators] have to be prepared to alter the reality … They [conspirators] had to mess with the film but to mess with the film, *they had to take their own film.* They couldn't wait after the assassination and say, "Gee, I wonder how many cameras there were in Dealey Plaza?" And [then] say, "Ms. Moorman, can we borrow your camera?" … No, you film it yourself, process the film, and then immediately you know what you're dealing with. [This would allow them to make corrections to the "official evidence" so that it matches with the "official crime."] That's a sophisticated way of doing it, and that's what I think happened here. That's how they knew what films to alter and when. But immediately, as you know, they gathered all the cameras. This is in the FBI record … These people were interviewed immediately. And when I think of the number of years it took me to analyze this, umm, the fact is it probably took them a similar amount of time to synthesize it [make it all jive], because there is a symmetric … relationship between analysis and synthesis. So, I'm analyzing something after the fact, but in doing so, we learn how they [conspirators] must have been thinking about it *before the fact*. And what that means is that from the beginning, in the minds of these criminals who did this, they ordered this as a … "body-centric" plot. That we're gonna murder the president … but that's not the end of it, then we gotta change the story of how he died. Why? To implicate Oswald. To make it look like the shots came from the southeast corner of the sixth floor window of that building. So, that's what's going on here … It's useful to have taken a course in writing a screenplay. Cuz, this thing is … not just a crime, it's a crime plus the manufacture of a false story of how he died [hence screenplay format]. That's not the same thing as "just a coverup." The manufacturing of a false story of how he [JFK] died is – it really captures the essence of it [the plot] ….

JH: Any other questions anybody has for Mr. Lifton?

PARTICIPANT ONE: Well … *Best Evidence* hasn't really been covered by the mainstream media – that I can tell – in the [United] States, certainly. But, it was in Canada – back in '83. *The Fifth Estate* did a really good [job] ….[216]

216   CBC News (Canadian Broadcasting Corporation), Toronto, Canada. See: CBC News. "About the Fifth Estate." CBC.ca. Retrieved 9/3/2023: https://www.cbc.ca/news/fifthestate. See

DSL: I don't know what year it is, but I have to jump in and correct the statement made: it [*Best Evidence*] *was covered* by the media. *Time* magazine-

PARTICIPANT ONE: Yeah.

DSL: Made *two full pages* in … a news account of it. They did not review it as a book. They treated it as a news story – which is remarkable. So, you open it up, and the big headline said, and this is in … the National Affairs section of *Time*, "Now A Two-Casket Theory." And, it's all spelled out … We use it [during presentations] frequently because the writer who did it visited me at home, and they sent a photographer out [too] … It was so well-written that I found it an excellent synopsis of what's in *Best Evidence*. What it doesn't cover is, "How the heck could this have been planned?" That's the kind of POV as they say in screenwriting – point of view – that's what's in *Final Charade*. [It's] the story of the synthesis – not the story of what happened. Because if you look at just what happened, you kind of get confused. "How could someone have planned this in advance?" Blah, blah, blah. The answer is, you can plan this in advance if you start the plan – not with the idea that you're gonna kill the guy – *but that his body is evidence.* And … a lot of people find that hard to accept. I must say that I, too, went through a brief period – and I put it in *Best Evidence* – when I first realized [that] this is a body-centric plot … I called my family at home, and I put that conversation into one of the chapters … I'm speaking to my mom or dad … cuz they had been … giving me money [and saying], "When is this going to get over?" You know, "We want [you] to get on with your life." And [then] saying, "I can't believe this. They altered the body." … Even the words "they altered the body" doesn't capture it because you've got to say, "Well, what do you mean by 'altering the body?'" … The answer is, "Well, I mean *the removal of bullets* and the alteration of the wounds to falsify the autopsy, to change the story of how he [JFK] died." And the idea that this was the mentality of those who planned this shows how clever they were. They're [conspirators] really smart people who came up with this. This [conspiracy] is not some idea of "Oh, we've got to kill the president. Let's get some shooters over here behind this wall and another one behind this bush" – and all that stuff. That's not what this is all about. This is about murdering the president and creating – in conjunction with that murder – a false story of how he

also: The Fifth Estate. "The JFK Files: The Murder of a President." YouTube, 2017, 00:35:44. This was originally broadcast in 1983. Retrieved 9/3/2023: https://www.youtube.com/watch?app=desktop&v=W-I23ec-4mc.

died – which permitted the vice president to become president under circumstances that appeared *accidental*; a quirk of fate. That's the whole key. If it hadn't appeared a quirk of fate, you'd have had God knows how many people saying, "Wait a minute. Lyndon Johnson can't become president with this kind of crap going on." But, if it looks credible – and it did [it will succeed] because they started with the body – and had this [near perfect] setup [Dealey Plaza]. Now, the setup malfunctioned. It didn't work the way it was supposed to work ... We can go through the things that went wrong ... One of the most important ones being the accidental or the unintentional shooting of Governor Connally. He's not supposed to be shot. Suddenly, they've got an extra body on their hands. So, then we get into that whole series. But, I can just tell you that it gets very complex, very quickly.[217] But at heart, the foundation of it, is a very, very clever plan and concept....

JH: Any other questions?

PARTICIPANT ONE: Yeah, I have another one ... [Josiah] "Tink" Thompson came out with a new book last year ... Basically, his thesis ... builds on his first one, that there was a shot much later than [Zapruder] 312.[218] Can you comment on that?

DSL: I can't comment on it because I don't know as much as you probably do from having studied his book ... Thompson and I ... remained cordial, but I never agreed with his analysis ... To synopsize the way he wrote *Six Seconds* ... here's what he did: remember, you've got the Dallas view of the body and you've got the Bethesda view of the body. And if you understand what I say in *Best Evidence*, and most people ... [do] whether they agree with it or not, in Dallas the body looked like it had been shot from the front, in Bethesda the body on the table looked like it was shot from behind. David Lifton says, "That's because somebody altered the body." *That's* not the way Tink Thompson approached it. Way back when in '68, he said ... by putting these two pictures together [Dallas wounds vs. Bethesda wounds], we have a double head hit. But, this is nonsense. You can't put the two pictures together. You can't add them up. You've gotta contrast them, and when you contrast the two pictures, you say, "Oh, somebody altered the body." You don't say there was a double head

---

217   With respect to the "extra body," Mr. Lifton seems to be alluding accidentally to "Godzilla" and the death of the Secret Service agent driving the car (i.e. not SSA X, not William Greer) – certainly not Governor Connally who survived. He did not want to discuss this theory publicly.

218   Thompson, Josiah. *Last Second in Dallas*. University Press of Kansas, 2021, 544 pages.

hit, but that was Thompson's error ... I don't think he's ever really backed off from that position....

PARTICIPANT ONE: Yeah, he has. Yeah. In the new book, he admits that the ... shot [that] supposedly pushed the president's head forward, didn't happen. It was ... his [Thompson's] mistake in measurements ... There was another shot later.

DSL: Yeah. Here's the problem: the reason why the shot looks like it pressed the head forward is that five seconds or more are removed from the Zapruder Film. So, the last frame – if you use this vocabulary – the last *pre-impact frame* is 312. The next *post-impact frame* is 313. But, there's time between 312 and 313. That's where one of the edits was made. Why do I know that? Because you've got over fifty people who think that the car – at least sixteen who said the car stopped, and if you start to relax the definition of the car stop a little bit, you get up to fifty people. And if you've been to Dealey Plaza – look, I interviewed the Newmans back in '72.[219] They were absolutely adamant [about the car stop] – this was before the Zapruder Film was shown – and the Newmans hadn't seen it certainly. He said [to me], "I don't care what anybody says at the [National] Archives. I was there. That car stopped right in front of me." And he turns to his wife, "Didn't it, honey?" ... She says, "Yes! We were right there. The car stopped." So, the problem is ... if the car stopped, then seconds go by and in those seconds, you can't omit that because if you omit that, you're omitting the car stop.[220] And the car stop then gets to the whole question of whether the driver was implicated and what happened ... The car stops in the middle of the shooting instead of hitting the accelerator right away? So, that's the kind of issue you get into.

JH: Excellent. Anyone else? Any other questions?

PARTICIPANT TWO: Umm, yes, I had a question ... Thank you, Mr. Lifton, for your work. I read *Best Evidence* when I was sixteen years old, and I've been fascinated ever since. If I could ask a slightly different angle

---

219   Bill and Gayle Newman and their two children witnessed JFK disembark from Air Force One at Love Field then rushed downtown to position themselves at the end of the motorcade route. They were positioned on the north side of Elm Street in front of the Grassy Knoll and had to shield their two boys from the gunfire. See: Dallas News Administrator. "Couple Who Witnessed JFK Assassination Recall Infamous Day the Shots Rang Out." *The Dallas Morning News,* November 9, 2012. Retrieved 9/3/2023: https://www.dallasnews.com/news/2012/11/10/couple-who-witnessed-jfk-assassination-recall-infamous-day-the-shots-rang-out/.
220   Hence the reason why the conspirators had to alter the Zapruder Film. They had to omit the car stop which allowed JFK to be fatally hit in the head – the sure sign of Secret Service complicity in the crime.

of a question: What is your view of Jack Ruby? What was his role and his motivation…?

DSL: Sure. I know the answer. I mean (Laughs), I have an answer to that. (Laughs) It depends on whether you want the three minute version, the ten minute version, or the one hour version. (Laughs) I'll try.

PARTICIPANT TWO: (Laughs) Probably three minutes.

DSL: I'll try. OK. The original assassination scenario does not involve Jack Ruby at all. The original assassination scenario depends on getting Oswald killed right after – within let's say fifty, ninety seconds of shooting JFK. So, there's a police officer that's going to run into the building and … encounter Oswald *and shoot him* … dead *thinking* – if I'm correct about how this police officer's mind worked – thinking that he shot the assassin and prevented the getaway, or some such nonsense. OK. That's what's supposed to happen. Oswald's gonna be dead within sixty seconds, ninety seconds. Instead, this guy [Motorcycle Officer Marrion L. Baker] screws up. First of all, he screws up because he runs into the building and Oswald … is drinking a Coke[221] in the lunchroom … So, he encounters (Laughs) Oswald, puts the gun up (Laughs) against his belly, and Roy Truly, the Superintendent of the [TSB] Depository says, "He's OK. He works here." That's what happened. So, then the officer is embarrassed. He fumbles, and he and Roy Truly go up to the roof – and this is in the sworn testimony of which gives you a lot of interesting evidence. [Enroute to] the roof, the officer says to Roy Truly, "We must be careful. This man will blow your head off."

PARTICIPANT TWO: Hmm.

DSL: That's (Laughs) in the Warren Commission's twenty six volumes. It's right there in the testimony of [Roy] Truly … And then the question becomes, and I … researched this very carefully – *before I made my discoveries about surgeries* – because I couldn't understand how this screwball Ruby, or whoever he was, got involved in a major assassination plot. How did this work?

---

221   Granted, whether Oswald was drinking a Coke (or even a Pepsi) or not – is disputed. One argument made is that Oswald grabbed an empty bottle and pretended to drink. Though his Warren Commission testimony does not state this, Marrion Baker was later asked to provide a "Voluntary Handwritten Statement" to the FBI on September 23, 1964, the day before the Warren Report was released, where he crossed out the phrase "drinking a coke" and initialed the alleged "error." Either way, it's clear why the Warren Commission would want to "erase" this from the record because it offers less credence to their claim that Oswald shot JFK just ninety seconds earlier, had time to run down the stairs, manipulate the Coke machine, open the Coke bottle, and apparently drink some Coke – all before Officer Baker arrived.

PARTICIPANT TWO: Uhh, huh.

DSL: And, uh, when I was working at *Ramparts* magazine, finished "The Case for Three Assassins" [1966], went back to UCLA trying to do my incompletes and finish all that, I got further involved in looking at Ruby's testimony ... It's in the ... course of looking at Ruby's testimony that I discovered what I believed to be *key passages* which explain his psychology ... Here's what the passages say: Ruby *demands* that he be flown to Washington to speak to President Johnson. He says ... "I know if I tell the whole story to Johnson, he'll understand." And then he says, "Because I know that you've been told that I was part of a plot to kill President Kennedy." And then he says ... "There's no greater harm [that] you can do to a member of the Jewish faith than to argue that he [Ruby] was part of a plot...."

PARTICIPANT TWO: Hmm.

DSL: In other words, he ... Ruby was looking at this from the point of a first generation Jew. You know, his parents had been born ... [in Europe]. But, it was very similar to my father who was born in Russia in 1905 ... So, that's the situation. Ruby was given this cock and bull story, he revealed what the cock and bull story was, but mostly it's been ignored by people who write about the assassination. I think that's the key to how Ruby was recruited. When Oswald was not killed on Friday afternoon the way he was *supposed to have been*, they [conspirators] had to come up with some scenario to get rid of him [Oswald]. If Oswald talks and says everything he knows, he'll reveal – not so much the truth – but the cock and bull story he was told as to: "What ... [was he] doing in the building with the rifle?" "Why was he behaving that way?" And the next thing you know, the whole story of Oswald's connection with Robert Kennedy, which I think is very important, will come out ... That's the last thing anybody [of the conspirators] wanted....

PARTICIPANT TWO: Thank you. And just one follow-up question: Are you familiar with the testimony of Seth Kantor, the [respected] Dallas newspaper reporter ... He testified in the Warren Commission ... that he saw Jack Ruby at Parkland Hospital that afternoon [when JFK died] ... [He] couldn't believe that the Warren Commission didn't believe his testimony that he was as sure as anything that Jack Ruby was actually at Parkland ... that afternoon [since he knew Ruby personally].

DSL: Yeah. I know Seth Kantor. He attended my news conference when *Best Evidence* was published the second week of January, 1981 ... He was very sympathetic and all that. But, let me tell you what I think is going on here ... First of all, I believe Seth Kantor. Jack Ruby was at the hospital ... [But] what was he [Ruby] doing at the hospital? And, I'll tell you what it was – in my opinion.

PARTICIPANT TWO: Uhh, huh.

DSL: I have [analyzed] peculiar theories or hypotheses [that] I don't give much credence to, [such as] ... he was there to plant the bullet. That's – none of that is true. Here's what's going on. Ruby ... was what we call in the Jewish Tradition a "white Jew." ... He's in a Dallas community that's not ... prominently Jewish. But, he's getting along fine. He runs his club and all the rest ... That was Ruby's situation. He wanted to show respect for the fact that he had great respect for Kennedy, and he wanted to make the deadline in ... the newspaper [to place] ... an ad ... Two newspapers in Dallas: the morning and the afternoon news: morning one is *Dallas Morning News*, afternoon is *Dallas Times Herald*. Ruby wanted to get [an ad] into the ... earliest paper with his little ad that said, "Carousel closed out of respect" – or something like that. So, he [Ruby] was at the hospital because he wanted to know *what had happened*. He wanted to know ... if Kennedy was going to live or are we dealing with a dead man? And at the hospital, he learned that Kennedy was in fact practically DOA, and he ran the ad ... as I recall – in the Friday afternoon paper ... It was his way of saying that he had this respect for Kennedy. I do not believe that Ruby was ... some part of an elaborate plot. However ... once Oswald's arrested alive, the clock is ticking. Look at what he [Oswald] was saying: "I do not know what these charges are about"; ... "I do not know what's going on here"; "I committed no act of violence." You know, this could get really bad [for the conspirators] ... I think he had a handler,[222] but suppose he had said, "Screw the handler! I'm gonna say what I think. I'm working for the United States Government. I was here on an assignment. I don't know what this is all about." That would have blown Johnson's chances to get the nomination in August 1964 – if he [Oswald] ever came out and said stuff like that. So, he [Oswald] had to be hushed up, and they had to get rid of him as soon as possible. And of course they did by arranging what the

---

222   I discussed this notion of a handler at length with Mr. Lifton. He believed Oswald was told things like, 'It's going to be OK. It's a misunderstanding. We'll get you out of this, Lee. Just be patient.' Of course, these were all lies designed to keep Oswald quiet and compliant until he could be silenced.

Warren Commission calls "the aborted transfer." ... That's the business that occurs on Sunday [November 24, 11:21 AM] when they transferred Oswald from city to county ... custody. [They] brought him downstairs. Had all those lights on, shining in his eyes, and Ruby had been given some story that if he didn't get rid of Oswald, Oswald was gonna implicate the Jews. Now, I tried to condense it [Ruby connection] as much as I can ... That's what's going on in ... Ruby's head. He's going to go "save the Jews." And that's what I call ... the Moses Hypothesis. He is gonna save the Jews....

PARTICIPANT TWO: Thank you.

JH: Anybody else? Any other questions...?

PARTICIPANT THREE: Yeah. I have a question. Mr. Lifton, you go into great detail about how the body has been altered medically, how the ... photographic evidence has been altered, and is primarily because there were shots from the front that needed to be ... obliterated ... Do you have any thoughts on why the overall plan for the assassination included shooters from the front?[223] ... Obviously, that leads to a lot of chaos that took place [for the conspirators] trying to cover up those shots....

DSL: OK ... I deal with this in detail – and I'll refer you to my Chapter 14 called "Trajectory Reversal."[224] ... The people who planned this, viewed the body – kind of holistically ... Look what they have to do: they have to kill the president which means shooting the president; but then they want to create a false story about how he died. And in Chapter 14, I try to show how complicated it gets if you start by shooting from the back because an entry wound is a small, little wound. An exit wound is a big – kind of like jagged wound. If you start by shooting from the back, you have no control over the number of the shots. It's [the entry wound] gonna determine whether it took two, or six, or seven shots to kill the president. *Whereas If you shoot from the front*, you have control. And here's why geometrically. It's very simple. A little wound can be changed into a big wound. A big wound *cannot be changed* into a little wound. So, if you want to go through

---

223   I hesitate to include this footnote, but I personally feel it has merit – and it partially addresses this woman's question. I believe confessed Grassy Knoll Assassin, James Files. To be clear, I did discuss this source with Mr. Lifton, and he dismissed it as not credible. See: Nitro Dubs. "JFK Grassy Knoll Shooter – Full Interview – Low-Level CIA/Chicago Mob Affiliated Hitman – 2003." You-Tube, 2021. Retrieved 9/9/2023: https://www.youtube.com/watch?v=1FiZ-x3l4ml. Interestingly, when James Files lived with his aunt and uncle in Round Lake Beach, Illinois, in the mid- to late-1980s, he lived some two blocks from where my father lived on Round Lake Drive.

224   See Chapter 14 of *Best Evidence*, "Trajectory Reversal: Blueprint for Deception," pages 338-379 of the Carroll & Graf edition.

this business of altering wounds, you want to be able to change an entry to an exit. You can't change an exit to an entry – unless you're going to sew him up and tell people to ignore the stitches.[225] So, that's why he has to be shot from the opposite direction of the story you're creating. The algorithm for this I call "trajectory reversal," and I discovered it two months after I discovered the stuff about surgery … I was up to my neck in courses about systems engineering, and algorithms, and all the rest, and I said to myself, "This is amazing that the people who did this … had this kind of insight that they … viewed the body as something to be altered to tell a false story." But, in order for that to work, *you have to shoot* from the opposite direction, because of a simple geometric fact that a little wound that is of entrance can be changed to an exit – a big, jagged wound. But, you can't do the reverse. So, if you shoot from behind, you're gonna mess up the blackboard on which you're trying to create the false story. The false story is two shots, one shot, maybe three shots, but that's what you want, and you don't want to go beyond that. If you start saying, "Oh, yeah, Kennedy was killed by a single assassin, but it took seven shots." Forget it! There's gonna be no credibility to it. It [false story] has to look credible, and to look credible, it has to have a minimum number of shots, and [for] the minimum number of shots, you've gotta … shoot from the other direction in order to be able to change an entry which is small, to an exit, which is large….

JH: Any other questions…?

PARTICIPANT ONE: Yeah, my cat [which was sitting on the chair behind his head] has a question. (Laughs)

DSL: (Laughs)

PARTICIPANT ONE: What can we do to help David – either generate more money or help in terms of research…? [The discussion quickly turns to his GoFundMe and the issue of the 45 filing cabinets in Orange County in a storage facility – which costs around eight hundred per month.]

DSL: The way this started was, you gotta go back to … December of '66 when I write the articles for Ramparts. Then I go back to UCLA to com-

---

225   In other words, you must hit the president precisely in the back of the *head* or jeopardize the opportunity to kill him according to "the official story." Shooting from the back *and the front* allows some "wiggle room" to kill the president according to the "official story" by merely including wound alteration to the overall assassination plot – if need be, which it was. According to James Files' account, he was told by Chicago mobster Charles Nicoletti to shoot JFK *only if necessary*. (Ibid, circa 01:00:00) If true, that supports Mr. Lifton's theory about a frontal shot. It was the "ace in the hole" if a rear shot to JFK's head did not materialize. See: Wikipedia: Charles Nicoletti and L. Fletcher Prouty.   161

plete my four incompletes, and that's how I made the discovery of surgery on the body. And what happened was … I remember this, first I had to buy a filing cabinet [for] in my … apartment. Then I had to buy a second one. Then, it got up to three. At some point, it reached eight … Eight filing cabinets! And if you entered my apartment near Brentwood, which is the same place that Marilyn Monroe died … I was in a very nice street … That's when I realized that people would come into my apartment and say, "Well, where do you eat?" You know, "Where do you sleep?" (Laughs) I'd show them my next room was my bedroom. That was an OK room. But not the living room. It was filled with these filing cabinets, and I didn't know what to do about it … At some point, I actually said, "I gotta get these cabinets out of here," and that's when I rented my first little storage area for $200 dollars. And then, it [storage area rental] got bigger, and it got bigger … When I [finally] did a full inventory, I had forty five cabinets. I had to put them somewhere. So, this company … gets this check from me every month, and believe me, it hurts. And it's unfortunate because that's the way I was living, with … these filing cabinets….

JH: This is definitely cool. Do you like doing this, Mr. Lifton…?

DSL: Well, yeah, I like to talk about the theory [trajectory reversal] … The hardest part I think of the whole case – and this was when I was writing *Best Evidence* also – is Chapter 14, "Trajectory Reversal." Cuz, people want to know "Why would you shoot from the front if you want to create the appearance he's shot from behind?" And the answer in one sentence is, because a little hole can be made into a big hole, but no hole can be made to disappear … I had these insights in December [of] 1966, two months after I discovered the surgery stuff. And, um, I was *astounded*. I mean, these people who did this were very smart … I went to Cornell in the engineering physics program, and believe me, it's a very unusual and hard program. I don't see how anybody who hasn't had a background in systems engineering, flow-charting, and all this other stuff, could have analyzed the screwed up record of the Warren Commission – unless you had this kind of training that I had.[226] So, the big unknown was, who the heck ever would think that it would take so long [to decipher]. Now, I got done

226   See: Lt. Col. L. Fletcher Prouty. *JFK: The CIA, Vietnam, and the Plot to Assassinate John F. Kennedy*. Birch Lane Press, 1992, 293 pages. In this book, he claims that the photograph of the Three Tramps walking past a well-dressed man in a suit is General Edward Lansdale – who was an expert in black ops. This claim is supported by a letter from General Victor H. Krulak to Prouty, dated March 15, 1985. (JFK. "Appendix D: Krulak Letter Re: Dealey Plaza Photos and Lansdale Identity." Ratical.org. Retrieved 9/9/2023: https://ratical.org/ratville/JFK/USO/appD.html. See also: Wikipedia: Edward Lansdale. Note that there is not one scintilla of reference to his alleged connection to JFK's Assassination.

by 1981, and it was published. But, since then – and I had resolved [that] I'm not getting further involved in this … I've learned other stuff about Oswald. Who he [really] was. What he was [really] doing in Russia? As some of you may know, I got to know his wife very well. We did filmed interviews with her. I got to know the [youngest] daughter very well. So, I got much more … knowledge now than I had then … It's a more complex situation than I would have ever believed … If you had told me decades ago, "Well, you'll be working on this until you're older than 70 years old," I would have said, "You're crazy. That's not gonna happen." And, um, but I was wrong…. (Laughs)

SATURDAY, FEBRUARY 26, 2022
The following was a Q&A Zoom sessions we held for some of Mr. Lifton's GoFundMe supporters…

JH: Any questions?

PARTICIPANT ONE: How did they [conspirators] get JFK's body out of the ceremonial casket on Air Force One – before it left Dallas…?

DSL : Yeah, I can answer that question … Johnson called everybody to the front of the plane. This is dealt with in Chapter 31 … of *Best Evidence*.[227] Johnson called everyone to the front of the plane for swearing-in. Everybody came to the front of the plane except one person: Godfrey McHugh, but he was running back and forth.[228] Anyway, he wasn't there [with coffin] all the time. But basically, the answer is the swearing-in was held amidship … There was a period of time when the Secret Service brought the body in … and … that's why there is only one person back there [from JFK's entourage] besides the Secret Service agents, and that was Godfrey McHugh … Everybody was called to the front, and that's basically how the deception worked. That's the only period they could have gotten the body out of the … coffin.

PARTICIPANT ONE: Would they have gotten it [the body] into the cargo hold or something? How would they have done that?

DSL: No. Once they get it out of the coffin, they put it on a … forklift truck which was brought up to the rear of the … plane. I have witnesses to the [presence of] the forklift truck … The forklift truck was used to get the body out, and then the forklift truck went about a hundred to two

---

227   See Chapter 31 of *Best Evidence*, "The 'When and Where' Problem Reconsidered," pages 673-690 of the Carroll & Graf edition.
228   Wikipedia: Godfrey McHugh.

hundred feet toward the front, and that's where they put it [body] into the cargo hold.[229]

PARTICIPANT ONE: Oh, OK. Wow.

JH: Good question.

PARTICIPANT ONE: Wow.

JH: Any other questions … ?

PARTICIPANT TWO: When the limo made the turn from the Triple Underpass to the Stemmons Freeway sign, David said that there were some people that witnessed something, and it's gonna be in the book. But also, another witness there [Triple Underpass] was Ed Hoffman … While … [he] was alive, did David interview him? Did he talk to him? Did he corroborate what the other witnesses said?

DSL: Yeah, I … watched Ed [speak] … at different conferences – specifically the … [JFK] Lancer conferences … and I'm going to tell you exactly what I believe which is not favorable to Hoffman. I felt the whole thing [his talk] was like an Amway meeting … where they're selling a product. It was a very strange experience. I watched it with reporter Robert Sam Anson.[230] … I know the guy [Hoffman] has problems, but that doesn't mean that we're not gonna be true to history … So, the answer to your question is that I don't believe Ed Hoffman was there or witnessed [what he claims] – or if he was there that he witnessed what he said he did. He did not come forward, as I recall, until 1967. Now that makes it soon from our vantage point [2022], but it's not quick from … the number of years that had passed. He did not come forward immediately [1963]. Three years he kept [quiet] before the story came out. I used to have a thick "Ed Hoffman" file because the whole key to this thing is when a person makes their statement. *If Ed Hoffman had said anything of the sort in 1963 or '4,* it would have been much more serious historically – but not when several years go by. Books were published and suddenly he comes out with this thing. That's why I never took it seriously.

---

229   Vince Palamara. "David Lifton: Lecture at Bismarck State College 11/17/13." YouTube, 2013, 57:46 minutes. Retrieved 10/12/2023: https://www.youtube.com/watch?v=zgL38AA8Ewc. In one of his most important presentations, Mr. Lifton lays out the evidence supporting the removal of the body from its coffin on Air Force One. The coffin was brought in at 2:18 and the swearing in ceremony was at 2:38. A forklift was used to move the body from the starboard side of AF1 to the forward luggage area. Blood was reported in the galley area, on Secret Service Agent Roy Kellerman's shirt, on Dr. George G. Burkley's sleeve, and even LBJ had to change his shirt. Lastly, it took seven hours to clean up AF1 at Andrews AFB. (Circa 45:00-50:00)

230   Wikipedia: Robert Sam Anson.

PARTICIPANT TWO: OK ... You said that you believe a Secret Service ... was killed ... during the assassination, and I'm trying to track that down ... I have multiple pieces of information. One says the Secret Service agent was killed in Dealey Plaza, the other information that he was killed elsewhere. Can you enlighten us on that?

DSL: Yeah ... the best ... I can do – I also tried to track it down, and here's the best I can do ... First of all, the most important piece of evidence that a Secret Service agent was shot is the original [UPI] Wire Service ... that was sent forth within ... [five minutes of the assassination]. And, it says ... "President Kennedy and a Secret Service agent were shot," blah, blah, blah. In other words, *the original transmission* ... mentions the death of a Secret Service agent. That's the way it starts. Second of all, when the car arrives at the hospital, there were reports of another body in the front seat. I'm talking about reports that went out on either the AP or the UPI wire. I have both of them ... about another body in the front seat. Third, that body was brought *inside* [the hospital] ... and it was placed on a stretcher with a sheet over it ... [Unfortunately], I don't have those documents right in front of me or I'd read them to you. But that ... [is proof] that something very serious occurred, and a Secret Service agent was shot. If you can get ... the original UPI and the original AP [reports] – as I have years ago, that file is very important and it was very useful.

PARTICIPANT TWO: Yeah, one thing I did go back and all of the news reports – the initial news reports – all of the major TV stations, and even Walter Cronkite said that a Secret Service agent *had been killed*. Is it possible, people just mistook Clint Hill – the fact that he was draped over the limo – as a Secret Service agent [who] was killed...?

DSL: No, I don't think so ... The reason I don't think so is as I recall, *Dan Rather* reported that [dead Secret Service agent] to KRLD within minutes [of the assassination].[231] In other words ... First of all, he takes a look inside the car [outside Parkland]. Then, he runs into the hallway, and he gets a telephone. There's a fight to get a telephone, I remember ... or he [had to co-opt] one of the nurse's lines. But, I believe that Dan Rather reported that immediately. When I say immediately, I mean within five minutes. And so, that's why I've always ... taken that [as] serious. What's more important, when I got involved in this work, and I was interviewing people, I heard that from more than one person ... There's some other work that I did, and ... that concerns the identity of the Secret Service agent who I believe was shot ... I can't do this from memory, but I'm gonna tell you this: that in the Fall [of 1963], President Kennedy was in North Dakota at a speaking engagement or some political event ... I believe that it's the Secret Service agent who was at that event ... and handling security at that event, who was the one that's shot [in Dallas]. But, whoever it was, they [Secret Service] removed his name. There is no official record as far as I know ... of the Secret Service agent being shot. Of course, the Secret Service is not gonna create a record that night and put it into the public files. The Secret Service files before the Warren Commission ... are very clear that there was nobody shot. So, if you were looking at the Warren Commission Secret Service records, it doesn't contain anything about anyone [in their ranks] being shot. But, if you look at the radio transmissions from Air Force One, it's a much different situation. I'll tell you exactly what ... raises questions. If you look at the radio transmissions, you'll find that three rows of seats had to be removed from Air Force One. These seats were taken out of the starboard side door, and they were placed along the runway there ... Aubrey Rike who I knew very well and ... [with whom] I had a beautiful interview ... He said, "Well, I knew they were making room for something, but I didn't know what." ... They put ... the coffin, I think it's just a shipping casket, in[side] which the Secret Service agent was shot – they put it right behind the ... first three rows of seats and tossed a tarpaulin over it ... It was officially referred to as "Lyndon's luggage." That's not a joke. That's actually what it was referred to as....

JH: Hmm. Hmm. Good questions.

PARTICIPANT TWO: Could you repeat one thing? He said something about North Dakota, but I had trouble hearing it....

DSL: I'm gonna name another event that's on film. When he went to visit his father who was in Florida recovering from a stroke, *that agent* – the one that ... I believe was the one who was shot – that agent appears in the North Dakota pictures, and he appears in the pictures when Kennedy visits his dad in ... Florida. I'm telling you that based on my own work, I think that's the guy [Secret Service agent] that got shot. And his name – he does not appear by name in the Secret Service records.

PARTICIPANT TWO: Hmm.

DSL: It's very bizarre.

PARTICIPANT TWO: But you believe he was a Secret Service agent...?

DSL: Yes. He was also – I could be wrong on this – but I think he's the same agent who ... was driving the car in Fort Worth, Texas, that morning. So, in other words, Kennedy gets up in the morning, he goes to the Fort Worth breakfast ... then he gets into the little motorcade that goes back to the airport ... And then, there's that eight minute flight from Fort Worth to Dallas, because this whole thing [plot] is designed around an airport arrival ... That's the Secret Service route. They arranged the routes starting with an airport arrival at Love Field. So ... the route was planned weeks in advance ... They had the motorcade going down Main Street, through Dealey Plaza ... I guess the question ... you haven't asked is, "Was the route changed at the last minute?" I don't believe that at all because ... Kennedy on November 22nd drove the same route that was test-driven by the Secret Service a week or two before ... It's kind of like assassination mythology. It's just not in the record. What's really important about the route is that it was planned so far in advance. In other words, Dealey Plaza – what happened there – was not something that occurred at the last minute. The motorcade goes down Main Street, right on Houston, and then that 135 degree turn at Dealey Plaza ... If there was a plot to kill President Kennedy at Dealey Plaza, and I believe there was ... and [evidence] corroborating what I just said. Think of it this way. Ask yourself this question: Was Oswald a pre-selected Patsy? How many people do you think went to the Soviet Union and defected ... Oswald was clearly pre-selected with his job at the building, blah, blah, blah. So, once you understand that Oswald was a pre-selected patsy ... [you can see] the geometry of this whole thing is arranged in advance ... He's not gonna be fished out at the last minute. *He's there!* He started working there October 16th, 1963....

PARTICIPANT THREE: The role of Admiral Burkley and Gerald Behn always fascinated me. Do you believe that they were part of the conspiracy?

DSL: My personal opinion [is] ... Admiral Burkley ... had foreknowledge, but if you're asking me if he was a designer of it, the CEO of the plot, no, I don't.[232] ... But, do I think he was knowledgeable about what happened and stood by [and did nothing]. I don't know what attitude describes his role. But he ... issued a false report that night about back wounds ... I guess I would say [he was] certainly some kind of a participant, but ... he didn't do any of the genuine "dirty work." As far as

Behn goes, I hope you understand that Behn did not go on this trip to Dallas. But, he was Head of the White House Detail when Air Force One returned to Washington.

PARTICIPANT THREE: I find it odd though that that's when he decided to take his first vacation.

DSL: Well, that's true … Maybe he wanted to distance himself from it and took a vacation. He said [to himself], "I don't want to have any part of this." … I don't know … It is interesting that he [Behn] did not go on the [Dallas] trip because he went on many trips with Kennedy, but he didn't go on this one….

JH: Any other questions?

PARTICIPANT FOUR: Yeah, I have a question … Hi, David … Dr. Burkley … when he … contacted the House Select Committee, and at that time he said … through his lawyer … that he had some information that he thought was pertinent to them … Have you been able to find out anything on that?

DSL: The short answer is no. When I called him, he wouldn't talk to me. When he realized who I was, he hung up….

SATURDAY, JULY 9, 2022

DSL : Fifty or sixty people stated the car stopped during the shooting momentarily. That proves the film has been altered. OK?

JH: And through your research-

DSL: There's at least fifty….

JH: And so … Who was "they?" And How did "they" edit the film…?

DSL: Well, that's a whole – there were books written about this … The Zapruder Film – the original – through the Secret Service was brought to an optical [printer] lab … and the film was altered using an optical printer. And so the result was that they [conspirators] had the prints ready … to be published in the first issue of Life magazine.[233] You can't alter the body of the president without altering the film also. There is a one-to-one relationship. So, if they mess with the body, they had to mess with the film. If you mess with the body, and you don't mess with the film, the film will give you an accurate record of what the body looked like. It's that

233   Wikipedia: Optical Printer. See: Egan, Daniel. "Zapruder Film of the Kennedy Assassination (1963)." Library of Congress. Retrieved 9/10/23: https://www.loc.gov/static/programs/national-film-preservation-board/documents/Zapruder-Film-of-the-Assassination.pdf.

good … That's what *Best Evidence* is all about. That's why I dealt with film alteration in some lengthy footnotes in *Best Evidence*. But [what's] more important, in that long essay I wrote called "Pig on a Leash" … it gets into the wider version of the assassination. You can't kill the president then plan to alter the wounds – unless you also alter that film of the assassination. You can't do one and leave the other unaltered because the films would then look different. *The wounds on the film* would be different than the wounds at Parkland Hospital.… They had to alter the film in order to create the [false story]. The main film they [conspirators] had to deal with was the Zapruder Film … The way it was dealt with was, there were four main films: Zapruder, Nix, [Bronson] … and Muchmore.… Basically, they had to take out the car stop … and shorten the assassination to six seconds or whatever.… [This] is basically a plot to alter … what we call "the best evidence" – only in the realm of cinematography.

JH: You talked about this before. Would you say that the Kennedy Assassination was [set up] almost like a movie plot with a screenplay … and actors…?

DSL: Umm, yes. I don't know how else to say it.

JH: It [plot] was all pre-planned … They literally had certain people in certain spots like you would in-

DSL: But if they planned to kill the president … it's a story. It was scripted … The autopsy [and] the other channel you might say of information was … the Zapruder Film.[234]

234   Martinson, Jon. "David Lifton on JFK." YouTube, 2013, 14 parts (Circa 200 minutes). Retrieved 10/10/2023: https://www.youtube.com/@davidliftononjfk2724. This is perhaps the best interview – and mirrors to a degree the conversations outlined in this book – where Mr. Lifton covers his latest research material destined for publication in *Final Charade*.

David Samuel Lifton
September 20, 1939
December 6, 2022
83 years, 77 days
You are sorely missed.
Rest in Peace....

EPILOGUE

TESTIMONIAL IN HONOR
OF DAVID S. LIFTON

Lifton's work on the crucial medical evidence was a paradigm shift for everyone."

–Vince Palamara[235]

Author and researcher David Lifton is, without question, one of the foremost pioneers in the serious study of the JFK assassination, in addition to being one of the most famous and best-selling authors on the case, as well. Lifton's work on the crucial medical evidence was a paradigm shift for everyone. His incredible book *Best Evidence* was not only a national best-seller that was reprinted many times over, but it also spawned a best-selling video *Best Evidence: The Research Video*, encompassing some of the most crucial interviews Lifton was able to garner with key eyewitnesses at both the Parkland and Bethesda end of the line.

Although I became somewhat interested in the case in 1978 at the tender age of 12, it was not until 1988, the 25th anniversary of the Kennedy assassination, that I began to truly become consumed with the greatest murder mystery of the twentieth century (if not for all time). In this regard, the paperback edition of Lifton's seminal book (which included some of the JFK autopsy photos, printed for the first time ever) was a landmark event for me, the research community, and the public, in general. Disturbing issues of body alteration, photo and x-ray tampering, and incomplete medical evidence issues came to the fore with lightning speed,

---

235   In this author's opinion, Vince Palamara is the leading "Scribe of the Kennedy Assassination." A former confidante of Mr. Lifton, Palamara has several portals of research which keep the public aware of the evidence in this famous case. His work can be reached at various online sites including but not limited to: Instagram, TikTok, Twitter (X), VincePalamara.com, and YouTube. Most importantly, Vince Palamara has authored several key works on the Kennedy Assassination including: *Survivor's Guilt: The Secret Service & The Failure to Protect President Kennedy, JFK: From Parkland to Bethesda, The Not-So-Secret Service, Whos' Who in the Secret Service* and *Honest Answers About the Murder of President Kennedy: A New Look at the JFK Assassination*. Coming on October 22, 2024: *The Plot to Kill President Kennedy in Chicago And the Other Traces of Conspiracy Leading to the Assassination of JFK – A Visual Investigation* (Trine Day)

as even the major PBS documentary Nova: *Who Shot President Kennedy* featured Lifton's work for all to see.

However, it was not until 1992 when, to my great surprise and pleasure, David Lifton contacted me out of the blue via phone to ask me many questions about my developing research. From that point on,

David would reach out to me (especially via e-mail and on The Education Forum) to ask me the identities of quite a few of President Kennedy's Secret Service agents, as this was an area of profound interest to me (I went on to author 5 books of my own regarding the JFK assassination, the medical evidence, and the Secret Service). It was a thrill to have a back and forth with someone I greatly admired.

David's sad passing on December 6, 2022, had such a profound effect on the research community that even those who believed Oswald acted alone, quite touchingly, gave tender and respectful tributes to David and his work. Yes – even those on the other side of the aisle, so to speak, tipped their hats to Lifton and acknowledged his important research. Even if one did not always agree with all his conclusions, few could possibly doubt his integrity and his scholarship.

During the years after the publication of *Best Evidence* in 1981, David Lifton worked in earnest on his follow-up book *Final Charade*. Sadly, he did not live to see both the completion and release of that work, although a family friend said that it will be published sometime in the not-so-distant future. I know we all await that day with great interest, to say the least.

If there was a Mount Rushmore of the greatest authors and researchers on the case, few could argue against the notion that David Lifton deserves an honored portion of that monument.

Index

Prouty, L. Fletcher 11, 19, 161, 162

R

Ramparts 55, 112, 113, 158, 161
Rather, Dan 165
RFK 38, 45, 46
Roberts, Earlene 91
Rogan, Joe 24, 60, 144
Romero, Robbie vi
Rosenberg, Ethel and Julius 113, 121,
    122, 123
Rowley, James Joseph 65, 131
Ruby, Jack 4, 55, 105, 156-160
Rush to Judgment 18, 19, 41
Ryder, George 127, 128

S

Salandria, Vincent 83, 84
San Antonio Express-News 114
San Antonio Light 81, 114
Scheinbaum, Stanley 113
Schultz, Howard 63
Scientific American 13
Shepherd, Peter 36, 124, 149
Six Seconds in Dallas 19, 152
Sorensen, Ted 5
Stone, Oliver 1, 3, 17, 18, 24, 60, 118
Storms, Harrison A. 14
Stroll, Irwin 45
Symington, Stuart 69

T

Talbot, David 83, 84
Thomas, Al 96
Thompson, Josiah 11, 19, 152, 155,
    156
Time 17, 69, 154
Tippit, J.D. 18, 58, 77, 80, 90-92
Truly, Roy 55, 79, 87, 88, 90, 157
Twain, Mark 63

V

Valentino, Linda 122
Valentino, Pat 122

W

Walker, Edwin 42, 74, 75, 76
Warren Commission viii, 1, 4, 18- 20,
    42, 55, 79, 84, 86-88, 90, 91, 99,
    109, 110, 114, 119, 141, 143,
    145, 147, 148, 157-159, 162, 166
Warren Report 19, 41, 66, 67, 83, 110,
    113, 157
Wecht, Cyril 11
Weisberg, Harold 11, 112
Westbrook, W. R 91
Whaley, William Wayne 27, 57, 58
Who Shot President Kennedy? 172
Willis, Phil 47, 138, 139, 140, 141

Z

Zapruder, Abraham 1, 3, 43, 52, 56,
    65, 77, 78, 83, 85, 112, 133-136,
    139, 140, 145, 151, 155, 156,
    168, 169
Zapruder Film 1, 3, 43, 52, 65, 83, 85,
    133-136, 145, 151, 156, 168, 169